Ian Sutton studied the history of architecture under Nikolaus
Pevsner, John Summerson and Peter Murray, before taking up a
career in art publishing. Since then he has written a book on the
architecture of theatres and co-edited *The Faber Guide to
Victorian Churches*.

World of Art

This famous series provides the widest available range of
illustrated books on art in all its aspects. If you would like
to receive a complete list of titles in print please write to:

THAMES AND HUDSON
181A High Holborn
London WC1V 7QX

In the United States please write to:

THAMES AND HUDSON INC.
500 Fifth Avenue
New York, New York 10110

Printed in Singapore

Karl Friedrich Schinkel
Gothic Cathedral on a River, 1813

Ian Sutton

Western Architecture
A Survey from
Ancient Greece
to the Present

456 illustrations

THAMES AND HUDSON

For Emily

British Library Cataloguing-in-Publication Data
A catalogue record for this book is available from the British Library

ISBN 0-500-20316-4

Designed by Derek Birdsall
Typeset by Omnific Studios

Printed and bound in Singapore by C.S. Graphics

Contents

7   Introduction

Chapter 1

10   **Prologue: Laying the Foundations – Greece and Rome**
The rule of the orders . The urban setting .
Rome, the heir of Greece . Vitruvius, a text for the future

Chapter 2

24   **The Christian Legacy of Rome**
Constantine and the New Rome . The Byzantine achievement .
The Byzantine legacy . Western Europe: darkness before dawn

Chapter 3

38   **Beginning Again: Carolingian and Romanesque**
The Carolingian Renaissance to *c.* 1000 .
Germany: the Imperial lands . France: diversity in unity .
The Normans in Britain . Romanesque in the south: Italy and Spain

Chapter 4

74   **The Gothic Centuries**
How Gothic began . The first Gothic century: France, 1150–1250 .
Gothic England . How Gothic ended . Secular and domestic

Chapter 5

126   **The Renaissance: Ancient Rome 'Reborn'**
Florence: the Early Renaissance . Rome: the High Renaissance .
The problem of Mannerism . A developing Renaissance .
The Renaissance outside Italy: Eastern and Central Europe .
England, France and Spain: problems of adaptation

Chapter 6

168   **Baroque and Anti-Baroque**
Baroque in Italy: the seed-bed . Central and Eastern Europe:
the flowering . Spain, Portugal and Latin America: the exotic
harvest . France: a special case . Flanders and the Netherlands .
England and North America

Chapter 7

224   **The Return of Classicism**
Phases of classicism: from Palladio to the Revolution .
Palaces, ministries and the Neoclassical city .
Privileged domesticity . Culture and commerce .
Classicism and Christianity . Four architectural portraits

Chapter 8

268   **'In What Style Shall We Build?'**
Why Neo-Gothic? . Architecture and morality .
Revivals and survivals . The new art . Houses and homes

Chapter 9

304   **After Style, Modernism**
Iron, glass and honesty . The doctrine of Modernism .
Modernism and national character . Alternatives to Modernism .
Three nonconformists

Chapter 10

354   **Epilogue: After Modernism, Style**
The legacy of Modernism . Ingredients of Post-Modernism .
Variety and scale . Present dilemmas

372   Glossary
375   Further Reading
376   Acknowledgments and Illustration Credits
377   Index

Introduction

Nikolaus Pevsner began his classic *Outline of European Architecture* (1943) with what he thought was a statement of the obvious: 'A bicycle shed is a building; Lincoln Cathedral is a piece of architecture.' In the event, no sentence in the book proved to be more controversial. Today, nobody would dare say such a thing. Architecture is no longer seen as a series of isolated great buildings, monuments, works of art: it is the totality of 'the built environment'. Cottages, farms, urban housing, factories and motorway junctions have now to be carefully researched and incorporated into architectural history (bicycle sheds still don't get much coverage). Pevsner's own *History of Building Types* (1976), which includes chapters on hospitals, prisons, warehouses, office buildings and shops, was itself an acknowledgment of the shift. The extreme of this new point of view is Reyner Banham's definition of architecture as 'that which changes land-use'.

A comparable shift has taken place in art history and literary history, where the so-called canon (the body of works traditionally recognized as 'great') has been rejected or downgraded and attention focuses instead on everything drawn, painted or written: folk-art, child-art, caricature, graffiti, videos, newspapers, broadsheets, pamphlets, advertisements, sermons, pulp fiction, pornography... The motivation behind these moves is the conviction that the canon (whether literary, artistic or architectural) is an unrepresentative and élitist selection chosen by a privileged, educated class to embody its own values and impose them on the rest of society.

Of architecture this is almost self-evidently true. One does not have to be a Marxist to see that the great castles and cathedrals of the Middle Ages, the palaces and country houses of later times, the parliaments and government buildings, even the theatres and museums, were all (whatever else) blatant expressions of authority and power and the desire to display that power. Should this be a reason for rejecting or downgrading them? That question must wait.

The main effect of such ideas, however, has been unequivocally positive: to bring architectural history closer to social history. We now have a better understanding of how buildings relate to communities and how economic and technical factors determine their form; and we have fresh insights into the urban fabric – how villages grow organically, how cities and suburbs develop and shape the lives of those who inhabit them.

Parallel with these approaches has gone the 'politicization' of architecture – the study of how ideologies have created buildings and in some cases demolished them. In 1789, Ledoux's *barrières* round Paris were so associated in the popular mind with the hated tax system that mobs attacked them and pulled some of them down. In the 19th century, the Gothic style became identified in the Rhineland with the Catholic, anti-Prussian party, and the completion of Cologne Cathedral in that style was undoubtedly a political statement. In our own times, the resumption of work on Gaudí's Sagrada Familia in Barcelona is likewise an assertion of Catalan nationalism. After the Second World War the old Berlin Schloss, a building of outstanding interest, was demolished by the East Germans because of its associations with Nazi militarism, a decision they now regret. And the fact that both the Nazi and Communist dictatorships favoured classical architecture still casts a baleful cloud over the orders, as the 1995 exhibition *Art and Power* in London demonstrated.

But most buildings outlive their original purpose. Castles no longer intimidate us. Country houses are no longer bastions of power. The Church no longer rules our lives. The accusation of élitism has to do only with the circumstances of their creation. The canon, by contrast, is based on the simple idea that architecture is an art, that certain buildings excel in that art, and that such excellence is to be (among other things) enjoyed. There is, of course, more to excellence than pleasure. Rather than venture into aesthetic theory, I fall back on a sentence from Robert Pirsig's *Zen and the Art of Motorcycle Maintenance*, a prolonged allegorical quest for excellence, which Pirsig calls Quality. Realizing that it can be neither objective nor subjective, he finally takes refuge in a sort of mysticism: 'Quality is the continuing stimulus which our environment puts upon us to create the world in which we live.' Is not this exactly what we hope architecture is doing?

A 70,000-word introduction to the entire history of Western architecture is not a place to look for new information or startling reappraisals. Nonetheless, this book is, and has to be, different from one written ten years ago. It is a truism that the present is conditioned by the past, but it is almost equally true that the past is conditioned by the present. If there had been no International Modernism, would anyone have paid attention to the Sheerness boat-store of 1859? If the Cold War had not ended, should we be looking so benignly on Stalinist architecture? If Post-Modernism had not happened, should we be so fascinated by Plečnik?

There is also the process of discovery – not so much discovery of facts as awakening to facts already known. In this sense Italian Baroque was 'discovered' in the 1930s, Central European Baroque in the 1950s, and that of Eastern Europe only in the 1980s. There is still no book in English on the Bohemian Johann Santini-Aichel, one of the world's supreme architectural geniuses.

One question that cannot be evaded is: Where does Western architecture begin? Some would say with ancient Egypt, or further back still with the early civilizations of Mesopotamia. There is a case to be made for these views. But if one is looking for a point that marks the start of a definable and continuous tradition, a tradition that was never forgotten and that has gone on determining the forms of architecture down to the present day, that point has to be Greece and Rome. That is where our history begins; the rest is prehistory.

Since this is written for students and the general reader, I have thought it best to concentrate on buildings, architects, dates, functions and styles rather than to attempt much in the way of social background or theory. This may be unfashionable, but unless the reader knows what Gothic architecture is, what Alberti thought, or what a church by Borromini looks like, he or she is not going to get much from a discussion of theory. That can come later. The views expressed here are therefore those generally accepted, though personal bias may have crept in sometimes. I hope so.

I. S.

London, 1998

A note on dates: For the sake of simplicity and easy memorizing, most buildings are here given a single date only, which is the date when they were begun. When they were finished is usually (though not always) unimportant, and anyway difficult to decide, so that no two books agree. Birth and death dates of architects are given in the index.

Prologue

Chapter 1:   Laying the Foundations – Greece and Rome

Students of the history of architecture need to know about Greek and Roman buildings, but are unlikely to spend much time looking at them. The reason is that so few of them survive. Of all classical buildings that are relatively intact and standing to their full height there cannot be more than a hundred, and a number of those have been converted to serve new purposes, like the Baths of Diocletian in Rome, now a church. If we add all the houses in Pompeii and Herculaneum, and count triumphal arches, monuments and aqueducts, the figure will doubtless rise, but generally speaking classical architecture is more important as an idea, as an inspiration to future ages, than as an experienced reality. This chapter will therefore concentrate on those aspects that were important and influential later, giving as much attention to the treatise by the 1st-century BC Roman writer Vitruvius, whose book all architects after the 15th century would have known, as to most of the buildings, which they may well not have seen.

It seems to have been realized by the ancient Greeks, certainly by Vitruvius, that the earliest temples were made of wood, and that the stone structures that succeeded them were masonry versions of timber originals. This explains several features that would otherwise be puzzling. The capital was originally a piece of timber between a vertical post and a horizontal beam. The pediment was the gable-end of the roof. The cornice was the eaves. The triglyphs (tablets with three grooves over the columns and in the spaces between them) were the decorated ends of the beams. The guttae (small studs under the triglyphs) were pegs or nails.

1. The Greek Doric order is unsurpassed as an expression of strength and solidity, emphasized by the slight swelling of the columns in the middle and narrowing at the top. The 'Basilica' (more properly the Temple of Hera) at Paestum in southern Italy, late 6th century BC, is among the earliest to have survived.

By the time the first stone temples were built (about 600 BC) they already followed a standard plan that was hardly to vary for centuries: the *cella*, a plain room, the seat of the god, was normally left empty except for an image; it was not used in worship. A room at the back served as a treasury. Smaller temples would be fronted by a portico with four columns; larger ones were completely surrounded by a colonnade (the peristyle), which had no function except to signal that this was a ceremonial and sacred building.

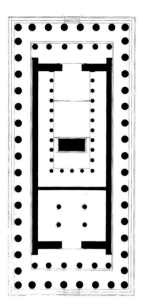

2. Opposite above, and above: the Parthenon (dedicated to Athena *parthenos*, 'the virgin') on the Acropolis of Athens, c. 440 BC, employs the same optical subtleties as the Paestum temple (ill. 1), but in a more refined form.

3, 4. Nearly every 5th-century Doric temple – here the Theseion in Athens (centre) and the Temple of Apollo at Bassae (below) – conforms to a standard design, though in each case the architect introduced variants of his own.

The rule of the orders

Columns are only one element, if the most important, of the three 'orders' of Greek architecture, which serve to categorize nearly all classical buildings: Doric, Ionic and Corinthian. The most obvious difference between them is their capitals, but an order includes the entablature (the horizontal area above the columns, consisting of architrave, frieze and cornice), the capital, the shaft itself and the base. It involves both design and proportion.

Chronologically, the Doric and Ionic orders came first. The Dorians were the early inhabitants of mainland Greece, while the Ionians lived on the coast of Asia Minor (now Turkey) and the islands. Doric and Ionic seem to have been equally ancient. The Doric order consisted of a fairly squat fluted column, swelling in the middle (*entasis*) and narrowing towards the top, with a capital like a cushion and no base. The columns were made up of drum-shaped sections held together by metal spikes. Above the columns the entablature was decorated by square panels incised with vertical grooves (triglyphs) alternating with other panels that could be blank or sculptured (metopes). The Ionic order was taller and slimmer, its capital was distinguished by scrolls or volutes at the corners, and it had a base. The third order, the Corinthian, the most ornate of the three, had a high base and a capital of acanthus foliage. With all three orders the triangular pediments were made the occasion for figure sculpture.

Temples were on a large scale from the beginning. The Ionic Temple of Artemis at Ephesus in Asia Minor was built about 560 BC. It had columns 65 feet (20m) high with bands of life-size figures around the bases. Of about the same date is the earliest preserved Doric temple, the 'Basilica' at Paestum in southern Italy, which has flat cushion capitals and very pronounced *entasis*. Both orders are represented by buildings of great beauty from the mid-5th century on the Athenian Acropolis – the tiny graceful Ionic Temple of Athena Nike and the sturdier Doric Parthenon, dedicated to Athena, one of the major temples of the Greek world. The Parthenon was unorthodox in having a continuous frieze of sculpture around the exterior of the *cella*, dimly visible high up within the colonnade. Inside, the roof was supported by a two-storey colonnade, with a 40-foot (12m) high gilded statue of Athena standing above a pool of reflecting water.

Below the hill of the Acropolis stands the almost contemporary 'Theseion' (more properly the Temple of Hephaestos), smaller but better preserved than the Parthenon. Outside Athens are a number of fragmentary Doric temples – Aegina (early 5th

1

2

3

century), Sunion (mid-5th), Bassae (late 5th). Bassae is unusual 4
in some respects; it had a sculptured frieze running around the
inside of the *cella* wall, and a single Corinthian column, also in
the interior.

Some of the best-preserved temples are in the Greek colonies
of Italy and Sicily. At Paestum, south of Naples, are three temples
side by side in a low, formerly swampy area near the sea: the
'Basilica', the 'Temple of Ceres' (late 6th century) and the 'Temple 1
of Neptune' (mid-5th). In Sicily, several temples still crown the
ridge outside Agrigento (the ancient Acragas), while the unfin- 5
ished temple at Segesta (late 5th century) reveals much about the
way these buildings were constructed.

By the 5th century Doric temples had become standardized
and extremely refined. Many of these refinements are detectable
only by careful measurement. Apart from the *entasis*, the columns
all lean very slightly inward. Corner columns are made slightly
thicker, since they are seen against the open sky. The platform or
stylobate on which they rest rises equally slightly towards
the middle. All these adjustments were intended to correct any
tendency to a feeling of top-heaviness or instability.

Even as ruins, these Doric temples are powerful and moving
evocations of strength and singleness of purpose. Their abstract
geometry is grasped at first glance, all the details merely reinforc-
ing the initial impact. In their original state, plastered and with the
details picked out in bright colours, their effect might have been

5. Lucidity, order, finite geometry
immediately comprehensible to
the eye and mind – these are the
key qualities of the Doric temple.
Enclosed, self-contained, there
is not even a hint of a way in:
the Temple of Concord, Agrigento,
Sicily, *c.* 430 BC.

rather different. Set as they are on craggy headlands overlooking the sea or amid sublime mountain scenery (to which the Greeks seem to have been profoundly indifferent), it is difficult not to see them through romantic eyes and react with emotions quite foreign to their builders. Such is the fate of all architecture as it recedes in time.

Far fewer Ionic temples survive than Doric. The Erechtheion on the Acropolis (late 5th century) is unique in its plan and many of its features, including the famous caryatid porch. The volutes of the Ionic capital (which can take several variant forms) convey grace as well as strength, and the taller, slenderer proportions give an elegance traditionally regarded as 'feminine'.

The Corinthian order came last and was not often used by the Greeks, though it was taken up with enthusiasm by the Romans. The remains we now see of the Temple of Olympian Zeus in Athens were built, on a vast scale, about 170 BC, at the very time when Greece was passing under Roman control. There were precedents for these extravagantly large proportions. At Agrigento, the triglyphs of the Temple of Olympian Zeus (late 5th century) are so large that an adult can comfortably lie down in one of the grooves. The building was to incorporate thirty or so giant Atlas figures holding up the walls. The Temple of Apollo at Didyma, in Asia Minor (3rd century), is 350 feet long, surrounded by a double peristyle of 108 huge Ionic columns, and so big that it could not be roofed.

6. The little Ionic temple of the Erechtheion (Erechtheus was a mythical king of Athens) on the Acropolis is an exception to all the rules. Built in the late 5th century BC, it has no peristyle but two porticoes; its most famous feature is the caryatid porch in the foreground.

7. The theatre at Epidaurus (c. 350 BC) preserves its circular *orchestra* for the chorus. The stage building beyond, probably of two storeys, has disappeared.

8. The Choragic Monument of Lysicrates in Athens (334 BC) reflects the form of a Greek *tholos*, a circular structure that goes back to Mycenaean tombs. The order here is Corinthian.

The urban setting

Temples were often only a part of much larger sacred precincts, whole complexes of buildings – shrines, altars, treasuries, theatres – linked by processional ways and lined by sculpture. Monumental as they were, there is an organic feeling about these precincts, a freedom from formality, that must have made them endlessly intriguing to move through. The Athenian Acropolis is such a space on a small scale. Much more elaborate, since they were in theory not the preserve of any single city or political power, were the centres of Delphi, Olympia, Epidaurus, Pergamon, Ephesus and the island of Delos. They show the Greeks to have had an instinct for imaginative planning to a degree that makes the Romans seem almost mechanical.

The theatres, which were also religious buildings, occupied sloping sites, with the auditorium hollowed out of a hillside. Originally, the dance-floor (*orchestra*) where the chorus stood was circular, as can still be seen at Epidaurus (mid-4th century). As Greek drama progressed, this area was made semicircular and the stage behind it grew more important. Behind the stage was a permanent architectural background with three doors, through which the actors entered.

Two other Greek buildings should be mentioned, not so much because they are important in themselves but because they survive prominently in Athens and were much imitated by Neoclassical architects: the Choragic Monument of Lysicrates and the Tower of the Winds. The first commemorates a prize won in 334 BC for providing a chorus in the theatre. Set on a square base, it consists of a cylinder surrounded by six attached Corinthian columns and a sculptured frieze. On the top a bronze tripod supported a cauldron. The second (1st century BC) was a clock tower, or *horologium*, incorporating a water clock and a wind vane, with sundials fixed to its eight sides. Around the top are reliefs representing the winds.

Rome, the heir of Greece

Aesthetically the Romans were content to follow Greek precedents; structurally they improved on them. Whereas Greek architecture can, not unfairly, be discussed largely in terms of temples, Roman demands a much wider perspective. But we may conveniently begin with temples, as they provide the readiest connection between the two.

Roman temples were not replicas of Greek. Typically they used the Corinthian or Ionic orders, almost never the Doric; they were raised upon a podium approached by steps; they usually had a portico one or two columns deep at one end and often attached demi-columns along the sides, rather than a free-standing colonnade all round. A typical Roman temple is the well preserved Maison Carrée at Nîmes in southern France (16 BC). 9

This was the standard. But after the 1st century AD Roman architecture grew freer, introducing forms that would have shocked earlier builders like Vitruvius (see pp. 22–23), ending with a phase that has been aptly christened 'Baroque'. The Temple of Bacchus at Baalbek, in Lebanon (early 3rd century AD), is surrounded by a peristyle (itself unusual) of unfluted Corinthian columns (also unusual), the ceiling of which is tunnel-vaulted and decorated with the busts of gods (even more unusual). Most unusual of all, it had an extremely lavish interior, lined with Corinthian demi-columns between arched recesses below and aedicule niches above containing full-size statues. The altar was an elaborate miniature building incorporating a 'broken' pediment, i.e. one that breaks off in the middle, leaving two triangular ends. All this brings it much closer to a church of the future than to any Greek temple of the past. 10

The contemporary circular 'Temple of Venus', also at Baalbek, is equally un-Greek. The Greeks did build circular structures, though they were not temples, and Roman examples are fairly frequent (often dedicated to Vesta, goddess of the hearth). What is peculiar about this one is not simply that it stands on a high podium reached by steps and uses the unfluted Corinthian order, but that its sides are pierced by niches and above the niches the entablature is correspondingly indented. It too has a large portico, again with a broken pediment.

The largest of all circular temples, completely outside the normal parameters, is the Pantheon in Rome (early 2nd century AD), dedicated to 'all the gods', or rather to the seven planetary deities. The interior was faced with coloured marble (the upper storey somewhat altered during the Renaissance, and all largely replaced by plaster in the 18th century) and covered by a vast coffered dome, with a central oculus open to the sky. Here, as nowhere else, one can experience a Roman building in its entirety. Unlike any Greek building but like virtually any Byzantine one, it is conceived from the inside out. The exterior is of no account: it is the interior that matters. Henceforward we shall see these two concepts, two ways of imagining structure and space, alternating, coming together and separating.

The Pantheon also introduces us to Roman technology. It is built of brick and concrete, materials that suggested new forms and opened up new possibilities. The Pantheon's dome, once the concrete had set, was rigid, exerting pressure vertically downward onto the circular wall. Concrete, arches and tunnel vaults were not strictly new inventions, but their combination was to produce structures on a scale never before seen in the West. The Basilica of Maxentius in Rome (completed by Constantine around 313 AD) comprised a central hall, or 'nave', covered with three quadripartite groin vaults (produced by the meeting of two tunnel vaults) resting on eight monolithic Corinthian columns. On either

9, 10. The Romans modified the concept of the temple in several ways. One was a new emphasis on direction, with a deep portico marking the entrance, and the rest of the peristyle 'recessed' into the wall (below: Maison Carrée, Nîmes, 16 BC); another was to enhance the status given to the interior (right: Temple of Bacchus, Baalbek, 3rd century AD).

11. The Pantheon, Rome, is virtually the only place where a complete Roman interior can be experienced (although even that is not quite true, since the middle storey was altered in the Renaissance). Built by the Emperor Hadrian between AD 118 and 128, its main cylinder is of brick, structured as a series of relieving arches which are visible on the exterior but totally concealed inside by marble-faced niches behind columns and (originally) marble veneer above; the dome is solid concrete.

side, arches led into tunnel-vaulted 'transepts'. All the vaults were coffered and the interior walls covered with marble veneer.

Basilicas (the name goes back to the royal hall of a king) were public assembly halls or law courts. That of Maxentius is exceptional in being vaulted. More normally, as in the Basilica of Trajan (early 2nd century AD), they consisted of buildings with a central nave flanked by aisles divided from the centre by rows of columns. The columns supported walls that rose above aisle height, containing windows (literally a 'clear storey'), and a wooden roof. There was often an apse at the end opposite the door.

Magnificent rooms in more varied shapes were to be found in the baths, very large complexes of buildings including hot and cold pools, fountains, dressing rooms, gymnasia and public assembly halls. There were several such complexes in Rome (those of Caracalla and Diocletian survive fairly intact) and at least one in all the major provincial towns, for instance at Pompeii in southern

Italy, Leptis Magna in Libya, and Paris (where large parts remain in the present Hôtel de Cluny). With most of these, the contrast between plain exterior and rich interior is again remarkable; from outside, the so-called Hunting Baths of Leptis look like a collection of air-raid shelters.

When so much Greek and Roman life was public, it comes as a surprise to find how private they were at home. This must partly have been due to the position of women, kept secluded as wives and mothers. From the street the house was virtually faceless. Inside the rooms opened off an atrium, typically open to the sky and surrounded by a colonnade, with a pool in the middle. In the country, villas had a more open aspect, but the planning was essentially the same. Roman domestic lifestyle and Roman baths are two aspects of the classical world which passed to Byzantium and then to Islamic civilization, where, having disappeared from the West, they still prevail.

Roman theatres followed Greek models fairly closely, though they did not rely on sloping sites but were built up on arches. The back of the stage, the *scenae frons*, became a highly elaborate architectural composition, which survives at Leptis and Sabratha in Libya, Aspendos in Turkey, Orange in France, and elsewhere. More exclusively Roman are the amphitheatres for gladiatorial combats, animal fights and general bloody entertainment. The

12. The Basilica of Maxentius, Rome (early 4th century AD). The central groin-vaulted 'nave' has disappeared and we are looking at the three massive tunnel-vaulted bays opening off one side; there would have been a matching trio opposite.

13. The Colosseum in Rome, built in AD 75–80 by the Emperor Vespasian, was the biggest amphitheatre in the world. Its major achievement was structural, but from the point of view of the future its importance lies in its use of superimposed orders – Doric, Ionic, and Corinthian demi-columns (unfluted) and Corinthian pilasters for the attic storey.

biggest and most famous, the Colosseum in Rome (1st century AD), is architecturally significant because it set the precedent (partially anticipated in the Theatre of Marcellus) for superimposing the orders one above the other, with Doric at the bottom, Ionic in the middle and Corinthian at the top, an arrangement that would probably have seemed distressingly vulgar to the Greeks. It was also the model for combining tiers of identical arches (structural) with a system of the orders supporting a flat entablature applied (non-structurally) to the wall, thus turning what had been a logical expression of function into a decorative sham. It was the beginning of a kind of architectural fiction upon which all the various classical revivals were to be based.

As a feat of engineering and planning, however, the Colosseum (and numberless other amphitheatres all over the Empire) is a triumph. Over 45,000 spectators could enter, enjoy the spectacle and leave without congestion or discomfort. It is ironic, but perhaps not unfitting, that this huge building, dedicated to such repulsive purposes, should have become the symbol of Roman greatness.

As engineers the Romans were not to be surpassed for centuries. Future ages looked with wonder at the aqueducts, bridges, walls, forums, markets and roads as 'the work of giants'. Many of these structures had a military function, and the same can be said of the founding and construction of whole new towns on regular chequer-board plans. At Palmyra and at certain North African towns such as Timgad and Leptis Magna one can wander for miles through Roman streets and appreciate the discipline of their layout. At Trier, in Germany, one can walk through the four-storey, double-arched town gate, the Porta Nigra. At Pompeii one can enter the homes of the wealthy middle classes, their luxurious way of life still vividly present. At Ostia, the port of Rome, one can penetrate the tall, dark tenements where the poor lived. In Rome itself one can stand inside the market of Trajan, its roof still above one's head and the shop-fronts on either side. At Tivoli one can lose oneself in the dreams of the Emperor Hadrian re-creating his past through the architecture of memory. At Split, across the Adriatic, most of the Emperor Diocletian's palace survives, now containing a small town.

Town-planning and engineering fall outside the limits of this book, but these vestiges of Roman power cannot fail to impress us. It is hard, for instance, not to regard the three great tiers of arches of the Pont du Gard, the aqueduct near Nîmes, as a work of art. Closer to the conventional definition of that term are the triumphal arches erected by the score to glorify emperors and generals, which often survive intact. Most consist of a single arch framed by the Corinthian order and surmounted by an attic storey with an inscription. Sometime there are three arches (a large central one flanked by two smaller) and a lavish use of sculpture. The most spectacular is the Arch of Constantine, in Rome (early 4th century AD), but one can find examples in every country of the Empire. Triumphal arches enjoyed an astonishingly long life throughout history, and appear in a variety of forms. 27

Vitruvius, a text for the future
Up to the 2nd century BC, classical architecture was, on the whole, fairly conservative. Things changed slowly and only in minor ways. It was therefore not difficult for writers on the subject to generalize and reduce it to a set of rules. We know from the text of Vitruvius that he was not the only such writer, but his treatise, written in the 1st century BC, is the only one to survive and so gained a perhaps undue degree of authority. Vitruvius gives us a certain amount of theory but most of his book is severely practical.

He covers basic topics such as building materials, foundations, walls, windows and roofs, and then goes on to the various types of building that an architect would be expected to design, including temples, theatres, forums, basilicas and houses. The qualities he recommends (archetypically classical) are harmony, symmetry, decorum and strength.

Only a small part of Vitruvius' book was relevant to later architects, notably that which dealt with the design of temples and the use of the orders. He is carefully, indeed tediously, systematic. He classifies temples according to the order used, the number of columns along the front and the sides, and whether the rows are single or double. Although he is ostensibly merely describing current practice, he naturally falls into prescriptive language: 'capitals *should be* proportioned...', 'the face of the volute *must* recede from the edge of the abacus...', 'the height of the capital *is to be* divided into nine and a half parts...' So there was always a tendency to read him as a schoolmaster laying down rules, despite the fact that many classical buildings did not conform to those rules.

It is to Vitruvius that we owe the characterization of Doric as reflecting the masculine, Ionic the maturely feminine and Corinthian the young girl. On the actual management of the orders he goes into minute detail, describing the exact form of the capital, the elements of the entablature, the proportion of height to diameter, the intercolumniation (space between columns), the degree of *entasis*, the number of flutes, the size of the base, and many other features. The subject, indeed, lends itself readily to this sort of rather pedantic discussion, so that one finds in later architects and critics prolonged debate over such questions as the positioning of the triglyphs of the Doric order when one comes to a corner: normally they are placed over the centre of the column, but if this is done with the last column in a row there will be a space between the triglyph and the corner. That can be avoided by moving the triglyph to the corner and slightly displacing the one next to it, so that it does not sit exactly over the centre of the column. This is merely one of many similar problems that arise in classical architecture. No part, however small, can be changed without entailing changes elsewhere. Lutyens called it 'the High Game'.

The break-up of the Roman Empire and the rise of Christianity changed the face of architecture. It was to be a thousand years before the High Game was played again.

Chapter 2:   The Christian Legacy of Rome

Constantine made Christianity the official religion of the Roman Empire in 326, and immediately set in motion an ambitious programme of church building in Rome and the East. Between then and his death in 337 six major churches were begun: Old St Peter's, Rome; St John Lateran, Rome; S. Maria Maggiore, Rome; Old St Sophia, Constantinople; the Nativity, Bethlehem; and the Holy Sepulchre, Jerusalem. The Holy Sepulchre was peculiar in having to incorporate the reputed tomb of Christ. The rest were all built to the same 'basilican' plan.

Constantine and the New Rome
Buildings of the type of the Basilica of Trajan, described in the last chapter, became the models for Constantine's churches. The word 'basilica' has come to be used confusingly in two senses – ecclesiastically for a church of a certain rank, and architecturally for a building with colonnades or arcades opening into aisles and a higher central vessel lit by clearstorey windows.

These first Christian churches were not small; they were almost as big as anything in the Roman world. Old St Peter's, which was demolished about 1500 but is well known from drawings, was over 350 feet (107m) long and had double aisles. There was a wide transept at the end and an apse where the altar stood. St John Lateran had a similar plan; it survives structurally but was transformed into a Baroque church by Borromini, though it retains its 4th-century octagonal baptistery. S. Maria Maggiore has also been altered, but not unrecognizably and still gives a good idea of its Early Christian appearance. Old St Sophia, Constantinople, has totally disappeared. The Nativity in Bethlehem, also double-aisled, was rebuilt in the 6th century but followed the original arrangement.

Not all of Constantine's foundations followed the same lines, though the more unusual examples have all perished. In Milan, the church of S. Lorenzo (370) survives in reconstructed form, a unique quatrefoil plan opening through concave arcades to a circular ambulatory. Even stranger was the martyrium of Qalat Siman in Syria (470), which had four long-aisled arms (four basilicas in fact) meeting at a central octagon.

14. The nave of Constantine's St Peter's, Rome, early 4th century, looking towards the entrance. The chief church of Western Christendom was a plain basilican structure with open wooden roofs: the central colonnade supported a flat entablature and small clearstorey, and was flanked by double aisles – an unusual feature. The inscription notes that it was 'demolished under Paul V'.

CONTIGNATIO·TECTI·PARTIS
VETER·BASIL·SVB·PAVLO·V·
DEMOLITAE·

The basilican plan remained standard in Italy, even after the Ostrogothic conquest in the early 5th century, since they were converted to Christianity (e.g. S. Sabina, Rome, 425, and St Paul without the Walls, Rome, begun in 480). But architecturally the initiative passed to the Eastern Empire centred upon Constantine's new capital of Constantinople. (The adjective 'Byzantine', from the old Greek name of the city, is used for the art and culture of this Eastern Empire.) Here the basilican form, seen, for instance, at St John of Studion, Constantinople (463), and St Demetrius at Salonika (late 5th century), soon gave way to a new concept of church-building based upon Roman brick and concrete structures and particularly the dome. Most Roman domes had been built over circular bases, e.g. the Pantheon and the *calidarium* (hot room) of the Baths of Caracalla. The so-called Temple of Minerva Medica in Rome (early 4th century AD) had broken new ground by placing a dome over a decagonal arcade and buttressing it with a ring of apsidal chapels. There were also, it seems fairly certain, eastern influences from outside the Empire. From the 3rd

15. S. Maria Maggiore, Rome, still keeps its Early Christian appearance. An earlier church was rebuilt by Sixtus III in 432. Later popes added the pavement (12th century), the ceiling (16th century) and the baldacchino over the altar (18th century).

century the Sassanians in Iran were capable of building domes over non-circular spaces. That of the palace at Bishapur (*c.* AD 200) had four sides opening into tunnel vaults and big niches across the corners, while the palace of Sarvistan used squinches (concentric arches of brick or stone) across the corners to convert the square into a circle.

Byzantine architects must have been familiar with these buildings, but it is still a matter for amazement that they could so quickly and confidently apply the new techniques on such a large scale. (Their confidence was in fact excessive and the first dome of the new St Sophia collapsed and had to be rebuilt.) Essentially, the Byzantine style was already fully formed by the accession of the greatest of the builder-emperors, Justinian (527–565).

The Byzantine achievement

St Sophia in Constantinople, or more correctly Hagia Sophia (the 16 Holy Wisdom), begun 532, is one of the high points of Western architecture, a building in which design and execution are perfectly matched and which never fails to give the authentic *frisson* of a work of genius. It was the first time that such a huge space (225 × 107 feet/69 × 33m) had been vaulted without intermediate supports. The architects – whose names are known: Anthemius of Tralles and Isidore of Miletus – seem to have been aiming above all at an effect of lightness. The reasons why the whole structure stands up are concealed. One has the feeling, as a contemporary put it, that the dome 'is suspended by a chain from heaven'.

In fact, of course, the system of supports is worked out with the greatest care. The dome itself rests on four arches springing from four massive piers. The corners of the resulting square are bridged by pendentives, a more sophisticated form of squinch, consisting of a concave triangle of masonry, or section of a sphere. The dome itself is dangerously shallow and is ringed at its base by a circle of windows, so that it does indeed seem almost weightless. The central space is apparently completely open at east and west (i.e. the altar and entrance ends), but is in fact supported by semi-domes which lean against the arches, transmitting the stress to a lower level and then by further stages to the ground. The north and south sides consist of two tiers of slender arcades and lunette walls pierced by windows – again clearly not load-bearing. But outside, hidden from within, are four massive buttresses that take the thrust of the dome in those directions.

The columns are of coloured marble, the capitals of white marble sculpted with the use of the drill, the lower wall-surfaces faced

16. Justinian's church of Hagia Sophia, Constantinople (532), was an achievement without parallel in world architecture, and one that was not to be equalled until the great age of Gothic cathedrals. Its structure concealed under marble veneer and mosaic, it admits light miraculously at every level, creating an atmosphere of heightened emotion in tune with the Byzantine liturgy that it served.

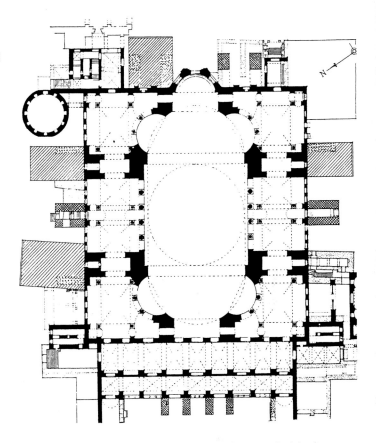

with marble veneer, and the upper originally covered with glass mosaic. The impact is still sensational and must have been even more so in Justinian's time, as a setting for Byzantine ritual and filled with Byzantine music.

There could be no second Hagia Sophia. Indeed no other Byzantine church ever approached it in scale; it remains unique. The church of St Irene in Constantinople (6th century, much rebuilt) is a reduced version of it, with two domes instead of one, giving a more longitudinal emphasis. St John at Ephesus, completed in 565, had three. Much later, Hagia Sophia's influence is evident on the great mosques built by the Ottoman Turks after they conquered the city in 1453 and renamed it Istanbul.

More immediately influential was another of Justinian's churches in Constantinople, the small SS. Sergius and Bacchus, begun slightly earlier than Hagia Sophia. Here the dome is built over an octagon, the sides of which open through triple arcades that are alternately straight and curved into a continuous

17

17. The church of SS. Sergius and Bacchus in Constantinople was another of Justinian's foundations, but on a much smaller scale than Hagia Sophia. The plan is equally inventive, seven of its eight sides opening by two-storeyed bays alternately straight and concave into a surrounding ambulatory. Only at the east end is the whole elevation given a single arch leading to the chancel. (When it was converted into a mosque the orientation was changed, making it look skew.)

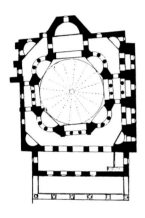

ambulatory going right round the church. This results in intriguing spaces and vistas, though the plan, a rough square, lacks regularity. When Justinian conquered Ravenna, the Ostrogothic capital in north Italy, he built S. Vitale, which is an improved version of SS. Sergius and Bacchus. Here the whole church is an octagon, the eight compartments under the dome opening symmetrically through concave triple arcades into the octagonal ambulatory. S. Vitale is especially noted for its mosaic decoration, which includes the famous panels of Justinian and Theodora.

19

Another of Justinian's churches, the Holy Apostles in Constantinople, had a Greek-cross plan and domes over the crossing and the arms. This was destroyed by the Turks but was probably the model for St Mark's, Venice, the most Byzantine of Western churches. The five domes, the coloured marble screens and the mosaics all look back to Byzantine precedents.

18

18. The Byzantine legacy in Italy. St Mark's, Venice, begun in 1063, appears to have been based on Justinian's Holy Apostles in Constantinople, now destroyed. Venice's strong links with the Eastern Empire give St Mark's a strongly Byzantine atmosphere.

19. S. Vitale, Ravenna, 6th century, is closely modelled on SS. Sergius and Bacchus (ill. 17) but now all the bays are concave. Ravenna was part of Justinian's empire.

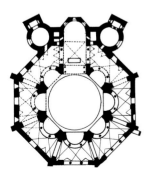

The Byzantine legacy

Within the Byzantine cultural orbit but (usually) politically independent was Armenia, a territory now divided between Turkey and the republics of Georgia and Armenia, formerly parts of the Soviet Union. Armenia was the setting for a brilliant architectural flowering which would figure much more prominently in the history books if it were not nearly all in ruins and virtually inaccessible. The Cathedral of Ani (10th century) is a longitudinal church of three bays given central emphasis by a dome over the middle bay; it has a claim to be the first building to use the pointed arch. Even more interesting is a series of smaller churches of the early 7th century with centralized plans. They are variants on S. Vitale at Ravenna, but circular instead of octagonal and with inner arcades, quatrefoil in plan, rising through three stages to a dome. Several small churches of the 6th century in what is now Georgia have quatrefoil, hexafoil and octofoil plans. Another frequent variant is a Greek-cross plan with four apses and four square chapels in the corners. It is hard to know whether these Armenian buildings are really as original as they seem. Excavations at Antioch in Syria have revealed a plan of the 5th century that is a quatrefoil-in-circle; another at Hierapolis (Pamukkale) in Turkey of the same date has an octagon-within-octagon. So there were clearly Byzantine precedents.

After Armenia, the European legacy of Byzantium comes as rather an anticlimax. When Constantinople fell the Eastern Church became the Greek Orthodox Church. The construction of churches was tolerated but not encouraged under Ottoman rule. They are tiny in scale and architecturally unremarkable, either longitudinally or centrally planned but nearly always domed. Their interior surfaces are so covered with mosaic or fresco decoration which totally ignores the structure that they hardly register as architecture. Their most striking feature is usually the iconostasis, a screen that shuts off the whole eastern part of the church, accessible only to the priest. Dark, intimate, mysterious, the faces of warrior saints glowing in the candlelight, they are still powerfully evocative of a Christian tradition that has changed very little in the last five hundred years. Most old Greek towns have such a church, specially notable ones being at Athens, Salonika and the monasteries of Mount Athos.

Further from Constantinople, in the former Yugoslavia, are more ambitious churches, following no standard plan but almost all with domes. One local variant, popular in Greece and Serbia, was the 'cross-in-square' plan, a square divided into nine, with a

20. One region where the Byzantine lead was followed most intensively was Armenia (now partly in Georgia, partly in Turkey). Here a whole series of highly ingenious churches was built, of which only fragments remain. That of Zwartnots (mid-7th century) looks back to SS. Sergius and Bacchus and S. Vitale (ills 17, 19), with its circular plan and concave arcaded bays opening onto an ambulatory. This reconstruction is based on its foundations.

tall dome over the crossing and smaller ones over the corners, leaving the body of the church as a Greek cross. Proportions are unnervingly tall, so that the narrow corner bays look almost like chimneys. Even so, their interior surfaces, like those of every other part of the interior, are covered with frescoes, often of the highest quality. The churches of Nerezi (12th century) and Gračanica (14th century) are notable examples of this type.

Byzantine Christianity came to Russia in 988, followed soon afterwards by Byzantine architecture. Its earliest monument of which any part survives is the Cathedral of Hagia Sophia at Kiev, built in the first half of the 11th century. It had one large dome and twelve smaller ones (symbolizing Christ and the twelve Apostles), probably elevated on tall drums with long windows. Within a few years the new style moved up the Dnieper to Chernigov, where the Cathedral of the Transfiguration is much better preserved (or was until the Second World War), and then to Novgorod, where at least three churches survive from before 1200, Vladimir (Cathedral of the Dormition, mid-12th century), Suzdal and Pskov. Most Russian churches of the period use variants of the cross-in-square plan with one or more domes. The Byzantine fresco tradition was also transplanted, so that their interiors are alive with intense colours and the spiritual gaze of apostles and saints.

21. Later Greek Orthodox churches were small in scale – there were never any rivals to Hagia Sophia – though they remain Byzantine in inspiration. The church of the Hodeghetria at Mistra, 14th century, is basically a square divided into nine smaller squares, with a large dome over the centre and smaller ones over the corners.

The tradition reached Moscow in the 15th century (Cathedral of the Dormition, designed, paradoxically, by an Italian) and continued without fundamental change right through the 17th, 18th and even 19th centuries, an extraordinary record of conservatism. But one change there was. Whereas Byzantine and Greek churches exist for their interiors, Russian ones soon came to be designed for exterior effect. Towers grew higher and extruded strange layers of overlapping ogee shapes like the scales of a dragon, called *kokoshniki*. Their tops sprouted golden onion domes. St Basil's in Moscow (1553) has eight of them, variously coloured. 'Moscow Baroque' became a recognized style. Many of the most picturesque examples form parts of the fortified monasteries that surrounded old Russian cities as a means of defence. The church of the Smolny Convent in St Petersburg (1748) by Rastrelli carries the same basic scheme into the age of Rococo.

22, 23. Transformations of Byzantium. Right: the church of Gračanica, Kosovo, a royal foundation on a grand scale, has a narthex preceding the main cross-in-square structure. Opposite: the end of the Byzantine tradition in 'Moscow Baroque' – St Basil's, Moscow, 1553. The main effort is now all directed to exterior effect, the interior being reduced to a series of small chapels.

Western Europe: darkness before dawn

In the West the architectural record for the four or five hundred years following the withdrawal of the Roman legions in the 5th century is not inspiring. In Italy basilican churches continued to be the norm, often more notable for their decoration than their architecture; for instance, S. Apollinare Nuovo, Ravenna (6th century).

In Spain it is known that the Visigothic kingdom was a major centre of Christian culture, with numbers of ambitious churches rich in every art. In most of Spain this was swept away by the Muslim invasion of 711, and today it is hard to find even the smallest fragment. The fervour of Visigothic Christianity was confined to the kingdom of Asturias, the strip of northern Spain never

24. The 9th-century church of S. Maria de Naranco, Oviedo, once formed part of the palace of King Ramiro I of Asturias, a province of northern Spain never conquered by the Moors. Though primitive compared with the buildings of imperial Rome (from which its vocabulary comes), it is relatively sophisticated for the time in Western Europe. Note the spirally fluted columns, the medallions in the spandrels hanging like seals from shallow projecting bands, and the tunnel vault.

conquered by the Moors, and here a number of highly accomplished buildings survive, including the church of S. Julián de los Prados at Oviedo (c. 820), a basilican structure with a wide transept and originally elaborate decoration apparently based on ancient Roman wall-paintings, and S. Maria de Naranco (848), once part of the royal palace.

The Anglo-Saxons and the Franks were both prolific builders and to judge from the written sources must have achieved impressive results. In Britain cathedrals were small but richly decorated. Evidence from Winchester, where the foundations of the early minster have been excavated, shows that there was no lack of ambition. Unfortunately, what survives does not match the chroniclers' enthusiasm. Churches such as Brixworth in Northamptonshire (680) or Deerhurst in Gloucestershire (early 10th century) have a certain naive strength, but nothing suggests much architectural sophistication.

The discrepancy is still greater in France. Gregory of Tours tells us that in 472 Bishop Perpetuus built a basilica in Tours dedicated to St Martin that was larger than any church north of the Alps (160 feet/49m long, 52 windows, 120 marble columns). There were major churches also at Auxerre, Paris, Lyons and Clermont. All trace of them has disappeared, destroyed by subsequent rebuilding. What survive are a few crypts and such modest efforts as the 5th-century baptistery of St Jean at Poitiers.

Germany was even more backward architecturally. There were memories of Roman rule west of the Rhine (Trier) and south of the Danube (Regensburg), but it would be hard to name any building dating from between that period and 800. Yet it was in this unpromising region that the revival of Western architecture was to begin.

Chapter 3: Beginning Again: Carolingian and Romanesque

On Christmas Day 800 Charlemagne, King of the Franks, was crowned Emperor in Rome by Pope Leo III. In practical terms this meant very little. There was no augmentation of the ruler's actual authority. But symbolically it meant a great deal. Charlemagne could now identify his empire as the successor to that of ancient Rome. (Two centuries later that claim would be formalized by the institution of the Holy Roman Empire.)

The Carolingian Renaissance to c. 1000
Architecture, together with art, literature and law, was a key part of Charlemagne's programme. But it is interesting to note that for his major building project, the palace and chapel at Aachen in the Rhineland, he turned not to ancient Rome but to the 'second Rome', Constantinople. His model for the chapel was Justinian's church of S. Vitale at Ravenna, vividly associated with the imperial idea through its mosaics, which Charlemagne would certainly have seen on his journeys south.

26

19

Much of the material – marble columns and bronze parapets – was actually brought from Rome. The bronze doors were classical in inspiration. But Aachen is S. Vitale simplified: while the exterior is also sixteen-sided and the inner arcade octagonal, the bays of the arcade are straight, not concave, producing a relatively obvious effect. Even so, with its contemporary fittings (throne, pulpit, corona), it is deeply impressive, its impact only slightly compromised by the late Gothic choir added in the 14th century.

The chapel (now the cathedral) was part of a large complex modelled on the Lateran Palace in Rome. Nothing of this survives, but elsewhere there are still a few architectural fragments going back to Charlemagne's time. One is the tiny chapel at Germigny-des-Prés, France (806), a cross-in-square plan with apses on all four arms. Another is the three-arched gateway to the monastery of Lorsch, in Germany (*c.* 800), probably based on a similar gateway in front of Old St Peter's, incorporating fairly classical composite pilasters and a quite unclassical triangular-headed blind arcade on the upper floor. Three more are the monastery churches of Niederzell, Mittelzell and Oberzell at Reichenau, Germany, all

25. Charlemagne's revival of Roman architecture marked an important turning-point, though the scale of his buildings was relatively modest. The start of work on the great 'imperial cathedral' of Speyer about 1030 signalled the beginning of a major new phase, Romanesque. The dwarf gallery and twin towers flanking the chancel appear also in Lombardy.

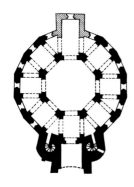

founded in the early 9th century, and all surviving with little alteration, in their idyllic setting in Lake Constance. They are basilican structures, Mittelzell with a large tower at the west end. Inside, much of the original fresco decoration remains. And finally the monastic church of Centula (St Riquier), near Abbeville in northern France, no longer extant but known from a drawing. Centula was even more ambitious than Aachen, and like Aachen contained material specially imported from Rome. It was a basilica, with a tower strangely rounded at its base over the crossing and another at the west end, which expanded into what became known as a 'westwork', a substantial block containing a narthex or vestibule on the ground floor and a chapel above, opening into the west end of the nave. At the east end were a transept, crossing and chancel, ending in an apse flanked by stair-turrets.

Centula is one of the great 'missing monuments' of architectural history. Had it survived, much subsequent history would be clearer. Charlemagne's reign was in a real sense the first Renaissance, a period when the values of ancient Rome were quite deliberately revived, and with them the idea that Europe was essentially a unity. He had managed to bring under his rule most of

26. Above and below: the chapel of Charlemagne's palace at Aachen is an overt, and no doubt ideologically intended, allusion to Justinian's S.Vitale at Ravenna (ill. 19), symbolizing the continuity of the imperial idea. Although simpler than the original, this was a striking statement, architecturally as well as politically, in early 9th-century Germany.

France, Germany and northern Italy. The idea remained even after his empire became divided under his successors, the Ottonian and Capetian dynasties, as almost every aspect of intellectual and artistic life bears witness. Links were also maintained with the still-existing Roman empire in the east (Otto II married a Byzantine princess). Not until around the year 1000 – the last Otto died in 1002 – did the various national groups begin to assume more definite cultural identities, a change that manifests itself more clearly in architecture than almost anywhere else. At that point we can most meaningfully mark the beginning of a new era called Romanesque.

What survives of 10th-century architecture in the Ottonian orbit are vestiges of a series of major churches in Germany and France. Many of them were monastic. This was the great age of monastic expansion. St Benedict had written his Rule and founded Monte Cassino in central Italy about 530, and the disciplined and well-ordered Benedictine communities soon became bastions of literacy and culture, many of them richly endowed and protected. By the 7th century there were Benedictine houses all over Europe. From about 820 we possess a unique document, a plan sent proba- 28 bly from Reichenau to St Gall in Switzerland. It is clearly not the plan of a real monastery, but it gives, in schematic form, a complete picture of what such an establishment would entail – not only the church, but all the ancillary buildings for a self-sufficient community: barns, sheds for animals, brewery, bakery, guest range, infirmary and cemetery. Already the typical monastic layout was formed, becoming standard all over Europe by the beginning of the 2nd millennium.

Corvey, in Germany, was an offspring of Centula, and its great 29 westwork, built about 880, survives intact, a massive building with a large, two-storey room on the upper floor. Two other similar churches in Germany belong to nunneries, Quedlinburg (early 10th century) and Gernrode (c. 960). Both are basilicas with arcades resting on alternating columns and piers, with clearstorey lighting and wooden roofs, and both have large westworks.

The years around 1000 are crucial to the story of architecture in the West but it is a story that can be told only inadequately because of the lack of documentation and the sparseness of the remains. The dozen or so major examples that survive in whole or in part in Germany and France are so varied and interesting that one is tantalized by the thought of what has been lost.

Two French buildings must suffice. St Bénigne at Dijon (1001) was a basilica with double aisles, transept, and a tower over the

27. Left: the Carolingian abbey of Centula (St Riquier), in northern France, begun in 789 and long demolished, seems to have been the prototype of a series of German churches featuring a 'westwork', or large tower-like structure at the west end (left, in this 17th-century print, copied from a lost medieval manuscript). Here one can already see the characteristic towered outline of Mainz and Worms (ills 32, 33).

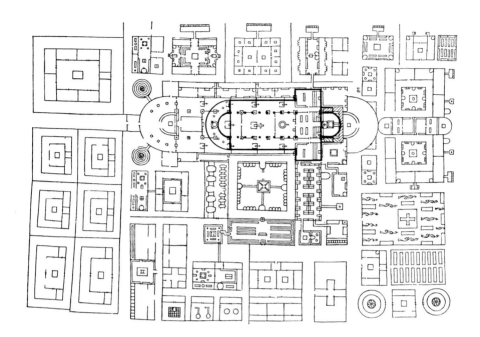

crossing. What made it unusual was its eastern termination, which was circular. Circular churches are often allusions to the Holy Sepulchre in Jerusalem, forming part of a symbolic pilgrimage. Of this rotunda only the crypt survives, and that has been so restored that it hardly counts as medieval.

At about the same time, or a little later, an intensive series of experiments in vault construction was being undertaken at Tournus, in Burgundy. The nave of St Philibert (1009) is covered with transverse tunnel vaults resting on transverse arches: that is, vaults that go across the church, bay by bay, instead of down the whole length (a system that is logical in that it avoids lateral thrust, but is not beautiful and was never repeated). The tall aisles have quadripartite groin vaults, a form that arises when two tunnel vaults meet. The two-storeyed westwork, or narthex, combines a longitudinal tunnel vault with groin vaults on the ground storey; on the upper storey the aisles have quadrant vaults, i.e. half a tunnel vault leaning against the arcade.

The church of St Michael at Hildesheim (begun c.1001) may take its place here as a fitting coda to the Carolingian/Ottonian story, for it looks back rather than forward, inspired by the same

28. This 9th-century plan in the library of St Gall in Switzerland seems to represent a sort of schematized blueprint rather than an actual monastery. The church (with two apsed ends) and cloister are in the centre. Around the cloister are the dormitory – with the latrines opening off a passage at the end – and refectory. Further out lie the infirmary and farm-buildings – everything needed for the self-contained world of the monks. The cemetery, near the bottom, right, is shown with flowers and a cross in the centre.

30

classical ideals as those of Charlemagne. Like Gernrode, its basilican nave alternates columns and piers and it has a large westwork. Its builder, Bishop Bernward, tutor to Otto III, had been several times to Rome. Two of the works he commissioned for his church were clearly based on classical models – the bronze doors with Biblical reliefs (the first to be cast in one piece since the end of the Roman Empire), and a bronze column illustrating the life of Christ, modelled, on a small scale, on the Column of Trajan. (Both have since been moved to Hildesheim Cathedral.)

There was nothing abrupt about the transition from Carolingian and Ottonian to Romanesque. It meant simply the end of a period of experimentation and the establishment of assured structural and stylistic conventions that would last for the next two centuries. The round arch would remain universal, both functionally, supporting and supported by thick walls, and decoratively. It would be used to span wider and wider spaces and, prolonged as a continuous surface, would create the longitudinal tunnel vault. By the early 12th century most ambitious buildings in continental Europe would be vaulted. Arcades would typically

29, 30. Below: Corvey, in Germany, probably comes closest to what Centula looked like, though the tops of the towers and the upper two storeys of the westwork were added in 1146. Below right: the nave of St Philibert, Tournus, in France, 1009, showing the very unusual transverse tunnel vaults of the central vessel and the groin-vaulted aisle beyond.

consist not of columns but of masonry piers. And they would be 3
articulated by increasingly sophisticated sculptural decoration,
something of which Carolingian and Ottonian builders had been
only sporadically capable. It also meant the formation of distinct
national styles, so that it becomes easy to 'place' a Romanesque
building in Germany, France, Britain, Spain or Italy – easier in fact
than at any time before or since.

Germany: the Imperial lands

The progress of Romanesque in Germany can be followed in the
three great Imperial cathedrals along the Rhine: Speyer, Mainz 3
and Worms. Begun about 1030 and finished about 1060, Speyer 3
has a long nave (twelve bays) on masonry piers with attached 3

31. The nave of Speyer Cathedral
(1030) now seems bare, but was
relieved originally by painted
decoration. A stone vault was
probably intended from the
beginning; the present one, with
domical bays of groin vaulting,
dates from soon after 1100.

32. Mainz, the second of the great
Kaiserdome (imperial cathedrals)
after Speyer, is roughly
contemporary with Speyer but has
been subjected to much more
rebuilding. It was altered in the
12th century and the two crossing
towers are 18th- and 19th-century
'restorations'.

shafts, a transept with octagonal tower over the crossing, a chancel flanked by square towers, and a westwork. In spite of alterations and restoration it retains the stark simplicity of its original style. Between the arcade and the clearstorey is an area of blank wall, probably intended for painting. The first ceiling was of wood, but a vault may always have been intended. The present groin vault was built before 1106.

Mainz goes back even earlier, but the first building was burnt down on its dedication day in 1009. The reconstruction, partly determined by the old foundations, went on through the 11th century, and the church did not reach its present form until 1137. Here the westwork has become transformed into another transept with an apse beyond, so that one end matches the other (to make it more confusing still the orientation is also reversed, so that the ritual east end is at the west). Mainz therefore has two sets of transepts, one with attached towers, and two octagonal crossing towers (both entirely rebuilt). The east end has two more lateral apses, forming a trefoil plan, an originally Italian idea much taken up in Germany. The 'dwarf gallery', a miniature arcade running round both apses, also derives from Italian models. Internally, the elevation has the same blank wall areas as Speyer.

The last of the three, Worms, was under construction from the 11th to the 13th century. It retains the same elements but they are differently proportioned. As at Mainz there are two crossings and two octagonal towers; there are two apses too (the western one concealed behind a straight wall), and both are flanked by towers. All of the details inside and outside – dwarf galleries, cornices, window surrounds, piers and capitals – are more imaginatively designed and carefully executed. Speyer's massive strength has been succeeded by a degree of conscious sophistication. 33

The extensive repertoire of elements now at the disposal of German architects included trefoil plans, octagonal towers, and smaller circular or square towers. The latter could be added to apses or transepts and were usually topped by 'Rhenish helms', tall pyramidal roofs growing out of four gables and descending to their bases, so that each face is lozenge-shaped. 34

To appreciate the full capacities of the style one has to go to Cologne. Here, before 1945, were eleven intact churches built between 1050 and 1200. All were badly damaged in the Second World War and have been restored with as much conviction as possible. Five have trefoil east ends (i.e. chancel and transepts all ending in apses), the most perfect being the Holy Apostles. Five have pairs of towers flanking the chancel. Several have octagonal crossing towers and square towers at the west end. St Gereon has an extraordinary oval, or more strictly decagonal, nave leading into a long narrow chancel flanked by towers. Great St Martin has a big square tower over the crossing with small octagonal towers attached to each corner. 34

German architects remained faithful to Romanesque long after it had yielded to Gothic in the rest of Europe, and with so much opportunity for variation and invention it is easy to understand why. (Is it too fanciful to see a parallel here with Gothic and then with Baroque? In both cases it was the German lands which, at a very late stage of these styles, took them to new extremes of originality.)

The drama of the exteriors must have been deliberate. It is common for churches to dominate their surroundings with four tall towers, sometimes more. Maria Laach, founded in 1093, follows the scheme of the Rhineland cathedrals, with two crossing towers and four smaller ones, two attached to transepts, two flanking an apse. Tournai Cathedral (1110) in Belgium groups five towers together in an arresting composition. Limburg-an-der-Lahn (1215) and Bamberg (1237), both rising on the crown of hills, make an even more spectacular effect. Many of these adopt 35

33, 34. The cathedral of Worms (far left) and the church of the Holy Apostles, Cologne – both seen from the east, and both mainly 12th century – show the whole repertoire of Rhineland Romanesque at its most accomplished, including polygonal and trefoil plans, curiously placed towers and decorative 'dwarf galleries'. The tower at the west end of the Holy Apostles is of 'Rhenish helm' form.

35. The abbey church of Maria Laach (mostly 12th century) has the same unmistakably German outline. It is entered by a small cloister or atrium at the west end, on the right.

36, 37. Opposite: the series of ambitious French churches built in the 11th century along the pilgrimage route to Compostela in Spain are sufficiently similar to have been given the name 'pilgrimage churches'. Santiago de Compostela itself (below left) is the grandest. Closely matching it is St Sernin at Toulouse (above, and below right); the clear, logical distinction of parts – crossing with (later) tower, transepts with chapels, apsidal east end also with chapels – is characteristic of the Romanesque aesthetic.

a feature that had already become established in France – a triforium or wall-passage between the arcade and clearstorey, giving a feeling of greater lightness. In common, too, with the rest of Europe, the piers of the arcade often alternate major and minor.

The Romanesque style was also tolerant – more tolerant than Gothic – of eccentric ornament in the form of bizarre animals (flanking the door of St Jakob in Regensburg, for instance), luxurious enrichment of window-surrounds (e.g. the apse of Bamberg) or weirdly unorthodox capitals (e.g. in Basel Cathedral, which consist of fierce beasts eating one another). Even when Gothic features, such as rib vaults and pointed arches, were introduced from France, Germany often chose to use them in totally un-Gothic ways. At Boppard on the Rhine, for instance, the pointed tunnel vault of the nave (part of a rebuilding of 1230) has in each bay sixteen ornamental ribs radiating from a central boss; they conspicuously fail to link up with any other linear members, so that no overall unity is created. Not until the late 13th century, with the building of Cologne Cathedral by a French, or French-inspired, master, did real Gothic take root.

France: diversity in unity

The major churches of the early Romanesque in France were those built along the pilgrimage routes to Santiago de Compostela. The discovery of the reputed bones of the Apostle James in this obscure north-western corner of Spain in the 9th century made it the most popular shrine in Europe. In 1078 a great new church was begun 36 on a scale quite unprecedented in that region, and the assumption is that a French master-mason was called in. This is made more probable by the fact that many of the French churches built along the routes to Santiago – each also possessed some relic or claim to sanctity, and pilgrims were expected to stop and make offerings – followed a common pattern. The most important of those that survive, apart from Santiago itself, are Ste Foy at Conques (1050) and St Sernin at Toulouse (1080). All had long naves (Conques is an 37 exception, being much smaller), with aisled transepts and apsidal 38 east ends with radiating chapels. All were tunnel-vaulted, but it is a sign of how cautious the builders were that they had no clearstoreys, the vault resting on the gallery. As a result they all tend to be dark, though the galleries themselves are lit by windows in

their outer walls. Ste Foy at Conques is the most complete and the least altered, and with its terrifying relief of the Last Judgment over the portal conveys more vividly than anywhere else the experience of medieval spirituality.

Another crucial factor in architectural development was the spread of Benedictine monasticism, which it is convenient to treat in a French context, though it originated not in France but in Italy. The monastic layout already appears in part in the St Gall plan; by the 11th century it was so standardized that a monk from Poland would have had no difficulty in finding his way round a monastery in Portugal. There was a square cloister, usually to the south of the church, which formed a covered passage connecting the various parts. On the east side was the chapter house, a vaulted room where the monks met on formal occasions, and above it the dormitory, a long room with evenly spaced windows between which the monks had their beds. On the side of the cloister opposite the church was the refectory with its kitchen, usually a solid building with large fireplaces and chimneys. The west, more public, side was normally reserved for guests and for the abbot's apartments. The infirmary, usually to the east of the cloister, was like a church, with nave and aisles for the beds and a chapel at the 'chancel' end.

38, 39. Ste Foy at Conques (1050) is the smallest but best-preserved of the pilgrimage churches (only the western tower-tops are 19th-century additions). Nestling in its remote valley, and still with its superb carving of the Last Judgment over the entrance portal, Conques evokes the authentic atmosphere of the Early Middle Ages.

40. The vast church of the abbey of Cluny (1088), in Burgundy, was largely destroyed at the French Revolution. Its plan (below) is certain, and its appearance in the early 12th century has been reconstructed, with its build-up of radiating chapels, apse, chancel, two transepts – both with apsed chapels – and crossing. Cluny was the mother-house of a powerful monastic movement working for reform and centralized control. Architecturally, too, it was innovative, already experimenting with the pointed arch.

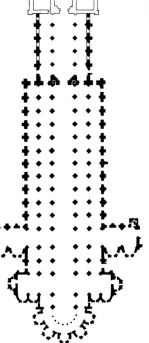

One monastery dominated all the rest through its energy and missionary zeal: that of Cluny, in Burgundy. Under a series of dynamic abbots, Cluny assumed a position of leadership, founding daughter-houses (eventually there were over a thousand of them) which owed obedience to the mother-house, a sort of order-within-an-order. Reformers, the Cluniacs reinvigorated the Benedictine Rule, searched out abuses, punished laxity.

The church at Cluny grew to be the largest in Europe. In 955 the original modest church (Cluny I) was replaced by a bigger, up-to-date building (Cluny II), basilican in form, tunnel-vaulted, with a tower at the crossing and two at the west end, and apsidal ends to the chancel and aisles. The monastery kept on growing and by 1088 a new church was begun on a new site, which lasted until the French Revolution. Cluny III was finished in 1121. It was over 600 feet long (counting the narthex). It had double aisles, two sets of transepts, both with eastern chapels, and an apsidal east end with radiating chapels. Like the pilgrimage churches, it was tunnel-vaulted, but it did not renounce the clearstorey. Significant for the future was the fact that its arcade arches were slightly pointed.

40

41, 42. Pontigny (above) and Fontenay (below), both in Burgundy, are among the earliest Cistercian foundations – 1114 and 1140 – and show the order's formal austerity. Fontenay keeps its early pointed tunnel vault and square east end; Pontigny was rib-vaulted about 1170 and given an apsed choir with flying buttresses around 1185–1210.

Cluny was always renowned for music (the capitals of the choir, still preserved, represent the 'tones' of medieval music), and the setting-out of the church made use of various mystical number-systems, including the so-called Pythagorean series of musical numbers (2, 3, 4, 6, 8, 9, 12), thought to be the basis of all harmony and beauty.

Cluny's influence was at its peak in the early 12th century. But wealth and power took their inevitable toll. The early ideals were compromised, luxury was allowed to creep in, and by the time Cluny III was finished the reformers were themselves ripe for reform. St Bernard of Clairvaux, spokesman of the newly formed Cistercian order, made bitter mockery of monks (who but the Cluniacs?) who allowed themselves worldly, extravagant and irrelevant ornament ('monstrous harpies' and 'unclean apes' – the very things we now most enjoy).

Cistercian monasteries were austere and functional; they out-lawed needless decoration but made use of any new technology that served their purposes, including the pointed arch. In many ways they are the precursors of Gothic.

The Cistercians' concentration on essentials and their puri-tanical avoidance of extraneous decoration were to win them the favour of many modern architects. It is ironic, therefore, that since they built mostly in wild, remote countryside, their ruined monas-teries have become clichés of romantic and picturesque beauty.

Architecturally, the buildings' merits are those of pure form. The Cistercians favoured square, not apsidal, east ends, two-storeyed elevations, and often quadrant vaults (half-tunnels) over the aisles. Cîteaux, the mother-house (founded 1098) has vanished; Pontigny (founded 1114) has been partly rebuilt; and the purest example of the early Cistercian style is now Fontenay (1140), though it lacks a clearstorey. The Cistercians proved immensely successful, founding houses in every part of Europe (by 1200 there were nearly 700), and flourishing until the Reformation and beyond. A number of other monastic orders, following slightly different rules, prospered at the same time but only the Carthusians (founded 1084) were sufficiently different architecturally to need a mention here. They had no dormitories, but lived solitary lives in individual houses grouped around one or more cloisters.

Apart from these monastic buildings and the pilgrimage churches, French Romanesque is strongly regional, each area being characterized by churches of a distinct type.

Burgundy, within the orbit of Cluny, could not escape its influence. Paray-le-Monial (*c.* 1100) is almost a miniature version of it.

43. French Romanesque divides easily into well-defined regional schools. Burgundy could hardly escape from the shadow of Cluny. Paray-le-Monial (*c.* 1100) has been called a 'pocket edition' of Cluny.

St Etienne at Nevers, a priory of Cluny, belongs to the same group. Autun (*c.* 1120) also has a three-storey elevation with a pointed tunnel vault, but is chiefly remarkable for the very Roman look of the full-scale fluted pilasters applied to the arcade piers (Cluny III had small ones at triforium level), a reminder that Roman remains were present throughout the Middle Ages and never ignored. Burgundy is also important for the revival of figure sculpture, itself classically inspired. The tympanum and capitals of Autun are among its masterpieces. So are those of nearby Vézelay (*c.* 1104), whose nave keeps to the round arch but dispenses with galleries and employs groin vaults rather than a tunnel. Rib vaulting, too, had begun to be an option in Burgundian churches for aisles, porches, but not yet for major high vaults. In many respects it is to Burgundy that we must look if seeking the origins of Gothic.

Classical influences were strongest in Provence. The façade of the church of St Gilles-du-Gard could almost be mistaken for a Roman structure, with its Corinthian columns, flat entablature and life-size figures of saints. To the west and north, in Aquitaine and Anjou, we are in a different world, where there was an un-explained fondness for domes. The otherwise unpretentious

44, 45. Burgundy led the rest of Europe not only in architectural experiment but also in the revival of figure sculpture, mostly on the tympana of portals and the capitals of arcade piers. At Autun (above) this is combined with fluted pilasters that look back to ancient Rome and pointed arches that look forward to Gothic. Vézelay (above right) is equally outstanding for its sculpture but retains the round arch.

44

45

46

cathedral of Cahors has two; Angoulême had four; Périgueux 47 (tragically over-restored in the 19th century) has five, making it the most Byzantine church west of St Mark's, Venice. In Anjou the bays are covered with dome-shaped rib vaults, functionally a logical solution, but disturbing to any feeling of spatial unity. (Angers 48 Cathedral is a late example, with vaults of *c.* 1150, but the lost church of St Martin in the same city had them a century earlier.) The Auvergne took its cue from the pilgrimage churches, but for some reason raised the height of the transept bays nearest to the crossing, so that the churches have 'shoulders' next to the 49 central tower. Supports are columnar, with big, dramatically carved and originally brightly coloured figural capitals. In Poitou we find yet another variant – tall naves with cylindrical piers supporting a tunnel vault, flanked by aisles of the same height, e.g. Notre Dame-la-Grande at Poitiers or St Savin-sur-Gartempe, the latter still with its original painted decoration, comprising 'marbled' piers and large Old Testament scenes occupying the whole length of the nave vault.

The Romanesque of Normandy is again a separate story, more so, indeed, than in other areas of France since it was an

46. Provence was, and is, rich in Roman remains, a feature that had its effect on the local Romanesque. At St Gilles-du-Gard the façade (mid-12th century) of a church since rebuilt is almost Neoclassical in both its architecture and its sculpture.

47, 48. Aquitaine and Anjou are distinguished by unusual vaulting techniques. Angoulême Cathedral (above) has Byzantinesque domes resting on pendentives. Angers Cathedral (above right) employs quadripartite vaults that rise in the centre giving a domical effect.

49. The peculiarity of churches in the Auvergne is the heightening of the bays flanking the crossing tower. Otherwise they follow the arrangement of pilgrimage churches (cf. ill. 37). Orcival (right) is typical.

independent duchy inhabited by Norsemen who had only recently adopted French language and culture. Norman churches impress by their scale and their unadorned strength, but they do not attempt technical innovation, spatial subtlety or decorative ornament of a figural character. The two great churches of Caen, La Trinité (1062) and St Etienne (1068), are basilicas with three-storey elevations. Both originally had timber roofs and both were given Gothic vaults in the following century. Both have two-towered façades (St Etienne's was later heightened with spires). The three elements of the interior elevation – arcade, gallery, clearstorey – are almost equal in height. The abbey church of Jumièges, near Rouen (1052), is similar, though the nave piers alternate major and minor. It is tempting to align with these churches certain others in northern France, in Picardy and Champagne. The churches of Normandy are ambitious in scale but they lack sophistication in their details, and show an almost total unconcern with figural sculpture. Certain aspects, such as the two-towered facade, were copied elsewhere in France. But their main progeny was to be across the English Channel.

50, 51

50, 51. Normandy pursued a path of its own, with large churches having three-storey interior elevations and twin towers at the west end. St Etienne at Caen (1068) was given spires to its already tall towers in the 12th century (below) and sexpartite rib vaults to its nave (below right).

The Normans in Britain

The Norman Conquest brought a complete restructuring of every aspect of English life – administrative, financial, social, legal and religious. The Domesday survey recorded the wealth and tax capacity of every town, village and farm, while a chain of strong castles, first of wood, later of stone, guaranteed unchallengeable military control (the Saxons had built virtually no castles). The religious restructuring was given equal, if not greater, priority; certainly it must have consumed as much of the country's resources. A new church was provided for nearly every parish. Saxon bishops were replaced by Normans, and the small Saxon cathedrals in remote rural areas by vast new ones in the major centres of population. It was one of the most intensive building programmes that history can show.

In the thirty years after 1066, the following new cathedrals were begun and carried near to completion: Canterbury, Winchester, Durham, Chichester, Worcester, Lincoln, London (Old St Paul's), Norwich, Rochester, Gloucester and York. To these we may add a number of equally ambitious abbey churches, many of which subsequently became cathedrals: St Albans, Bury St Edmunds, Tewkesbury. Most of the remaining British cathedrals followed in the two decades after 1100, including Southwell, Peterborough, Chester, Ely, Hereford and Dunfermline.

Architecturally, the Normans took practically nothing from their Anglo-Saxon predecessors. The scale, the style, often even the stone, came from Normandy, as no doubt did the master-masons. The cathedrals followed a formula already worked out in France. They were exceptional only in their extreme length. All had three-storey elevations, the arcade, gallery and clearstorey given roughly equal emphasis (some exceptions are noted below). The roofs were nearly always of wood. Figure sculpture was generally not attempted, and decoration was confined to a few abstract motifs such as the zig-zag or chevron, billet and beak-head. East ends soon gave up the apsidal plan and became straight.

All the buildings named here have been substantially altered and added to in later times (this is more consistently true of English great churches than those of any other country), and in particular have been given Gothic vaults. The great exception is Peterborough, where the painted Romanesque ceiling remains, a unique survival.

In the matter of vaulting, Normandy and therefore England were for long unadventurous. There is not a single high tunnel vault in England; even groin vaults are used sparingly and on

52, 53. The development of Romanesque in England. Below: the north transept of Winchester Cathedral (1079), one of the earliest of major Norman buildings, is plain, unadorned, elemental. Peterborough (opposite) does not change the system but by now (the 1120s) the proportions are more sophisticated and the details more refined. Alone of English cathedrals, Peterborough has kept its original painted wooden ceiling.

52

53

58

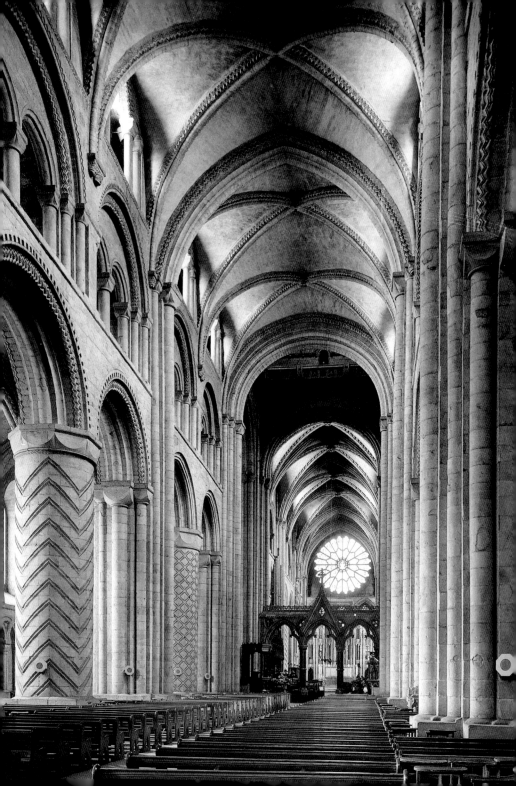

a small scale. Then suddenly, about 1100, England leaps ahead with the first high rib vault in Europe. The present choir vault of Durham is a replacement of about 1120, but it seems certain that the original of the 1090s was similar to that of the nave, vaulted about 1125, which remains intact. That is divided into double bays by transverse arches which are slightly pointed. Two of the key elements of the Gothic style are thus already present. Even flying buttresses are prefigured in the half-arches beneath the gallery roof which serve to support the vault at crucial points.

Durham is exceptional also in the design of its arcade. The major piers are complex clusters of shafts, but the minor ones are fat cylinders on which abstract patterns (zig-zags, lozenges, etc.) are incised and were probably once picked out in colours. It is not excessive to call Durham the *locus classicus* of English Romanesque, for its design quality, for its spectacular position on a cliff overlooking the River Wear next to the bishop's castle, and for its almost perfect state of preservation.

54

55

54, 55. Durham, begun in 1093, is the most dramatic of English cathedrals. Its situation, on a promontory high above the River Wear, guarded by the ancient castle of the bishops, is unsurpassed. Architecturally it matches expectations. Its arcade consists of compound piers alternating with fat cylindrical pillars incised with abstract patterns. The choir vault, later rebuilt, was originally similar to that of the nave and was almost certainly the earliest high rib vault in Europe.

56, 57. Tall cylindrical piers are one of the few regional variants of English Romanesque. They occur in several major churches of the West Country, including Tewkesbury Abbey (above) and Gloucester Cathedral (above right). Both have been given later vaults.

The cylindrical pier comes into its own in a group of churches centred on the West Country. At Gloucester, Hereford and Tewkesbury they are immensely tall, pushing the gallery and clearstorey into insignificance. At Oxford, the gallery is squeezed, rather unhappily, inside such an arcade.

Façades were often two-towered, as in Normandy (Durham, Canterbury), but equally often had no tower, or one single one (still to be seen at Ely). Lincoln is unusual in having three great niches and a screen of blind arches running in front of two towers, something which became a favourite solution in English Gothic. There was usually a tower over the crossing.

During the mid- and late 12th century English Romanesque grew more delicate and refined, with a wider repertoire of ornament, but no important technical innovations were made. The example of Durham's rib vault was not followed until the rebuilding of Canterbury (see the next chapter), and then the model was continental, not English. In these later Romanesque buildings, however, there is a sense of assurance, even of playfulness, that contrasts with the severity of the early years: compare the transepts of Winchester (1079), for instance – heavy, austere,

57

56

52

almost grim – with the Galilee of Durham, a porch and chapel 58 built in front of the west façade about 1170, using slender piers of quatrefoil section and very pronounced chevron ornament in all the arches. Rows of blind arcading, sometimes intersecting, are a common decoration both internally and externally, e.g. at the west end of Ely or the chapter house of Bristol.

Many late parish churches have the same vigour, though few survive structurally intact and none (apart from a few fragments) retain the vivid painted decoration that once covered their walls. Ornament is usually concentrated on door surrounds, sometimes with three or four concentric rows of zig-zags or twisted cable. The same motifs occur on chancel arches, which thereby announce the approach to the holiest part of the church. In rare cases figure sculpture is attempted (e.g. Barfreston in Kent, or the Prior's Door at Ely), and here the influence seems clearly to be Burgundian rather than Norman. Unique are the capitals in the late Romanesque crypt of Canterbury, of which the source appears to be manuscript illumination.

58. The so-called Galilee porch at the west end of Durham Cathedral, added in 1170 in a decorative style characteristic of late Romanesque.

59. The Transitional style in England is marked by unrepeated one-off experiments. The nave elevation of Worksop Priory (above) of about 1180 alternates wide and narrow openings at gallery level, undermining the sense of strength and solidity that had been the essence of Romanesque.

60. Castle Hedingham, Essex (above right), dates from about 1140. Norman castles consisted of a strong usually square keep on a mound (the motte) surrounded by a wall of secondary defence enclosing subsidiary buildings (the bailey). The keep was not intended as a residence, though it often incorporated a ceremonial hall. Entrance was at an upper level reached by steps that could be dismantled.

At the very end of the Romanesque period, between 1170 and 1200, we encounter a style known rather lamely as Transitional, which incorporates Gothic elements, notably the pointed arch. It reflects not so much a real transition, however, as a desire for novelty. At Worksop, in Nottinghamshire, for instance, the gallery alternates wide and narrow openings, the narrow ones over the piers and under the clearstorey windows. This is an interesting period, which abounds in rather eccentric ideas before succumbing to the discipline of Gothic.

Norman keeps, the strongly fortified, typically square towers at the centre of defensive works, tell the same architectural story, from stark strength (the Tower of London, very much reconstructed, or Colchester Castle) to elegant finesse (Castle Hedingham or Norwich). Most keeps had a large chamber on the upper storey spanned by a wide arch: this, the most richly decorated part, was the lord's hall. One separately built hall survives at Oakham in Rutland, with round-arched arcades. Westminster Hall in London was originally of this type. Durham Castle retains a splendid, over-decorated doorway into its hall.

Romanesque in the south: Italy and Spain

Italian Romanesque is even more regionally differentiated than France, which is understandable in view of the fact that what is now one country was so sharply divided politically and culturally. We have space here to look only at five areas – Lombardy in the north, Tuscany and Rome in the centre, and Apulia and Sicily in the south.

In some ways 11th- and 12th-century architecture of Lombardy belongs earlier in this chapter, since it was an important influence in Germany and France. The double-ended plan (with an apse at east and west) and the dwarf gallery under the eaves, later popular in Germany, appear to have originated in Lombardy. The motifs of the trefoil plan and twin towers flanking the apse, on the other hand, seem to have been imported in the opposite direction. S. Abbondio in Como (1063) has the two towers and also experiments with rib vaulting in the chancel.

Rib vaults come into their own at S. Ambrogio, Milan. Here 61 the nave appears (the evidence is problematic) to have been vaulted between 1080 and 1093, which would make it earlier than Durham. S. Ambrogio, however, is much lower and has no clearstorey, so the achievement is not quite so impressive. The vault is domed-up, as in Anjou, though not so steeply. S. Ambrogio was 48

61. S. Ambrogio, Milan, (founded by and later dedicated to St Ambrose) was the most important Italian church outside Rome in the 11th century. Lombardy was, in fact, the only region of Italy really interested in structural experiment, and S. Ambrogio's rib-vaulted nave (around 1090) marked an important advance in building technique.

62, 63. At S. Zeno, Verona (far left), and S. Miniato al Monte, Florence (left), the chancel is raised up, leaving a space underneath for a crypt. Typically, both vary the rhythm of the arcade, the first into two, the second into three arches per bay.

historically important, for it was here that the emperors were crowned on their way to Rome. The church of S. Sigismondo at nearby Rivolta d'Adda has similar domed-up rib vaults dated to 1089, though on a smaller scale. Others in the same area took up the idea, and most of the 12th-century cathedrals – Parma, Piacenza, Cremona, Verona, Ferrara – have rib vaults built after a disastrous earthquake in 1117. Relatively low and wide in their proportions, these churches lead without a break into Italian Gothic (see the next chapter). The fact that many equally large churches preferred roofs of timber was not necessarily a sign of conservatism: S. Zeno at Verona (1123) has a highly sophisticated wooden roof that is trefoil in section.

62

A feature of many of these buildings was a very tall, square bell tower or *campanile* with a pyramidal roof and with the typical feature of window openings increasing in number towards the top. S. Zeno has a fine *campanile*; that of the abbey of Pomposa, with nine storeys, is perhaps the most spectacular.

Across the Apennines, in Tuscany, we might be in another world, where architects seem blissfully untroubled by thoughts of vaulting or structural innovations of any kind. From an engineering point of view there is no advance on Early Christian times – the same long rows of columns (carrying round arches, not a flat entablature), the same unadventurous wooden roofs. So classical, indeed, are these churches that when Brunelleschi wanted to make contact with ancient Rome he did not need to look much farther than his own Florentine Romanesque.

The church of S. Miniato al Monte, Florence, was finished by 1062. Its interior is divided into three by diaphragm arches resting on piers with attached demi-columns. Between these, longitudinally, are columns supporting triple arches. The same rhythmic arcade motif is applied to the slightly later façade. Both interior and exterior are clad in patterned marble.

63

The same aesthetic is taken further in a much larger building, Pisa Cathedral (1013), whose whole exterior is wrapped in miniature arcading of exquisite white marble (the façade not finished until the 13th century), which migrates to the neighbouring Baptistery (partly Gothic) and runs riot on the eight-tiered *campanile*, the famous Leaning Tower. Pisa Cathedral, like San Miniato al Monte, is wooden-roofed (the present one is not original); the dome over the crossing was built later (1380). Several contemporary churches in Pisa are almost replicas of the Cathedral, and the style was adopted at nearby Lucca, retaining the same essential features even when translated into Gothic.

64

64. Pisan Romanesque delighted in rows of miniature arcading covering every surface. The famous group at Pisa – Baptistery, Cathedral and Leaning Tower – was planned together and built from the late 11th century onwards; the upper parts of the Baptistery with their pointed canopies are later, but in keeping with the earlier design.

65. S. Clemente, in Rome, could easily be mistaken for an Early Christian church like S.Maria Maggiore (ill. 15). It was in fact built about 1100, but the marble choir enclosure was retained from an earlier building.

The architectural history of Rome between Early Christian times and the Renaissance is curiously uneventful. The only memorable buildings are a series of 12th-century churches, of which S. Clemente and S. Maria in Cosmedin are the most ambitious. They continue the earlier arrangement virtually unchanged, with a colonnade below a clearstorey and wooden roof; as in Tuscany, however, the columns are sometimes interspersed with piers, and they support arches. Many of them have picturesque brick *campanili*. S. Clemente is remarkable in preserving much of its old furnishing from the previous building, including the 6th-century marble screen enclosing the chancel within the body of the church. Patterning in inlaid coloured stone and marble, derived from ancient Roman examples, is associated with the Cosmati family (second half of the 12th century), who were extremely prolific in Rome and widely copied throughout Europe.

Apulia, the heel of Italy, was, like England, conquered by the Normans in the 11th century. Its architecture does indeed show some memories of the north (not only Normandy), but was also subject to influences from Lombardy, Byzantium and elsewhere. The result is a series of buildings about which it is difficult to generalize but which are of special interest because for so many centuries afterwards the region remained poor and undeveloped, leaving them remarkably intact, with their superb, if often savage and unnerving, stone-carving and metalwork. The Norman Crusaders who conquered this country – Tancred, Robert Guiscard, Bohemond (whose mausoleum still stands at Canosa di Puglia) – were not gentle characters, and in Apulia one feels close to the harsh reality of early medieval Christianity.

The earliest and largest of the Apulian churches is S. Nicola at Bari (1039). Its interior generally conforms to a plain basilican scheme. The aisles have groin vaults but the nave roof is of wood. Other Apulian churches follow S. Nicola fairly closely: Barletta, Bitonto and Ruvo, all begun before 1200. One technical feature that is almost unique to Apulia is the quadrant vault, a half-tunnel vault that acts like a continuous buttress. (We have encountered it once at St Philibert, Tournus.) It is used in the aisles of Molfetta Cathedral (12th century) and in the smaller church of S. Francesco, Trani.

The troubled history of Sicily in the early Middle Ages made it the meeting place of three civilizations – Western European, Byzantine and Islamic. The Normans conquered the island in 1061–91, but at their cosmopolitan court Muslim and Byzantine artists were valued and welcomed. In 1194, together with most of southern Italy, it became part of the Holy Roman Empire under the Hohenstaufen.

From the Norman period the major monuments are the Palatine Chapel (1132) in the royal palace of Palermo, and the cathedrals of Cefalù (1131) and Monreale (1174). They each

67

66

66, 67. Sicily uniquely combined influences from the classical world, northern Europe, Byzantium and Islam. Below: the apse of Monreale Cathedral (1174) is decorated with interlacing pointed arches whose hybrid origins almost defy analysis. Below right: the Palatine Chapel, Palermo (1132). The columns look to ancient Rome, the stilted arches and pendant wooden roof to Islam, and the mosaics to Byzantium.

take elements from all three civilizations, the Palatine Chapel – a basilica with an arcade of stilted arches on classical columns – more explicitly than the others. The side walls and east end are decorated with Byzantine mosaics, while the wooden ceiling is a masterpiece of Arabic carpentry.

Cefalù, on a much larger scale, has features that look to northern Romanesque – the two-towered façade (1240) filled with miniature intersecting arches, the groin vault in the chancel and tunnel vaults elsewhere. But Cefalù's nave, with arcades on columns and a wooden roof, is more Byzantine, and the great mosaic of Christ in the eastern apse completely so.

Monreale is essentially similar but more richly conceived. Here too the mosaics of the interior are purely Byzantine, but the exuberant intersecting arcades around the exterior of the east end, picked out in two colours, are more Islamic than Romanesque. 66 Its very pretty cloister continues the mixture of styles, with Romanesque capitals, miniature shafts inlaid with coloured marbles in a style derived from Cosmati work in Rome, and stilted arches.

Three smaller churches in Palermo, S. Giovanni degli Eremiti (1132), the Martorana (1143) and S. Cataldo (1161), combine basically Byzantine schemes with Islamic domes. A unique secular survival is the castle of La Zisa (1154), also in Palermo, built by Muslim craftsmen for a Norman king, where an austere exterior encloses an interior from *The Thousand and One Nights*.

Finally to the last outpost of medieval Europe, the Iberian Peninsula. Charlemagne's name will be forever associated with the struggle against the Moors through the great legendary epic *The Song of Roland*. Soon afterwards St James of Compostela gave his supernatural aid. By the end of the 9th century the Christians had advanced as far as the Douro and the upper Ebro. By 1050 they were south of Ávila, by 1100 across the Tagus, and by the late 12th century two-thirds of Spain had been reconquered. It is against this background of a never-ending crusade that Spanish architecture must be seen. The tide of Romanesque, like the tide of war, moves from north to south and ebbs out just beyond Toledo.

By the 10th century, Christian architects were drawing ideas freely from their Muslim enemies, in particular the horseshoe arch, which appears for instance in the very assured churches of Santiago de Peñalba (919) and S. Maria de Lebeña (924). Northern Spain, though in many ways a frontier region, did absorb some architectural innovations: both the churches just mentioned are tunnel-vaulted, as is S. Pere de Roda (consecrated 1022,

68. The monastery church of Ripoll (completed in 1032) shows no advance on Old St Peter's, on which it seems to have been based; here we are looking at the east end with the choir apse in the centre and the transept with its chapels extending on either side. Spanish Romanesque before Santiago could be grand in concept and spectacular in decoration but remained essentially conservative.

though perhaps finished later), which has quadrant vaults in the aisles.

The largest church in Spain before the building of Santiago de Compostela was that of the monastery of Ripoll (finished 1032). Though lavish in its decoration, it was not adventurous technically, looking back to Old St Peter's in Rome rather than to anything more modern; it has double aisles, thick masonry piers supporting a plain clearstorey, originally a wooden roof (the present vault is modern), and a T-shaped eastern transept with chapels.

Santiago itself was, of course, the major monument of early Romanesque in Spain. Because of its many links with France, it has already been discussed in a French context, and indeed it stands very much alone in Spain. Considering its size and fame, one would expect it to have been more influential, but further French influences seem to have come from other sources. One major church, the cathedral of Pamplona, in the north-east, on which one of the Santiago masons is known to have worked, is lost, so a vital piece of evidence is missing. As we move east, towards the Mediterranean seaboard of the Peninsula, French and Lombard influences become more insistent. Seo de Urgel (1131) follows Ripoll in its plan, but has more refined piers and clearstorey windows and a tunnel vault. Its crossing carries the first of the characteristically Spanish ribbed domes. Subsequent Catalan architecture depends very much on French models, in particular Cistercian churches, reaching forward into 'half-Gothic' – with shafted piers, rib vaults and pointed arches. Examples are the cathedrals of Tarragona (1171) and Lérida (1203), both of which remained faithful to their original design throughout a long building history.

A more distinctive form of Spanish Romanesque developed in the central regions of Aragon, León and Castile. Jaca Cathedral (*c.* 1054) is a basilican church with alternating supports, tunnel-vaulted transepts and a ribbed dome over the crossing. It is tempting to relate these domes to Muslim precedent, which is clearly the case at S. Miguel at Almazán (12th century), where the vault is based on one bay of the mosque at Córdoba.

It is a scholarly pastime among Spanish historians of Romanesque to attempt to distinguish French features from those indigenous to Spain. But whatever the Spanish architects borrowed, they made their own. S. Isidore at León (late 12th century) has a tunnel-vaulted nave and transepts but lobed Moorish arches. The cathedral of Ciudad Rodrigo (1165) has domed-up vaults reminiscent of Anjou. S. Vicente at Ávila (1109) has a rib-vaulted nave, but its three apses project from the sheer, windowless wall of the transept in a way that could only be Spanish.

Spanish Romanesque reaches its climax in the cathedrals of Zamora and Salamanca. Both were begun about 1150 and both are

69, 70. The proximity of the Moors led to several idiosyncratic features in Spanish Romanesque, the octagonal crossing towers of the Colegiata of S.Maria at Toro (below) and elsewhere, and the lobed ornament around the windows. Moorish influence is clearest of all at S.Miguel, Almazán (below right), where the ribs of the dome echo the mosque at Córdoba.

structurally close to the Cistercian formula. Most remarkable are their crossing domes. That of Zamora, raised on a single-storey drum, originally had sixteen small windows, divided by sixteen ribs inside and out. Soon after it was finished, four round turrets were added at the corners, blocking four of the windows. (The tower of S. Maria at Toro is almost a replica.) Both the main dome and the turrets are covered with a scaly surface of overlapping circles. The crossing dome of the Old Cathedral at Salamanca, which still stands modestly next to the vast new Gothic cathedral erected in the 16th century, has two storeys of windows but the same corner turrets and the same scaly decoration on the outside, where it rises to a stunted pyramid.

69

Many relatively marginal areas of Romanesque Europe have had to be omitted from this survey, including Ireland (Cashel of the Kings with Cormac's Chapel, 12th century, within the Norman orbit); Scandinavia (the unique and fascinating wooden stave churches of Norway); Poland (which evolved an interesting brick Romanesque of its own); and, most regrettably, the Holy Land, where the military orders of the Knights Hospitallers and Templars were responsible for many buildings powerfully expressive of both the cross and the sword. Templar architecture, in particular, had repercussions on Europe. As their name implies, the Templars were the guardians of the Temple Mount in Jerusalem. Here the most conspicuous building was the Muslim Dome of the Rock, equated by the Crusaders with Solomon's Temple, which became the model for a whole series of round Templar churches. (Somewhat confusingly, round churches are also the hallmark of the Hospitallers, in their case based on the church of the Holy Sepulchre, which the Muslims may well have been copying when they built the Dome of the Rock.) Perhaps the most impressive of all the Templar churches in Europe is that at Tomar, in Portugal (1162), with a central octagonal arcade surrounded by an aisle with sixteen ribs.

It may have been noticed that one more region which might be expected to figure prominently is conspicuous by its absence, and that is Paris and its surroundings, in or near the Ile-de-France. The reason seems to be that most of the religious centres there – certainly St Denis, Chartres and Beauvais – already had major cathedrals built in the Carolingian age and there was therefore no need to rebuild or replace them. When that time did come, however, in the mid- and late 12th century, it was precisely this area that would consequently be most receptive to architectural innovation. That story begins another chapter.

Chapter 4:   The Gothic Centuries

The Gothic style has nothing to do with the Goths. It was a name coined in the 17th century to describe a style that by then seemed primitive and barbarous. But it stuck and is by now impossible to replace.

How Gothic began
The change from Romanesque to Gothic is usually explained in structural or engineering terms. And this is right. The combination of the pointed arch, the rib vault and the precisely placed buttress transformed the possibilities open to architects. The pointed arch meant that spans of different widths could be given the same height; the rib vault meant that thrusts could be channelled onto specific points; and the buttress in its evolved form, the flying buttress, meant that these thrusts could be transferred to the ground without the need for thick walls. The result was a system based on forces held in equilibrium, a concept not completely new to architecture (it had been applied, for instance, at Hagia Sophia), but never exploited so eagerly and deliberately. Each of these three features had occurred in Romanesque, but in combination, and articulated clearly by precise mouldings, they led not only to a new structural approach but to a new way of conceiving spaces and volumes which architects were quick to exploit. This in turn led to a new aesthetic, an aesthetic of line rather than mass. In a Gothic building not only is space defined by line, but this line seems to possess dynamic force. Clearly articulated shafts rise from floor to ceiling, meeting and mingling in the pattern of vaults and traceried windows in a way that irresistibly suggests that this is how the building stands up. The 19th-century French architect and historian Viollet-le-Duc did in fact evolve a theory in which all these members had a structural function. Modern engineers are more doubtful. The important point is that they satisfy the eye: they seem to be working, even if the role of some parts is a fiction.

Gothic architecture lasted for a very long time – from roughly 1150 to roughly 1550 – but during that time no fundamental structural innovation took place. In the following pages we shall see how the main phases of Gothic succeeded each other, and how regional styles evolved differentiating the Gothic of France,

71. Bourges Cathedral, begun about 1195, is a perfect expression of the Gothic impulse to verticality, the articulation of forces through line and the integration of every element into an overwhelming unity. Here we are looking from the nave to the inner aisle, which is so tall that it has a complete three-storey elevation of its own. Typical of the subtlety of the Bourges master is the way the wall above the piers swells slightly, as if to suggest that they continued upward within the masonry.

England, Germany, Spain and Italy. All of these distinctions are essentially matters of the variation of parts, multiplication of vaulting ribs, enrichment of decoration, tracery and sculpture.

The great majority of buildings to be examined in this chapter are churches and cathedrals. Christian worship was the driving force for every cultural activity in the Middle Ages – philosophy, art, architecture, literature and music. Preoccupied to the point of obsession with the fate of the soul after death, medieval men and women devoted a large part of their assets and their energy to the glorification of God, to gratitude to Christ for his redeeming sacrifice and to endless appeals for intercession to the Virgin and the saints. Architecture is at the centre of this mental world.

Until the 19th century, the great cathedrals and churches were widely regarded as anonymous buildings which seemed in some strange way to have arisen spontaneously from their social and cultural background – through the 'spirit of the age'. The way that many cathedrals grew piecemeal over the centuries, accumulating parts in a variety of styles (and indeed being admired all the more for that reason by later generations), encouraged such a view. But without question they were all begun to the design of a particular professional master-mason (or, as we should say, architect), whose name in many cases we now know; and the same applies to every alteration and addition.

From the middle and end of the Gothic period we have drawings prepared by architects for their patrons and workmen. 72 Presumably the same was true earlier, although in the actual process of construction all the parts would be drawn out full-scale on the floor. In the case of major buildings like cathedrals, which might take a century or more to complete, the architect could expect his work to be taken over by a successor, who would not necessarily follow his original design. The choices open to the second architect (and after him, the third and the fourth) were, however, not unlimited. What had already been built largely determined what could be built next. Strict systems of proportion were learned as part of the architect's training, based partly on geometry, partly on what was known of the strength of materials, and partly on a form of mystical numerology (no longer fully understood). An architect who, for instance, inherited an arcade of a certain height and bay-width could continue with a gallery conforming to certain norms, divided into a certain number of openings and leading to a certain formal progression on which the next storey would have to be based. Much of this knowledge was a professional secret which masons were forbidden to reveal to

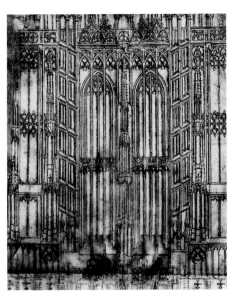

ıſt dıe tʒunge aller erden vnd

outsiders. But at every stage, the architect could make a choice. The result was a harmonious whole, though it might be the product of many minds.

We cannot reconstruct this secret knowledge (or, more properly, these technical guidelines), but we can see its effects. The building history of Chartres Cathedral has been analysed into over thirty campaigns overseen by nine master-masons, some of whom returned at intervals, and each of whom could at every stage have decided differently from the way he did. But the end-product is a building that conforms to consistent criteria, and (apart from the disparate west towers) could easily have been designed in one go from the ground up. Much later, at the end of the 15th century, the designer of Bell Harry Tower at Canterbury, having carried the work up to a certain point, told his patrons that he could continue in one of two different ways, and gave them the choice. In this case documentary evidence happens to survive, but it must have occurred over and over again. In the absence of documents, the proportional and geometrical systems used by medieval architects have to be deduced from the buildings themselves. The plans of St Maclou in Rouen and Orford Castle, in Essex, have revealed an almost incredible complexity which only careful measured drawing brings to light.

Numerous contemporary manuscript illustrations show Gothic buildings under construction and the machinery that was

72. Above: detail from one of the rare architect's drawings to survive from the Middle Ages, Matthäus Böblinger's design for the tower of Ulm Minster, c. 1480. The tower was not built until the 19th century, when the original drawing was used.

73. Above right: a 12th-century German miniature showing masons at work. The heavy stones, held by pincers, are raised by cranes worked by treadwheels.

73

available. The material was always high quality cut stone or in the Baltic region, brick. Treadwheel cranes hoisted the stones to the positions where they were needed – a few of them still survive, walled up in the vaults that they had helped to build. Scaffolding was primitive, and was preferably fixed progressively into the completed parts of the building rather than resting on the ground. A technique was evolved for building rib vaults without elaborate centering, allowing the web or cell to be filled in between them. Roofs were generally built before vaults, serving as protection for the masons.

By far the most circumstantial account of the construction of any medieval building is that left by the monk Gervase of Canterbury in the 12th century. He tells how in 1174 fire had destroyed the old choir of the cathedral a few years after the murder of Thomas Becket; how the assembled monks sought a master-mason; how they chose a Frenchman, William of Sens; and how for six years he supervised the building of the present choir. While the work was still in progress, William fell from the scaffolding and was so badly injured that he had to retire. His place was taken by another William, 'the Englishman', who carried it to completion. Gervase does not say so, but it is quite clear that the second William altered the design of the first. The whole campaign was remarkably fast, lasting only about twelve years altogether. We cannot be sure that the story of Canterbury was typical, but there is no reason to think that it was exceptional.

The first Gothic century: France, 1150–1250

In the 1140s all the key elements of Gothic came together to produce a work that was recognizably new. By a general consensus of historians, that work was the new east end of the abbey of St Denis, just outside Paris, begun in 1140.

74

St Denis owes its importance not only to the fact that it was technically and aesthetically innovative, but also to its prominence and prestige. Whatever was built there would be noticed immediately and be influential everywhere. Its patron, Abbot Suger, was one of the great men of France, Louis VII's chief adviser and deputy, and his abbey one of the richest in Europe. Suger was not a modest man, and he saw his new abbey church as a means of asserting his status. We are lucky to have his own account of the building of St Denis – a unique document that brilliantly illuminates a medieval churchman's view of himself and the world. Suger boasts of the amount of money he spent, of the gold and jewels that adorned the reliquaries, of the mystical significance of the

74. The ambulatory of St Denis, looking east (c. 1140). The way the spaces are unified, flowing into each other without partition or division, has no precedent in Romanesque architecture. In Abbot Suger's eyes, light had a mystical quality symbolic of the divine. 'Bright is the noble edifice', he wrote, 'which is pervaded by the new light.'

75, 76. The experimental 12th century: Notre Dame of Paris, and Chartres Cathedral. The original four-storey elevation of Paris (late 1170s) was restored by Viollet-le-Duc in three bays at the crossing. By the time of Chartres (1194) the three-storey elevation was established, with triforium subsidiary to arcade and clearstorey.

77, 78. Opposite: the mature 13th century. Reims (left) and Amiens both employ piers consisting of columns with shafts in the main directions, of which one carries the vaulting shafts. Reims (1211), the prestigious coronation church of the French kings, first used bar-tracery, to be followed at once by Amiens (1220). Amiens has a classic plan (below), with short transepts and a cluster of radiating chapels, though the projecting Lady Chapel is unusual.

coloured glass and the imagery of the saints, and of his cleverness in finding all the right materials. But he does not describe the architecture in detail, nor mention the architect. Presumably he wanted the best, and he got it.

For the time being, Suger left the old Carolingian nave standing, and added a chancel with a semicircular ambulatory and radiating chapels. There are double aisles, the arches are pointed and the bays rib-vaulted. Unfortunately, everything above the arcade level was taken down and replaced after 1231, so that nothing is known about the high vaults or whether flying buttresses were used. What is certain, however, is that the building of St Denis was the signal for a burst of major architectural activity that consolidated the new style and produced a series of cathedrals which for boldness, originality and imagination are unrivalled.

These cathedrals – all (with two exceptions, Coutances and Bourges) in or close to the Ile-de-France region – are: Sens (begun in 1143), Noyon (1145), Laon (1160), Paris (1163), Bourges (1192), Chartres (1194), Reims (1211), Le Mans (choir, 1217), Amiens (1220), Coutances (1235), and Beauvais (1247). Each is a highly individual building, reflecting the ideas and personality

75

76, 77

78

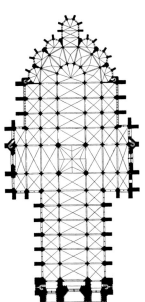

of its master-mason, but they are all essentially variations on a common theme. They all (except Bourges) have cruciform plans, with a nave, crossing, transepts and chancel with apsidal ending (Laon was later altered to square). Sometimes the transepts project beyond the line of the aisles, sometimes not. In elevation they are either three- or four-storeyed: that is, always with an arcade, gallery and clearstorey, and sometimes with an extra wall-passage, or triforium, thrown in between gallery and clearstorey. (These terms are not used consistently in architectural books. The middle level between the arcade and the clearstorey is often called a triforium. This becomes confusing when there are four storeys, and it seems best to call the middle level a gallery when it is as wide as the aisle underneath and has a roof, and a triforium when it is just a passage in the wall.) The arcade piers are either cylindrical or more typically comprise a cylinder with four shafts in the main directions, the line of the innermost shaft rising the whole height of the building. Vaults are either quadripartite (each compart-ment, divided into four, covering one bay) or sexpartite (each com-partment, divided into six, covering two bays). On the exterior there are usually two towers at the west end; very often more

79. Coutances, in Normandy, lay outside the orbit of the Ile-de-France and its cathedral incorporates several regional peculiarities, including wall-passages in front of the windows, seen here in the ambulatory of the mid-13th-century choir.

80. Beauvais (1248) marks the end of the era that had begun with St Denis just over 100 years before. It is the highest of all Gothic cathedrals. With an appropriateness that seems almost like retribution, its vault collapsed in 1284, though whether excessive height was to blame has never been established. This engraving shows the chancel in its rebuilt state. The crossing and transepts were eventually completed in the 16th century, but the nave never.

towers were planned but never built (Chartres was to have nine, Laon seven). Bourges, Le Mans and Coutances are exceptional in having double aisles, of which the inner is higher than the outer and is given a complete elevation of its own, an effect which at Bourges is quite breathtaking, since there seem to be complete churches on each side of the nave. Beauvais has the distinction of being the highest Gothic cathedral ever built – so high in fact, that its vault collapsed in 1284 and had to be rebuilt in a strengthened form. It never progressed further than the crossing and stands today as a vast but poignant witness to an unrealizable ambition.

81, 71

80

81, 82, 83. The evolution of the French Gothic west front. Laon (above, 1190) still retains elements of Romanesque – the round arches, the way the levels of the central bay differ from those of the towers and the deep, cavernous porches projecting from the wall. Three-dimensionality is emphasized by the diagonally placed tabernacles on the corners of the towers from which oxen peer out.

Amiens (opposite, 1220) keeps the three deep porches and gables but aligns the horizontals and incorporates a sculptured gallery of kings below the rose-window (whose tracery dates from the 15th century). This pre-1914 photograph shows how for centuries the great cathedrals dominated their surroundings.

At Reims (above right, c.1255) the central porch gable has begun to invade the rose-window, and the gallery of kings has risen to the uppermost level.

By the middle of the 13th century, indeed, French Gothic had become international, and for a while in the later 13th century it is possible to find French features in almost every European country. In Germany, Cologne (begun 1248 – only the choir and the base of one tower were built in the Middle Ages) is virtually a French building, while the masters of Regensburg, Magdeburg and Limburg-an-der-Lahn had clearly been looking across the Rhine. In Spain, Burgos and Toledo have decidedly French features, and León may well have been designed by a Frenchman. At Westminster Abbey the supposition is even stronger. 106 118

Among the most impressive features of these churches are their west fronts – ceremonial entrances to the house of God. The two-tower façade, taken over from the Romanesque of Normandy, reflects the interior structure of nave and aisles, and provides the setting for three or more deep porches filled with sculpture in the form of free-standing figures and scenes in relief. Laon is a powerful early essay (its towers bizarrely peopled with oxen gazing out over the countryside). Paris, Amiens and Reims take the form to its climax. 81 82, 83

This account has necessarily had to omit smaller-scale buildings, which are often the occasion of the most inventive designs

84, 85. Tracery came into its own in the 13th century, when the Rayonnant style, epitomized by the rose-window of the new south transept of Notre Dame, Paris, begun by Jean de Chelles in 1258 (above), made it a dominant element in the total design. The Sainte Chapelle, Paris (above right), begun in 1242, is a Rayonnant building whose rose-window was replaced in 1485 in the Flamboyant style.

and the richest workmanship. Most notable of all is the Sainte Chapelle, the private chapel of the kings of France (begun 1242), built to house a relic of the Crown of Thorns, a cage of stained glass glowing with colour and sculptured decoration. Its double structure (dark lower chapel; high, light upper chapel) was copied a few years later in London at the equally prestigious St Stephen's Chapel, Westminster.

After the middle of the 13th century in France, however, the great age of experiment was over, and the process was to be one of refinement. In one aspect only is development obvious, and that is the design of window tracery, a feature that gives its name to the succeeding styles. The earliest Gothic windows have no tracery. Around the late 12th century, a form known as plate-tracery had evolved – two paired lancets and a circle are punched through the wall and set within a moulded frame; large rose-windows are made in the same way. By about 1215, at Reims, the sections of wall are reduced to mere lines of stones and we have arrived at bar-tracery. As windows grew larger, bar-tracery grew more elaborate, but in this first phase it is always based on a limited geometrical repertoire of pointed arches and circles, usually cusped. Rose-windows (e.g. the transept ends of Notre Dame in Paris) provided the greatest opportunity, with an ever-growing number of lights radiating from the centre, giving its name to the classic phase of French Gothic, Rayonnant.

The assured mystery of the Rayonnant style is characterized by the way tracery becomes totally integrated into the whole design, with hardly an inch to spare; by a readiness to experiment with uneven numbers of lights, new shapes (triangles and squares with curved sides) and double tracery; by eliminating mass, reducing the elements to a skeleton; and by glazing the triforium, as in the rebuilt nave of St Denis (1231) and the choir of Amiens (1250). And there were master-masons who craved to do things no one had done before, like the designer of the choir and transept of St Urbain at Troyes (1262) which is full of eccentricities including syncopated double tracery and a porch that seems to grow out of flying buttresses. In the mid-14th century this gave way to a style in which the tracery bars weave and flicker like flames – the Flamboyant style. The ultimate source of Flamboyant Gothic was England, and to this country we must now turn.

86. The unknown designer of St Urbain at Troyes (begun in 1262) was an avid explorer of new spatial effects. On the inside he experimented with syncopated tracery (i.e. one pattern over another); on the outside he created skeletal gables in front of the window walls, and balanced his south porch on buttresses whose main attention seems to be elsewhere.

English masons were aware of what was happening in France but they were slow to commit themselves to the new style in cathedral-scale buildings until a Frenchman showed them the way. This was William of Sens, already mentioned as the architect of the new choir of Canterbury.

Canterbury Cathedral occupied as prominent a position in England as St Denis did in France. Not only was it the seat of the primate but from 1170 onwards it was a pilgrimage centre whose shrine – of the murdered Thomas Becket – rivalled any in Christendom. So it was not long before William's innovations were being taken up all over England. (William was not, in fact, given a completely free hand. He had to fit his new choir into the shell of the old, a task that he managed with some ingenuity.) At Canterbury, arches were pointed, vaults sexpartite, thrust balanced against counter-thrust by concealed buttresses in the galleries.

It is extremely rare at this time to find comment on architectural design, but the chronicler Gervase was clearly aware that the choir was something new, and he tried hard to define what it was:

The pillars of the old and new work are alike in form and thickness but different in length. For the new pillars were elongated by about twelve feet. In the old capitals the work was plain, in the new ones exquisite in sculpture. No marble columns were there, but here are innumerable ones. There, in the circuit around the choir, the vaults were plain, but here they are arch-ribbed and have keystones. There, there was a ceiling of wood decorated with excellent painting, but here is a vault beautifully constructed of stone. The new work is higher than the old...

The 'marble columns' that Gervase mentions are black Purbeck marble; they serve to define the lines of shafts with great clarity. This had some precedent in Flemish Romanesque (Tournai marble is also black) but not in France. It is, however, very much in the spirit of Gothic and was destined to have a long life in England.

The story of cathedral building in England is harder to tell than that in France, for one simple reason. Whereas in France bishops were on the whole ready to demolish their old buildings and start afresh, in England (mainly because they had spent a fortune not long before in building their Romanesque cathedrals) they were more cautious – adding a new choir or modernizing a nave, but rarely allowing a master-mason to realize a total vision. There are only four English Gothic cathedrals that can be judged in terms of a consistent aesthetic approach. All the others are hybrids – Romanesque structures with, for instance, a Gothic vault (Gloucester, Norwich) or a Gothic crossing and choir (Ely), or structures where Gothic rebuilding took place at widely separated intervals (Canterbury). This does not make visiting an English cathedral less rewarding than visiting a French one, but it does make it different.

The four 'new' major churches are Lincoln, Wells, Salisbury and Westminster Abbey. They all belong to the first phase of English Gothic, traditionally known as 'Early English'. Of the next phase, 'Decorated', there is Exeter apart from its Norman towers, York apart from its Early English transepts, and the choir of Bristol. Of the third and most characteristically English, phase, 'Perpendicular', there is no complete example (except Bath, finished much later), only a remodelled choir (Gloucester) and two rebuilt naves (Canterbury and Winchester). These stylistic labels, invented in the early 19th century, serve well to distinguish the three quite easily recognizable styles.

87. The choir of Canterbury Cathedral (1174), whose building history can be followed in unique detail in a contemporary account, marked the decisive beginning of Gothic architecture in England. Its first architect was French, William of Sens. The classically inspired columns and sexpartite rib vaulting (over the foreground bays, not visible) come from France; but much of the ornament and the use of Purbeck marble are English. The curious 'pinched' look is caused by the need to retain Romanesque towers on each side of the original apse, beyond which the Trinity Chapel – by William the Englishman – opens out to house the shrine of St Thomas Becket.

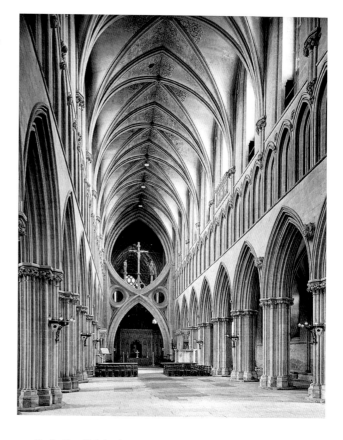

88. At Wells, begun only a few years after Canterbury, the influence of France is considerably less. Instead of emphasizing verticality (compare Bourges, for example, ill. 71), the English designer seems to want to stress the horizontal. No shafts rise from floor to ceiling and the gallery arcade runs from end to end without a break. The 'strainer arches' which brutally interrupt this movement at the crossing (we are looking east) were added about 1338.

Early English is closest to French Gothic, though right from the beginning English architects followed their own tastes.

While Canterbury choir was still under way, in 1180, a new cathedral was begun at Wells. Although every element here is Gothic, we are immediately aware that we are a long way from the Ile-de-France and that many of the preferences that typified English Romanesque still operate. By French standards the nave is too long and too low. Horizontality, not verticality, is empha-sized. The division into bays is blurred. The vaulting shafts, instead of rising from the ground, begin just below the clearstorey, while the gallery openings run without a break from one end of the nave to the other. The internal height is only 67 feet/20m (Amiens is 140 feet/43m). Clearly, the English designer was not aping any French model. The same is true when one comes to the west front, which, instead of signalling the entrance by vast gabled porches, seems almost to conceal the fact that there are doors at all. It is a screen for the display of sculpture.

88

90

In 1192 an even more ambitious building was begun at Lincoln. Here the intention was progressively to demolish the old Romanesque cathedral and replace it with a Gothic one. (This was done, except that funds ran out when work reached the old west front, which was allowed to remain.) The patron at Lincoln was the energetic Bishop (later St) Hugh. As his architect he appointed a man (probably called Geoffrey de Noiers) fully as exceptional as himself. While keeping the basic stylistic vocabulary of Canterbury, the Lincoln master indulges in a whole repertoire of personal quirks: crocketted shafts inside other shafts, double overlapping miniature arcades along the aisle walls, and a strangely proportioned polygonal east end (later destroyed to make way for the Angel Choir). For the vault he chose neither quadripartite nor sexpartite but a mixture of the two which results in an odd, asymmetrical pattern, dubbed the 'crazy vault' by a modern historian, never seen before and never repeated again. St Hugh's architect died before the cathedral was half built and the nave is the work of his successor. Though not eccentric like the choir, it initiated two novel features in the vault destined to have a long career in England: the tierceron and the ridge rib. Tiercerons are extra ribs, extending from the wall to the crown of the vault: at Lincoln,

89, 90. Lincoln: the choir looking west (below) and the nave looking east (below right). The eccentric 'crazy vault' of the choir, with its irregular, disturbing, rhythm, developed into the first fully formed tierceron vault of the nave. A ridge rib now runs along its whole length, again stressing the horizontal.

instead of three ribs springing from the same point (the transverse rib and two diagonals), we have seven. The ridge rib runs along the crown of the vault from beginning to end. Like the treatment of the gallery at Wells, both these features have the effect of playing down the division into bays, so dear to the French, and making the whole vessel one continuous space.

Salisbury, begun in 1220, is without quirks, an exercise in formal logic, though just as English in its proportions. Purbeck marble forms a major design feature, giving it a linear quality and (combined with a total absence of sculpture or foliage capitals) a certain plainness. On the exterior, however, Salisbury makes an unforgettable impression, building up through a sequence of clearly defined volumes to culminate in the great central tower and spire.

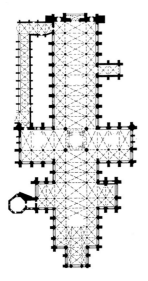

With Westminster Abbey (begun in 1246) French influence reasserts itself. Its architect, called 'Henry of Reyns' in the documents, may well have come from Reims, which is its closest model. Its patron, King Henry III, saw it as a demonstration of Plantagenet prestige and with its wealth of sculptured decoration, intricate mouldings, fine materials and double tracery it was probably one of the most expensive buildings of the Middle Ages. In the choir stood the shrine of Edward the Confessor, which was to be surrounded by the tombs of English kings. The proportions – tall and narrow, with the emphasis on verticality – and the details of arcade, gallery and clearstorey are close to French precedents, and for the first time in England the windows are given tracery corresponding to Rayonnant patterns in France, including the great (though much restored) rose-windows at the ends of the north and south transepts and the very latest innovation from Reims, the so-called spherical triangle or triangle with convex sides. Westminster is the culmination of the Early English style and its influence can be traced in numberless churches and additions to cathedrals through the country, from the new choir at Lincoln (the Angel Choir) to the Chapel of the Nine Altars at Durham. But already by 1280 England was on the brink of a development that would give it the architectural leadership of Europe – the Decorated style.

92

The name is not inappropriate because the style is highly decorated, but it does not tell the whole story. Gothic architecture broke free from formal geometry and the logic of apparent function, and entered a world of untrammelled imagination that would lead (though not in England) to an exuberance and an excess of fantasy that would have seemed madness to the master of St Denis.

Lavishness of decoration was a symptom. In the classic first phase of Gothic, ornament is a product of function, in that it serves to mark and emphasize key points of structure: the capitals of columns, corbels from which vaulting ribs spring, bosses where the ribs meet. By the 1280s such enrichment is spreading to walls and window-surrounds; altar reredoses become complex compositions full of statuary; wall-shafts can disappear into niches and emerge the other side; vaulting ribs multiply from seven to nine and then to eleven, so that they project over the interior space like giant palm branches, and from these ribs (tiercerons) sprout yet others (liernes) beginning and ending where fancy, not structure, dictates; a new form of arch, the ogee, consisting of two S-curves, begins to appear everywhere; the tracery of windows casts off obvious obedience to the ruler and compass and begins to curve and weave unpredictably, leaving shapes and spaces for which new names ('mouchettes') have to be invented.

Most radical of all, space itself begins to be conceived in new terms. When the central tower of Romanesque Ely collapsed in 1320, it was decided to rebuild it not as a conventional lantern tower with straight sides, but as an octagon, cutting off the adjoining bays of the choir, transepts and nave with diagonal walls – something without precedent in the history of Christian architecture. For the retrochoir of Wells Cathedral the architect devised a system of interlocking vaults that made nonsense of the very idea of distinct bays. At Bristol in 1306, the master-mason made the nave and aisles equal in height (i.e., no gallery or clearstorey), carrying the thrust of the vault across the aisles on little stone bridges; in a nearby chapel he built a vault consisting only of ribs, a skeleton with no flesh on it.

The Decorated style, the most exciting phase of Gothic, lasted roughly seventy years, from 1280 to 1350. During or shortly after that time, it seems fairly certain that architects from the continent visited England and were impressed by what they saw. But England, as though wearied by the effort of imagination, turned to a completely opposite style, the rectilinear Perpendicular, which – astonishing as it can be on its own terms – seemed to contradict everything that went before.

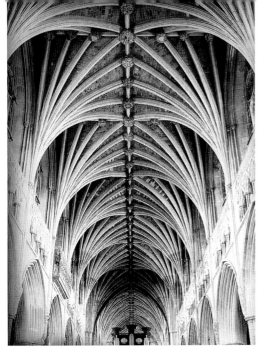

93. Exeter Cathedral, the nave (1328). Here the urge towards unity is carried further than in any French design. Clusters of ribs like palm branches (eleven springing from one point) virtually abolish the division into separate bays. This is a symptom of new free-flowing spaces of the Decorated style.

94, 95. The Ely octagon and the aisles of Bristol are two of the leaps of spatial imagination that make the English Decorated style unique. At Ely (below left) the crossing area, damaged by the fall of the tower, was thrown into a single space covered by a wooden octagonal lantern and lit by diagonally placed windows. At Bristol (below) the thrust of the main vault is carried across the choir aisles by miniature bridges with complete vaults of their own.

How Gothic ended

The final phase of Gothic is a confusing story and there is no way of simplifying it. This is because one can no longer make general rules. Every European country goes its own way, apparently without reference to the others. It is the period that is most neglected by architectural historians, but in some ways the most exciting.

We return to *France*. The classic, international style established by the series of cathedrals up to Beauvais continues to develop, but without major changes. The proportion of window to wall increases. Beginning in the 14th century, Flamboyant tracery blossoms into luxuriant growth (St Wulfran, Abbeville, and the rose window added to the Sainte Chapelle in 1485), but is not reflected in the vaulting patterns, which remain stubbornly quadripartite. Piers, however, abandon the simple forms and become bundles of linear members. On the exterior, blank tracery becomes ever more popular, reaching up into the towers in the form of tall niches and elongated panels. The west front of La Trinité at Vendôme or the south transept of Beauvais are so covered with Flamboyant patterns that it is hard to tell window from wall. Rouen has two churches, St Ouen and St Maclou, which rival English Decorated in both planning and decorative complexity. (St Ouen was originally designed with diagonally turned west towers, an experiment hardly ever repeated.)

8

9

96. The west front of La Trinité, Vendôme (1499) represents the take over of architecture by Flamboyant tracery.

97. The cathedral of Albi, in the Languedoc (below right, 1282), was built in the aftermath of the Albigensian wars; its closed surface – seen here from the east – evokes a fortress. The severity was later relieved by a Flamboyant south porch.

There were also regional variations partially surviving from the earlier local Romanesque. In the south-west, recently devastated by the Albigensian wars, there are churches that look like fortresses. The brick-built Albi Cathedral (1282) presents a defensive face to the world, its buttressing system internalized in the form of walls across what would be aisles. At the very end of the period, when Renaissance motifs were already entering French architecture, Gothic experienced a sort of late flowering, with such exotic blooms as the pendant vaults of St Pierre at Caen (choir 1518).

England, as we have seen, embraced the Perpendicular style. As early as the 1330s, first the south transept and then the choir of Gloucester Cathedral were remodelled by placing a stone grid against the walls, concealing the Romanesque structure and continuing into the vault in the form of a tight network of ribs and across the vast east window in a pattern of straight glazing bars extending the full height with straight mullions crossing them. For whatever reason, the logic of Perpendicular appealed to 14th-century England more than the exuberance of Decorated. For two centuries, innumerable parish churches (most notably in the rich wool counties of East Anglia and Gloucestershire) followed the same formula: tall, wide arcades with simple mouldings, often uninterrupted by capitals, and large,

98. In 1337 the Romanesque choir of Gloucester Cathedral was remodelled in the new Perpendicular style. A grid of tracery and panelling was placed over the walls, a complex vault built, and a vast new window opened up the east end.

99. Below right: looking west in the nave of a typical East Anglian Perpendicular parish church, Saffron Walden, Essex (early 15th century).

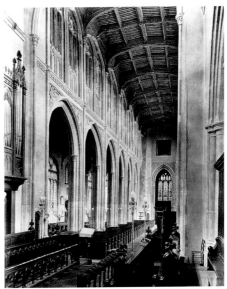

100. The rebuilt nave of Canterbury Cathedral (1379) is an epitome of the Perpendicular style: lines are clean, spaces uncomplicated, decoration restrained. It is the total effect that matters.

bright windows with rectilinear tracery. In cathedral building, the naves of Winchester and Canterbury are the major works, structures carefully organized to make the maximum effect at a single glance. The effect of austerity is often offset by blind panelling at dado level and sometimes even on the jambs and soffits of arches. Two other features, apart from the rich decorative effect of stained glass and colour, give Perpendicular some extra glamour. One is towers: the central towers of Canterbury and Gloucester or the west towers of many Somerset churches are

101, 102. The fan vault was the last creative invention of the Perpendicular style. At King's College Chapel, Cambridge (below, c. 1515) it takes the classic form of half-cones meeting at the centre. In the Henry VII Chapel, Westminster Abbey (below right, 1503), full cones with pendant bosses appear to hang from the roof.

among the glories of the Middle Ages. The other is fan vaulting, an exclusively English invention. Structurally, a fan vault is a solid stone ceiling carved into a pattern of radiating ribs in the form of inverted half-cones. King's College Chapel, Cambridge (complet- 101 ed in 1515), is the most lavish example. In special cases, pendant bosses are suspended from the cones in apparent defiance of gravity, as in Henry VII's Chapel at Westminster Abbey, begun 102 as late as 1503.

In *Germany*, Romanesque did not surrender to Gothic until well into the 13th century. The first innovatory ideas were all French, but by the 14th century specifically German forms of Gothic are clearly in evidence. Prague Cathedral, the most 103 ambitious church east of the Rhine, was begun by a Frenchman, Matthew of Arras, but in 1356 was taken over and completely transformed by Peter Parler, the most outstanding of a dynasty of German architects. Unrestricted, he might have chosen the hall-church form, the favourite German type throughout the 14th and 15th centuries. By giving up gallery and clearstorey, architects risked depriving themselves of the soaring verticality of French Gothic, but in fact the churches are often so high that this does not happen, and they achieve unprecedented effects of width and

103. Peter Parler took over Prague Cathedral from the more conservative Matthew of Arras in 1356, when he was only twenty-three. His vaulting system – the so-called scissors vault – (1380s) is decorative rather than functional. Note how the triforium passage elegantly bends out to accommodate the openings through the piers.

104. Freiburg-im-Breisgau (above right) has the most accomplished of those German openwork spires that came to completion in the Middle Ages.

105. The choir of Cologne Cathedral (1248), with its tall clearstorey and glazed triforium, belongs with the cathedrals of the Ile-de-France as the final statement of the Rayonnant style.

106. Only the lower part of Cologne's right-hand tower was built in the Middle Ages, but the design (*c.* 1300) survived and was carried out in the mid-19th century.

spaciousness. Hall-churches are almost universal in central and eastern Europe, from St Elizabeth at Marburg (1257) to St Stephen's Cathedral in Vienna (*c.* 1300 onwards), and in fine parish churches such as Schwäbisch Gmund (1351), Landshut, Ulm, Soest and the two great churches of Nuremberg, St Sebald (1361) and St Lorenz (1439). For the façades, German architects particularly loved openwork spires, built at Freiburg-im-Breisgau (*c.* 1300) and intended (though not built until the 19th century) at Cologne, Regensburg and Ulm.

    One reason for the German fondness for hall-churches must have been that they were more favourable to complex vaulting

104

106

patterns, since ribs could spring in all directions instead of only inwards. Vaulting is the outstanding feature of German late Gothic. It is tempting to look for connections with English Decorated (the 'star vault', common all over Germany, may derive from English polygonal chapter-house vaults; and Peter Parler's 'scissors vault' at Prague is anticipated – by pure chance? – at Ottery St Mary in Devon), but the style soon takes off into a world of autonomous fantasy. Perhaps the most exquisitely beautiful is that of St Anne's at Annaberg in Saxony, of 1525, but it is by no means the most extreme. At the Marktkirche at Halle the ribs fly free from the vault; at St Mary's in Ingolstadt (1520s) they twist into stone pretzels and blossom into stone flowers; at Pirna, near Dresden, one rib simply spirals off on an adventure of its own without even a pretence of a destination. At Brunswick in 1474, and in a few other churches, the unity of the design is reinforced by twisting the columns, so that the ribs writhe away from them as if they were prolongations of the pier mouldings. At the very end of the 15th century a new variant was invented, in which ribs are arbitrarily cut off in mid flight, a form taken to its limit by Benedikt Ried, the virtuoso designer of St Barbara, Kutna Hora, and the Vladislav Hall in Prague Castle. What began as an experiment in structural engineering has ended as a game.

108

107

109

107, 108. The favourite German Gothic ecclesiastical form was the hall-church, in which the aisles are as high as the nave. It generated an amazing variety of rib vaults, linked to the arcade by spiral shafts, as at St Blasius, Brunswick (above left) of 1474, or blossoming into radiant petals as in the nave of St Anne's, Annaberg (right), of 1525.

109. In its final phase German Gothic vaulting playfully draws attention to its own artifice by having ribs that overlap and are arbitrarily chopped off when no longer needed. The Vladislav Hall of Prague Castle (1493) is the masterpiece of Benedikt Ried.

110, 111. Bohemia, Silesia and East Prussia, now parts of Poland, produced their own forms of vaulting. Below: nave aisle of St Mary on the Sands, Breslau (Wroclaw), showing so-called jumping vaults, or triradials, a system of triangular cells with three ribs. Below right: St Mary, Danzig (Gdańsk), with 'cellular' vaults, in which ribs or groins are fashioned on the surface and have no practical function.

The northern and eastern parts of the German lands have vaulting features of their own. Silesia (now western Poland) favoured a type called the 'jumping vault', which consists of a sequence of triangular compartments with three ribs radiating from a boss, creating an irregular rhythm. In Bohemia ribs may be dispensed with altogether; these 'cellular' vaults, of brick covered with thick plaster (apparently the invention of Arnold of Westphalia), look like crinkled paper. Both vaulting types were diffused in central Europe. Absence of stone also led to the technically bold use of brick in northern Germany, even for such details as glazing

110

111

mullions. The brilliance and daring of some of these great brick churches (e.g. Schwerin), many erected by the Franciscans and Dominicans, with narrow windows 90 feet (27m) tall and gables with brick tracery patterns of quite fairy-tale imagination, are among the boldest achievements of medieval architecture.

The Gothic churches of *Flanders* and the *Netherlands* took the classic French formula (still fairly intact at Utrecht, 1265) and developed it in yet other ways. Arcade and clearstorey almost squeeze out the middle storey, which becomes merely a band of patterned masonry. Some of these churches are extremely ambitious. Antwerp Cathedral has not just double but triple aisles and a tower 403 feet (123m) high. Other towers went even higher. Mechelen (Malines) would have had the tallest tower in the world,

112. Characteristic Netherlandish Gothic: the south transept of St John, s'Hertogenbosch, c. 1430. Most of the tracery, including the eccentric inverted arches on the heads of others, is a reconstruction of the 19th century, but accurate.

113, 114. Two Italian churches whose Gothic qualities are compromised not only by the width of the bays but also by the use of tie-rods or beams: Florence Cathedral (above, 1334 onwards), and SS. Giovanni e Paolo in Venice (above right, 1260 onwards).

at 550 feet (168m), but work stopped when it had gone half way. St John at s'Hertogenbosch (begun *c.* 1430) is notable for the lavishness of its decoration, including the intricate tracery of the south porch and the rows of tiny figures (all now restored) that sit astride the flying buttresses. The region of Brabant also evolved a particular ornamental motif, the 'round-topped ogee', whose closest parallel is contemporary female head-dress.

Nothing can prevent the northern visitor's first reaction to *Italian* Gothic from being one of disappointment. It is not a question of success or failure, but of a different aesthetic. Instead of the complex spatial experience of northern cathedrals, with their dark, close-set piers, their linear complexity and their overall feeling of verticality, there is a spaciousness and a clarity that seem to renounce all mystery and mysticism. The nave of Florence Cathedral is much longer than that of Salisbury, but where Salisbury is divided into ten bays, Florence has only four. The result is that it feels shorter. There is also no suggestion of forces held in balance. Italian architects had no objection to stretching iron tie-rods across the main vessel to hold the two sides together, something that contradicts the whole spirit of northern Gothic. This applies in varying degrees to all the great Italian vaulted churches – Siena Cathedral, S. Petronio at Bologna, S. Francesco at Assisi, S. Maria Novella at Florence... All except one: Milan.

The story of Milan Cathedral is immensely complicated. It is a northern cathedral on Italian soil – but is it really a northern cathedral? Its plan is not unusual: a nave with double aisles, almost as wide as it is long, transepts with aisles, and a polygonal east end. Both the nave and the inner aisles have clearstoreys, but so small that they do little to make it lighter; it is as if the cathedral aspired to be a hall-church. The main arcade piers are composite and their vast capitals are surmounted by circlets of niches in which stand over-life-size statues. The vault is simple quadripartite. In the apse the huge windows have patterns that are like Flamboyant tracery stirred into a vortex. The exterior is a forest of pinnacles and statues culminating in an octagonal cupola over the crossing. The material throughout is white marble.

This great, weird building is the result of a century of argument, indecision and compromise followed by three centuries of interrupted construction. It exemplifies all the problems of medieval building methods, but also how they were solved. It was begun about 1385. Within ten years the authorities began to have doubts about its stability. A series of conferences were held.

115, 116. Milan Cathedral, begun *c.* 1385, is unlike any other church in Italy or indeed in Europe. Its wide, spreading proportions reflect the very tall double aisles which considerably reduce clearstorey lighting. The ornate exterior (below) was designed in the 1390s though completed centuries later. Inside (opposite), the rings of canopied niches that take the place of capitals frustrate the effect of verticality which is the hallmark of Northern Gothic.

Altogether some fifty architects, many from France and Germany, including one of the Parler family, were consulted. The records of these conferences give us our most detailed knowledge of masonic techniques, the alternative ways of producing an elevation from a plan (by basing it on a square, 'ad quadratum', or a triangle, 'ad triangulum'), and the diverse views of Italian, French and German experts on such topics as buttressing and strength of materials.

Next, to *Spain*, a country to which many architectural roads lead but from which none return. The earliest French-dominated phase of Spanish Gothic has already been briefly mentioned. León 118 comes closest to the French ideal (and its full complement of stained glass makes it comparable with Chartres). Toledo, which

117. The western spires of Burgos Cathedral were designed *c.* 1440 by 'Juan de Colonia' – Johannes of Cologne – and it is clear that he was inspired by drawings for the then-unbuilt spires of that cathedral (ill. 106).

118. León is the most French of Spanish cathedrals. Begun *c.* 1255, it is almost a textbook example of the Rayonnant style.

119. The Chapel of the Constable, Burgos (below right, 1482), by Juan de Colonia's son Simón. The glazing of the centre of the vault is a modern alteration.

closely followed it, has the Bourges feature of double aisles with complete three-storey elevation to the inner aisle. But before long other influences become apparent. The openwork spires of Burgos 117 were designed about 1440 by a 'Juan de Colonia', i.e. Johannes of Cologne, and he must surely have seen the drawings for the spires – then unbuilt – of the cathedral in his native city. His son and grandson stayed at Burgos, designing the richly decorated Chapel of the Constable and the central tower, both quintessentially 119 Spanish. One should not forget that in Spain Christianity never lost the character of a crusade. The southern part of the peninsula remained in the hands of the Moors until the middle of the 14th century (Granada, a lonely outpost, did not fall until 1492), and this gives Spanish religious architecture an emotional intensity that can still be felt.

When, in the south, Spanish Gothic acquired a true character of its own, its most immediately noticeable feature is width – an openness that does not sacrifice mystery because of the extreme richness of decoration that covers the surfaces and because the space became filled (or was filled until the disastrous reorderings instigated by the Second Vatican Council of 1962–65) with screens and grilles that reduce the interior to a series of shadowy recessions. Window tracery and vaulting ribs are as exuberant as in English Decorated, sometimes amounting to a frenzy that left its legacy to Spanish Baroque.

120, 121. Late Gothic in Catalonia is marked by a preference for extreme width. S. Maria del Mar (above, 1324), close to the port of Barcelona, is a hall-church almost exactly as wide as it is long, giving an impression of spaciousness. The same qualities are carried to their extreme in the cathedral of Palma de Mallorca (above right; begun in 1306, nave 1360). Here width is matched by height, for the whole nave was raised in the process of building. Here we are looking south-east; a great rose-window fills the space between nave and choir vaults.

122. Something similar to Palma occurred at Gerona (right), where in 1416 it was decided to scrap the earlier scheme of the choir (1312) and open out the whole space into one very wide nave.

The most typical of Spanish great churches are those where the width of the central vessel and consequently the span of the vault are pushed to the limits of structural possibility. The architects of Catalonia and Andalusia were particularly reckless in this respect. Two churches in Barcelona – the cathedral and S. Maria del Mar – prepare us for the cathedral of Palma de Mallorca, where the builders took a fresh draught of inspiration after the east end and when they came to the nave almost doubled the height and the width. At Gerona, which had been begun in the early 14th century in a conventional style with choir and aisles, gallery and clearstorey, work was taken over in 1416 by Guillermo Boffiy, who, with unprecedented bravado, threw the whole space into one – as wide as choir and aisles together and much higher – and covered it with the widest of all Gothic vaults. To stand at the west end and look east is to see a demonstration model of one phase of Gothic superseded by another.

The largest of Spanish cathedrals, and indeed the largest medieval cathedral ever built, is that of Seville, begun as late as 1402 and not completed until 1518, with the explicit ambition, as one of the building committee put it, of making 'those who should see it finished think we were mad'.

120
121

122

123

123. Seville (1402, finished 1518) is among the last Gothic cathedrals and the largest. Its width is emphasized by double aisles, but the impression of lowness given by the exterior is belied by the soaring height of the interior elevation.

124, 125. Two extreme – but typically extreme – examples of the last phase of Portuguese Gothic, known as Manueline. Above: the monastery church of Belém, outside Lisbon (1499). Above right: the chapter-house window of the Cristo Monastery, Tomar (c. 1520).

For the last flourish we must go to *Portugal*, where the Gothic style, some would say, did finally take leave of its senses. Under King Manuel I (1495–1521) the Portuguese empire in the Indies enjoyed its greatest period of expansion. Suddenly enriched, Portugal began to build churches and monasteries to reflect its new wealth, in a style that came to be called 'Manueline'. The piers of arcades begin to twist like barley sugar, and imagery drawn from exploration and the sea – anchors, seaweed, shells, nets – proliferates. The window of the chapter house of the Cristo Monastery at Tomar, as large as a three-storey house, is festooned with such motifs. Most common of all is rope, which encircles buildings as if they were giant parcels. At Viseu Cathedral the vaulting ribs are rope, with knots as the bosses.

By the time this was built the Italian Renaissance was already a century old and the new St Peter's was rising in Rome.

Secular and domestic

It is not unfair to judge medieval architecture primarily in terms of churches and cathedrals. Not only were they overwhelmingly the major building type, commanding a large proportion of national resources, but they were also the focus of experiment and change. However, there were other objects of masonic skill and we should look briefly at the wide range of non-religious buildings.

Castles were nearly as expensive as cathedrals, but their form was governed by the science of defence more than the art of architecture. In early examples the tower is retained as a place of last resort, situated at a point where the castle was most vulnerable. It would be complemented by a 'bailey' defended by walls which themselves incorporated towers. Outside there would be a moat or dry ditch. In the 13th century the keep became less important and the defenders relied more on the curtain walls, which might be doubled, forming concentric rings. It was the gateways which now became the most heavily fortified parts and were treated like keeps themselves, as at Harlech in Wales. Every large town, too, had its ring of walls punctuated by towers, a few of which impressively survive today, from York in England to the north to Ávila in Spain to the south. Sometimes these defences, like castles, incorporated a double or triple line of walls, still to be seen at Carcassonne in south-western France. 126

126. The citadel of Carcassonne, in south-western France, preserves its double circuit of defensive walls. The inner ring goes back to Merovingian times; it was extended and added to up to the 14th century and restored in the 19th.

127. The castle of Marienburg (now Malbork, Poland) was the headquarters of the Teutonic Knights, a Christian military order waging war on the pagan Slavs.

128. Beaumaris on Anglesey (1283), never finished, was the most geometric of Edward I's castles built to subjugate the Welsh.

129. Castel del Monte, the Emperor Frederick II's castle in Apulia (1240), is the most formally perfect of such structures. Its pedimented doorway bears witness to Frederick's classical ambitions, anticipating the Renaissance by two centuries.

Every strong seat of power was fortified, but the most revealing castles are those built in areas of continuing war or unrest, where royal resources had to be expended. Edward I's castles, built to subdue the Welsh in the late 13th century – Harlech, Conway, Caernarvon and Beaumaris, the last the most formally perfect – are textbook examples of current strategic thinking. That thinking came largely from the experience of the Crusaders in the Holy Land, a testing ground for methods of warfare for several centuries, and the site of some of the grandest of all castles, such as the Hospitallers' Krak des Chevaliers in Syria (13th century). Less well known and more idiosyncratic are the castles built by another military order, the Teutonic Knights, as part of their campaign to Christianize the Slavs, culminating in the headquarters of the Grand Master at Marienburg (now Malbork, in Poland), a huge complex of buildings that broods threateningly over the flat plains of the Vistula. At the other end of Europe, Spain's long struggle against the Moors produced scores of castles, once in the front line, now bare and empty in the dry landscape of Castile. Spanish castles did not go through the same evolution. They were usually compact, combining the functions of stronghold and palace. In the remarkable castle of Bellver, Mallorca (14th century), which seems to have been planned

128

127

130. The great hall of Barcelona, the Tinell, shows the same passion for width as Catalan ecclesiastical architecture. Begun in 1359, it uses diaphragm arches to support a wooden roof.

almost as an exercise in abstract geometry, the two aspects are clearly separated, the palace consisting of a circular courtyard with a two-storey arcade, the stronghold of a smaller circular tower linked only by a bridge, where the garrison lived. Elsewhere the typical *alcázar* (e.g. of Segovia or Toledo) is a single block relying for its strength largely on its site. The most spectacular is Coca (Segovia), built of brick in the 15th century and decorated in such a way as to make it clear that it was as much for show as for war.

This is not the place to analyse the military aspects of castles, but we may draw attention to certain aesthetic qualities. It is clear that where topography allowed architects did not suppress their natural instinct for symmetry and proportion. The results can have a powerful beauty of their own. The Emperor Frederick II's Castel del Monte in Apulia (1240) is a perfect octagon punctuated by eight identical towers. In England, Warkworth Castle, Northumberland (*c.* 1400), has a complex Greek-cross plan, the various rooms fitted into it, around and above each other, with extraordinary ingenuity.   129

Castles during this period shared many of the functions of palaces; residential and ceremonial parts of the building developed alongside military. The 14th-century castle of the French kings at Vincennes, just outside Paris, contained lavish reception rooms and a chapel. Marienburg had a large chapel and splendid vaulted halls. Very often great halls were constructed of wood within the castle precincts and have not survived.

Palaces like those of Whitehall or Westminster in London or the Vatican in Rome were not unified, designed structures but random collections of buildings serving various purposes. The Kremlin in Moscow is the best existing example. Only rarely does a medieval palace survive in anything like its entirety. The Palace of the Popes at Avignon (begun in 1334), where the popes lived during their exile from Rome, is one. Another is the Albrechtsburg at Meissen (1411) whose sequence of rooms covered by fantastic late Gothic vaults by Arnold of Westphalia brings it close to the Vladislav Hall in Prague.

131. Westminster Hall, London, originally a Romanesque structure, was transformed in 1394 by the addition of the great hammerbeam roof by Hugh Herland, one of the glories of medieval carpentry. The central section rests on the hammerbeams whose ends are ornamented with angels; the wide arches unify the space aesthetically.

Prague is one of a number of cases where a great hall has survived virtually on its own. Others are the hall of the Counts of Poitiers in that city (13th and 14th centuries), Henry III's hall at Winchester (1222), and the hall of the counts of Barcelona, the Tinell (1359), a wide space spanned by diaphragm arches. Largest is Westminster Hall, London, in the 12th century probably provided with two rows of posts down the middle but in the late 14th century covered with the vast hammerbeam roof that we see today.   109   130   131

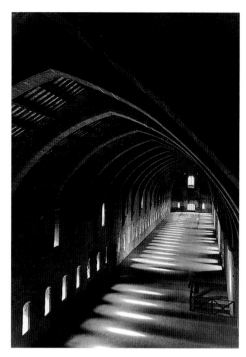

132, 133. Monasteries were among the most demanding of architectural patrons, and their buildings remain monuments of sober imagination. The refectory of Maulbronn, Germany (above, 1224), and the dormitory of Poblet, Spain (above right, late 12th century), were both built for Cistercian communities.

134. Right: the roof of the chapter house of Wells, England (c. 1280). Octagonal chapter houses were peculiar to England, giving spectacular opportunities for the development of vaulting.

The layout of monasteries remained the same as in Romanesque times, and only a few of the communal buildings registered much change. Cloisters were given open tracery, some of it of great elaboration. The cloister of Lérida, in Spain, is rather taller than the church to which it is attached. Refectories too grew grander and were sometimes divided by a row of columns down the middle supporting vaulting (e.g. Maulbronn, in Germany, 1224). Dormitories were rarely vaulted, but could have diaphragm arches to hold up the roof, putting them almost on a level with the halls of the nobility (e.g. Poblet, in Spain, late 12th century).

A peculiarity of English monasteries, and some non-monastic communities, was the circular or octagonal chapter house, often with a central column and a great umbrella of radiating ribs, as at Wells (*c.* 1280). Infirmaries also grew in scale and quality, and became the models for secular hospitals, of which examples survive at Angers (1174) and Beaune (1443), both in France.

Inevitably, over the centuries, the old disciplines were relaxed. The Cistercians forgot St Bernard. Abbots built themselves palatial apartments. Towers, prohibited by the old rules, were allowed. That of Fountains, in Yorkshire, built in the 16th century on the eve of the Reformation, is like a parable of the sin of pride.

Universities and colleges were like secular monasteries, always with a chapel, and often a cloister and domestic quarters grouped around it. Most of the ancient universities of Europe have lost their medieval buildings; England is lucky to have not only fine examples at Oxford and Cambridge but also two schools for younger students at Eton and Winchester.

132

133

134

135

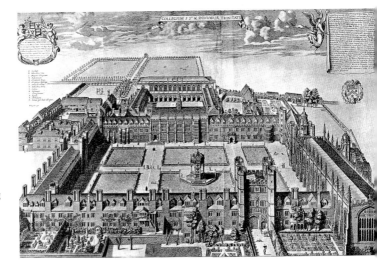

135. Trinity College, Cambridge, in the 17th century was still close to what it had been in the Middle Ages. The Great Court is entered through an elaborate gatehouse. The chapel is on the right, with the hall – its oriel window marking the dais or high-table end and balancing the asymmetrically placed door – between the two courts. (Wren's much later library, ill. 250, is in the far distance.)

119

136. Civic pride was manifested by lavish town halls, whose bell-towers (*campanili* in Italian) often rivalled cathedral spires as dominant elements in the city. That of Siena (1289) fronts onto the great open space where the medieval Palio is still held.

137, 138. Venice evolved a form of lace-like secular Gothic that was never used for churches (and was therefore recommended by Ruskin as suitable for 19th-century civic buildings). Opposite, below: the Doges' Palace (1343). Below: the Ca' d'Oro (1423), a highly-wrought private palace.

Finally, to civic and commercial buildings, town halls and exchanges. The most splendid of these, naturally enough, are in the free cities of Italy, Flanders and Germany, where communal pride was strongest: in Italy the Palazzo Pubblico of Siena (begun in 1289), the Palazzo Vecchio in Florence (1299) and the Doges' Palace in Venice (begun in 1343); in Flanders the cloth hall of Bruges, with its towering belfry (14th and 15th centuries), and that of Ypres, destroyed in the First World War but accurately rebuilt, and the town hall of Leuven or Louvain (1448); in the German sphere the town halls of Brunswick (14th and 15th centuries) and Breslau (now Wroclaw, Poland). Spain has a number of spectacular exchanges (*lonjas*): that of Valencia (1483) has rib vaults carried on a double row of tall twisted columns.

Of grand private houses few survive, and of those even fewer of major architectural importance. In France, the houses of the financier Jacques Coeur in Bourges (1442) and of the Abbot of Cluny in Paris (1485) bear witness to the luxury that the rich could enjoy. Large numbers of houses belonging to the lesser gentry and merchants remain, especially from the later Middle Ages, built of stone, brick or (most commonly) timber. They follow standard

136

137

139

139. The silk exchange (Lonja de la Seda) of Valencia (1483) comes close to Portuguese Manueline style, with its vigorously twisted columns and complex vault.

140. The dense streets of pre-war Danzig (Gdańsk), with houses on long, narrow plots, are typical of medieval cities. The great parish church of St Mary (see ill. 111) rises high above the gabled roofs, outscaling the towered town hall; warehouses of the great Hanseatic city are clustered on the island across the river.

plans which persisted until the 16th and 17th centuries. The nucleus was the hall, which had a raised dais at one end, where the master dined (often lit by a bay window), and a screen at the other. The entrance porch led into the passage formed by this screen, and was therefore at one end, not in the middle, of the façade. Doors led from this passage to the kitchen and buttery. At the lord's end a staircase led to his private apartments.   135

Town houses had simpler plans, often in England with oversailing upper storeys and in central Europe with a projecting oriel called an *Erke*. The interiors of such houses were for convenience, not for show, but the exteriors would be painted and decorated and *en masse* presented a magnificent spectacle. Civic buildings such as town halls would often belong to the same vernacular tradition. Before 1939 Europe possessed many beautiful, virtually intact medieval towns, Danzig (Gdańsk) and Nuremberg perhaps   140 the best of all. But they have been sadly depleted by war. Venice remains, its fabric still largely late medieval, employing a particular local form of Gothic which was – uniquely – exclusively secular: generally two upper storeys of intersecting ogee arches enclosing lobed quatrefoils, lighting the *gran salone*. The Ca' d'Oro   138 (1423), on the Grand Canal, represents the style at its best.

Timeline showing the overlap between Gothic (in bold type) and Renaissance architecture

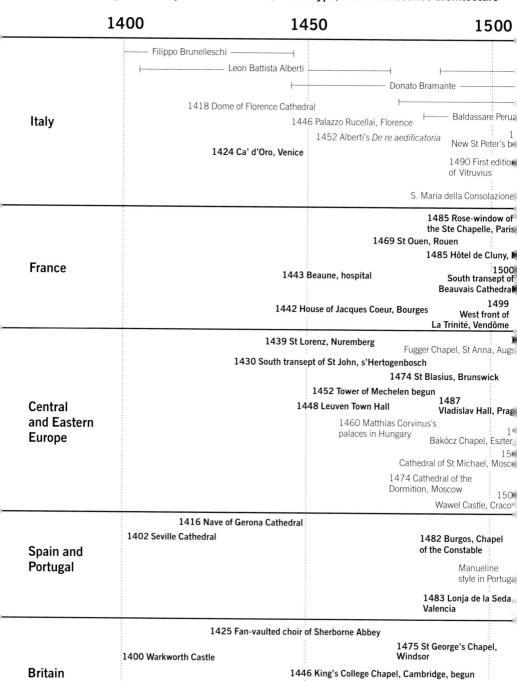

	1400	1450	1500

Italy

Filippo Brunelleschi ————

Leon Battista Alberti ——————

Donato Bramante ——

1418 Dome of Florence Cathedral

1446 Palazzo Rucellai, Florence

Baldassare Peruz

1452 Alberti's *De re aedificatoria*

1

New St Peter's b

1424 Ca' d'Oro, Venice

1490 First editio
of Vitruvius

S. Maria della Consolazione

France

**1485 Rose-window of
the Ste Chapelle, Paris**

1469 St Ouen, Rouen

1485 Hôtel de Cluny, ▶

**1500
South transept of
Beauvais Cathedra▶**

1443 Beaune, hospital

**1499
West front of
La Trinité, Vendôme**

1442 House of Jacques Coeur, Bourges

**Central
and Eastern
Europe**

1439 St Lorenz, Nuremberg

▶

Fugger Chapel, St Anna, Augs

1430 South transept of St John, s'Hertogenbosch

1474 St Blasius, Brunswick

1452 Tower of Mechelen begun

1448 Leuven Town Hall

**1487
Vladislav Hall, Prag**

1460 Matthias Corvinus's
palaces in Hungary

1

Bakócz Chapel, Eszter.

15

Cathedral of St Michael, Mosc◀

1474 Cathedral of the
Dormition, Moscow

150
Wawel Castle, Craco▶

**Spain and
Portugal**

1416 Nave of Gerona Cathedral

1402 Seville Cathedral

**1482 Burgos, Chapel
of the Constable**

Manueline
style in Portug

**1483 Lonja de la Seda,
Valencia**

Britain

1425 Fan-vaulted choir of Sherborne Abbey

**1475 St George's Chapel,
Windsor**

1400 Warkworth Castle

1446 King's College Chapel, Cambridge, begun

150

Henry VII's Chapel, Westminster Abb◀

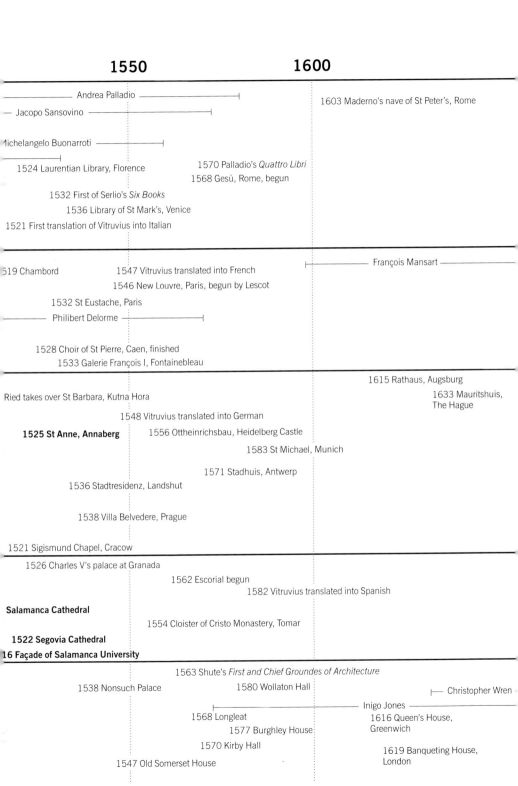

1550

1600

—————— Andrea Palladio ——————|

— Jacopo Sansovino ——————|

1603 Maderno's nave of St Peter's, Rome

Michelangelo Buonarroti ——————·
————|
1524 Laurentian Library, Florence

1570 Palladio's *Quattro Libri*
1568 Gesù, Rome, begun

1532 First of Serlio's *Six Books*
1536 Library of St Mark's, Venice
1521 First translation of Vitruvius into Italian

519 Chambord   1547 Vitruvius translated into French   —————— François Mansart ——————

1546 New Louvre, Paris, begun by Lescot

1532 St Eustache, Paris

—————— Philibert Delorme ——————|

1528 Choir of St Pierre, Caen, finished
1533 Galerie François I, Fontainebleau

1615 Rathaus, Augsburg

Ried takes over St Barbara, Kutna Hora

1633 Mauritshuis,
The Hague

1548 Vitruvius translated into German

1525 St Anne, Annaberg   1556 Ottheinrichsbau, Heidelberg Castle

1583 St Michael, Munich

1571 Stadhuis, Antwerp

1536 Stadtresidenz, Landshut

1538 Villa Belvedere, Prague

1521 Sigismund Chapel, Cracow

1526 Charles V's palace at Granada

1562 Escorial begun
1582 Vitruvius translated into Spanish

Salamanca Cathedral

1554 Cloister of Cristo Monastery, Tomar

1522 Segovia Cathedral

16 Façade of Salamanca University

1563 Shute's *First and Chief Groundes of Architecture*

1538 Nonsuch Palace   1580 Wollaton Hall

—— Christopher Wren

—————— Inigo Jones ——————

1568 Longleat
1577 Burghley House
1570 Kirby Hall
1547 Old Somerset House

1616 Queen's House,
Greenwich

1619 Banqueting House,
London

Chapter 5:   The Renaissance: Ancient Rome 'Reborn'

The Renaissance brought about a sharp break in architectural history, a break not only in style but in professional practice and client expectation. This is not to say that the process was a sudden one. It took two hundred years to spread across Europe. But wherever and whenever it established itself, one entire tradition was replaced by another. Renaissance architecture, it must not be forgotten, was only one aspect of a much larger cultural movement, and cannot be understood in purely architectural terms.

In Italy, where it began, the break was less abrupt because the two traditions were closer together. But even here, continuity of practice was interrupted. Architects no longer learned their craft from their masters, passing it on from one generation to the next. Instead of inheriting a system of assumptions, beliefs and conventions from their own past, they had to assimilate those of a civilization separated from them by time, culture and religion, the civilization of ancient Rome.

The Renaissance originated in the movement known as humanism, which began in Italy in the 14th century as a revival of interest in classical literature and philosophy. As it broadened socially and intellectually it took in classical law, history, art and architecture, until the ambition of humanist courts seemed to be to re-create ancient Roman culture. Architects, therefore, were obliged to become archaeologists and scholars. They read Vitruvius, and measured classical ruins. They were no longer practising master-masons, but intellectuals.

Florence: the Early Renaissance

Architecturally, the Renaissance is always taken to begin in 1418 with Brunelleschi's dome of Florence Cathedral. This is slightly odd because the dome owes practically nothing to classical architecture and a great deal to Gothic. A second oddity is why Brunelleschi came to be chosen in the first place, since his training,

141. Brunelleschi's S. Spirito in Florence was new in the purity of its line, the harmony of its proportions and the classical correctness of its mouldings and capitals. But in its basic form it was wholly traditional. Renaissance architecture was not a sudden interruption of normal usages, but an adaptation of the Roman idiom to modern needs.

142

142. Technically the dome of Florence Cathedral (designed in 1418, begun in 1420) was a *tour de force*, depending partly on a quasi-Gothic rib system, partly on an unusual method of bricklaying in a herringbone pattern forming not separate layers but a continuous spiral. The most classical features, the lantern and the exedrae (the semicircular bays at the base of the drum), were the last to be built.

according to later biographers (who were concerned to stress his classicism), had been that of a goldsmith and sculptor and his architectural knowledge confined to examining Roman ruins. It is, however, conceivable that he had been to France, Germany and even England, since during his boyhood his father had visited these countries in his capacity of recruiting officer for mercenary soldiers. At any rate, he must have acquired some traditional masonic knowledge, since he understood the 'acute fifth', a calculation governing the curvature of pointed arches known to Gothic builders but not to Roman, and he used the medieval method of drawing out architectural elements full-scale on the ground. The basic shape of the dome had already been settled in the 14th century. A painting of 1368 shows it very much as it looks now, only without a drum. It was certainly an ambitious design, but the problem that preoccupied the building committee was how it could be built without ruinously expensive scaffolding. Brunelleschi solved this problem, as well as inventing new hoisting machines and conceiving the idea of tying the whole base together with timber and iron 'chains'.

Had Brunelleschi built nothing but the dome of Florence Cathedral he would not be remembered as the father of Renaissance architecture. But his other works confirm that title. All are in Florence: the loggia of the Foundling Hospital, the Old Sacristy 143 of S. Lorenzo, the churches of S. Lorenzo and S. Spirito, the Pazzi 141 Chapel (probably), and the lantern and exedrae added to the dome 142 after it was finished. All show classical elements. The loggia and the arcades of the two churches use fluted pilasters and columns with Composite capitals; in the churches in addition there are slabs of entablature (dosserets) above the capitals supporting round arches and flat, coffered ceilings. The Old Sacristy and the Pazzi Chapel have shallow domes on pendentives; the lantern and exedrae scroll-buttresses and egg-and-dart mouldings.

The classical vocabulary had never quite disappeared in the Middle Ages. Volutes, Corinthian capitals, arcades of round arches outlined in grey limestone or *pietra serena*, all have precedents in Tuscan Romanesque, of which many examples survived in Brunelleschi's time; some still do (SS. Apostoli, S. Miniato al 63 Monte, the Baptistery). But, as ensembles, Brunelleschi's buildings struck contemporaries as new, Roman in spirit, and part of that ancient culture which they wished so passionately to join. In the unfinished church of S. Maria degli Angeli he experimented

143. The loggia of the Foundling Hospital in Florence, the Ospedale degli Innocenti, built simultaneously with the Cathedral dome (1421), was a much purer exercise in the classical style. Between the arches are the famous swaddled babies in glazed terracotta roundels by Luca della Robbia.

with a centralized sixteen-sided structure which reflected the Renaissance preoccupation with geometry and proportional systems. Of course the architects of the Middle Ages had done the same, but whereas masonic geometry had been esoteric and concealed, that of the Renaissance was open, explicit, Euclidean.

The next generation is represented by a man from a quite different background. Leon Battista Alberti was a scholar, fluent in Latin and with some knowledge of Greek, well-read, trained as a lawyer, and expert in all the accomplishments expected of a 15th-century gentleman, including music and horsemanship. A connoisseur of the arts, he made himself the leading authority on Roman architecture. His book 'on matters to do with building', *De re aedificatoria*, became the modern Vitruvius, and inevitably he was invited to design buildings himself.

Equally inevitably, Alberti approached the task from a position quite unlike Brunelleschi's. He was the first 'architect' in the modern sense, that is, a man who makes a design on paper and then leaves it to someone else, the contractor or clerk of works, to build.

Alberti was a pioneer in a number of ways. He was the first architectural theorist of modern times, the first to codify the rules of classical architecture, the first to show how specific features of Roman architecture (the orders, the triumphal arch, etc.) could be adapted to modern requirements, the first to formulate the principle, so fundamental to the classical style, that in a harmonious building 'nothing could be added or taken away except for the worse'. Unlike Brunelleschi, Alberti can be understood purely and consistently in terms of Roman prototypes. His façade for the Palazzo Rucellai, in Florence, was the first to use the orders – Doric, Ionic, Corinthian – superimposed in the 'correct' way. His remodelling of S. Francesco at Rimini as a memorial to Sigismondo Malatesta applies the Roman triumphal arch motif – here three equal arches – to the façade of a church. In his façade for the Gothic church of S. Maria Novella, in Florence, he introduced scroll-buttresses to mask the transition from high nave to low aisles, another idea that was to have a long life. The only two works in which Alberti was not restricted by previously existing buildings were his two Mantuan churches, S. Andrea and S. Sebastiano. The first, on a cathedral scale, features a triumphal arch motif (in this case a large arch flanked by two smaller ones) on both the façade and the interior elevations of the nave; this meant that instead of an arcade with aisles behind, there was a series of self-contained chapels whose solid walls functioned as the

144, 145. Leon Battista Alberti, most scholarly of Renaissance architects, was particularly adept at re-inventing ancient forms: the triumphal arch as a church façade (S.Francesco, Rimini, 1446, above) and the superimposed orders on the front of a palace (Palazzo Rucellai, also 1446, above right).

buttresses supporting the big coffered vault (copied from Roman baths). S. Sebastiano was not completed; it had a Greek-cross plan, with square spaces in all four directions, fronted by a portico.

Alberti died in 1472. In the years that followed he was the most powerful single influence on contemporaries and younger architects – men such as Michelozzo and Giuliano da Sangallo in Florence, Bernardo Rossellino in Pienza, and Luciano Laurana in Urbino. Michelozzo, in fact, was slightly older than Alberti. In the 1440s Cosimo de' Medici employed him to build the Palazzo Medici, a building close to the traditional Florentine *palazzo* (a large town house rather than a palace in our sense), but with an open arcade to the street – later filled in – and a wide projecting cornice, and a courtyard surrounded by Brunelleschian arcades. Giuliano da Sangallo is remembered for the small centralized church of S. Maria delle Carceri at Prato, a clever combination of Alberti's S. Sebastiano and Brunelleschi's Pazzi Chapel.

Bernardo Rossellino had actually worked with Alberti; and when Pope Pius II commissioned him to build a whole miniature city centre (named Pienza in his own honour), he seized an unprecedented opportunity to put Alberti's principles into practice. The group comprises a cathedral, a town hall, a papal palace and an episcopal palace, carefully graded – religious, civic, domestic – according to a hierarchy explained by Alberti. At the same time a comparable ensemble was rising not far away at Urbino, redeveloped to express the power and taste of another autocrat, Duke Federigo da Montefeltro. Federigo's architect was Laurana, who, though denied the same overall freedom in the site, designed a palace that remains the most complete surviving setting for a humanist court, with its graceful courtyard, cool rooms with giant fireplaces, and intimate *studiolo* lined with marquetry panels. Rome, soon to take over the architectural leadership of Europe, could boast only one building to compare with these: the Palazzo della Cancelleria, for which no architect has yet been discovered. There are two orders of pilasters on the façade and two courtyards with two-storeyed arcades.

It must by now be obvious that, however fervently Renaissance architects and patrons admired ancient Rome, their buildings are not merely – indeed, not primarily – imitations of classical ones. How could they be? Rulers and churchmen of 15th-century Italy did not want temples, forums, amphitheatres or baths. They wanted churches, public buildings and *palazzi*. The classical style could only ever be an adaptation to unclassical uses. In any case, Renaissance architects were not wholly under the spell of the past; as we have seen, they were also fascinated by something only indirectly connected with ancient Rome – geometry. In church-building this led to a situation where geometry was no longer the servant of ecclesiastical requirements, but their master. The architects themselves saw no conflict since, in Platonic theory, perfect forms (square, cube, circle, sphere) were aspects of divine perfection. Ancient Rome and modern geometry were to come together with intriguing results in the greatest of all Renaissance architects, Donato Bramante.

Rome: the High Renaissance
In about 1500 Bramante moved to Rome from Milan. His own background had been the court of Urbino, a centre of inquiry into mathematics, perspective and the creation of ideal spaces, both fictive and real. His early work as a painter and an architect reflects these interests (S. Maria presso S. Satiro, Milan, was given a whole choir in fake perspective – a built fictive space), and his friendship with Leonardo, whom he had known in Milan, no doubt stimulated his ideas about centralized churches, evident in the domed crossings he built for Pavia Cathedral and S. Maria delle Grazie, Milan (1492).

But it was in Rome, at the age of 56, that his real career began. Here, in the fourteen years that remained to him, he designed five buildings that were to set their mark on the whole subsequent history of architecture. They are the courtyard of S. Maria della Pace (1500); the Tempietto of S. Pietro in Montorio (1502); the Belvedere Courtyard in the Vatican (1503); the new basilica of St Peter's (begun in 1506); and the House of Raphael (*c.* 1510).

The first two are small in scale, but by looking at them in detail one gains vivid insight into Bramante's mind. At S. Maria della Pace he built a courtyard with two storeys, the lower one consisting of Doric piers supporting round arches, with applied Ionic pilasters supporting a frieze above, the upper one of a flat entablature on Composite pilasters, subdivided by a smaller order of Corinthian columns. At the corners, where the more usual method was to close the arcades with a full pilaster, Bramante leaves a mere thread to show where it would go if there were room.

The Tempietto, built as a Roman 'memoria' to a Christian hero, St Peter, is Bramante's most complete resolution of the two cultures, and he found himself facing a series of problems to which there were no conventional answers. It takes the form of a round

146

147

146, 147. Two of Bramante's first Roman experiments in the classical language, begun in 1500 and 1502: the courtyard of S. Maria della Pace (arch-plus-entablature, pilaster-plus-column) and the Tempietto of S. Pietro in Montorio (circular peristyle-plus-pilaster).

cella surrounded by a circle of columns. Since the circumference of the colonnade is greater than that of the wall inside it, the pilasters (which are 'projections' of the columns onto the wall and therefore of the same dimensions) have to be closer together. Between these pilasters are doors and windows which, too, have to incorporate their proper elements and observe proper proportions. Bramante met these demands by, for instance, squeezing the window frames into the depth of the openings. The building repays analysis on these lines almost *ad infinitum*. When Serlio and Palladio came to illustrate the masterpieces of ancient Rome as models for architects of their own time, they included this work as an honorary classic. Bramante had challenged the Romans and equalled them.

Of the last three buildings on our list, one has been demolished and the other two altered almost beyond recognition. The demolished one is the House of Raphael (*c.* 1510), a town palace which united elements from both ancient Roman and Italian traditions. The ground floor, containing shops, was built of huge rusticated blocks of masonry (actually concrete); the upper floor was a smooth ashlar composition of paired Doric columns with entablature, separating large windows. Functional and elegant, the design was taken up by Palladio and over the next three centuries was adapted to a myriad of country houses and street façades.

148. In the Palazzo Caprini or House of Raphael (*c.* 1510, acquired by the painter in 1517) Bramante modelled the rusticated ground floor on Roman shops and for the upper used coupled columns supporting a Doric frieze, with pedimented windows between. A comparison with the Palazzo Rucellai (ill. 145) makes clear how much more three-dimensional and monumental Bramante's generation is than Alberti's.

Raph Vrbinas ex Lapide Coctili Rome, exstructum.

149. Bramante's foundation medal, issued in 1506, is one of the few clues to his design for St Peter's. By drawing inferences from this, and from a plan by Bramante showing one half of the building, Serlio and later commentators were able to reconstruct his presumed original design as having four apses (one of them the entrance), four corner towers, a peristyle drum and a hemispherical dome based on that of the Pantheon.

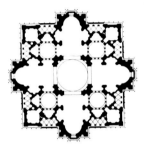

The Belvedere Courtyard, commissioned by Pope Julius II, aimed to lend ancient Roman grandeur to the grounds of the Vatican Palace by linking it to the Belvedere, a villa about 300 yards to the north. Bramante laid out a rectangular open space divided into two by ramps and staircases to accommodate a rise in ground level and ending in a semicircular exedra. The lower courtyard had a three-storey elevation on the long sides (an open arcade on a Doric order, then Ionic and Corinthian above), the upper courtyard a single storey only. Some features, such as the exedra, look back to Roman precedents, e.g. the temple-complex of Palestrina (Praeneste); but in others, like the spiral staircase at the northern end of the site, Bramante had to exercise his own ingenuity.

Overshadowing all these works and preoccupying Bramante for the last ten years of his life was the new St Peter's. This project, 149 initiated in 1505 by Julius II – to tear down and rebuild the mother church of Christianity which had stood for over a thousand years – still seems almost unbelievably presumptuous. But for Bramante it meant a chance that few architects could ever dream of.

Unfortunately, the surviving documents establish neither the pope's exact brief nor Bramante's definitive design. On the crucial question of whether he intended a Latin-cross or Greek-cross plan, the drawings are tantalizingly ambiguous. But most probably, as Serlio (for one) certainly believed, what he began was a centralized Greek-cross church, with four apsidal arms opening off a domed central space. The scale was huge, but the interior was ingeniously broken up by a series of chapels in the corners of the cross. Four giant piers supported semicircular arches upon which the dome rested – a hemisphere on a drum, rather like the Tempietto. Work was begun in 1506 and carried up to the level of the four main arches, but it is all now encased in the much more massive masonry added by Michelangelo fifty years later. An idea of Bramante's exterior can be gained from the foundation medal, 149 and of the interior from Raphael's *School of Athens*, where it is used as a setting for the meeting of the great men of antiquity.

Bramante stands out as a man totally dedicated to architecture, the very opposite of the dilettante. To him, more than to any of his predecessors, the classical style was a discipline, a logical system, which dictated its own formal solutions. At the same time, it was both an art, a vehicle for the imagination, and a part of the real world, in which patrons expected buildings to serve specific functions. Because classicism was being asked to perform tasks for which it was never intended, almost all of Bramante's commissions brought problems of reconciling these demands. What should happen when two arcades meet at right angles? What should happen to the relationship between intercolumniations and wall-openings when the building is circular? What should happen to the hierarchy of the orders if they are being used on a spiral staircase? None of these problems would have bothered a Gothic architect. One cannot help thinking that they bothered Bramante very much. Superficial attractiveness was not enough. What he was striving for, as even Michelangelo, an unfriendly witness, recognized, was 'the truth'.

The problem of Mannerism

The eighty or ninety years after the death of Bramante in 1514 have long been a problematic area for architectural historians. This is not because the facts are in dispute but because they are subject to two contradictory interpretations. An older school of thought, represented by Rudolf Wittkower and Nikolaus Pevsner in the 1920s and '30s, held that in the first quarter of the 16th century architecture and the other arts reached a point of balance and harmony expressed to perfection by the generation of Raphael and Bramante. The Reformation and in particular the Sack of Rome (1526) induced a malaise and crisis of faith, epitomized in the overwhelming personality of Michelangelo, who subverted this harmony by rejecting the certainties of the High Renaissance and substituting doubt, tension and distortion, leading the whole of the next generation to follow him. This movement they called Mannerism.

It must be admitted that Giorgio Vasari, Michelangelo's disciple and biographer, does give some grounds for such a judgment. Of the Medici Chapel he says, 'He made it very different from the work regulated by measure, order and rule, which other men did according to normal usage and following Vitruvius and the ancients, to which he would not conform…Therefore the craftsmen owe this man infinite and everlasting obligation, because he broke the bonds and chains of usage they had always followed.' It seems clear, nevertheless, that Vasari did not regard Michelangelo as subverting the classical 'rules' but as taking them further, extending them to discover new 'beauties' and 'graces'. Later architects, similarly, saw themselves as elaborating and refining the example of Bramante and ancient Rome, not as turning their backs on it. A consensus now seems to be emerging which would maintain that there never was a Golden Age of orthodoxy in which the rules were clear and universally observed. From Brunelleschi onwards the process was one of continual experiment, adaptation and innovation. Reverence for Vitruvius and Roman precedent was never undermined but it never hardened into dogma. The two most influential manuals of the century, Serlio's *Architettura* (Architecture, first part published in 1537) and Vignola's *Regola dei Cinque Ordini* (Rule of the Five Orders, 1562) are both based firmly on the authority of the ancients. But as Serlio, in fact, remarks, 'Nowadays men hanker after novelties, especially when they are made by rule and reason' (Book VI, f. 23).

'Novelties' could take many forms, and not every architect could resist the temptation to be outrageous. When Bernardo Buontalenti, for instance, chopped a classical pediment in half and swapped the two halves round over a doorway in the Uffizi in 150 Florence (1580), did he mean it to be amusing? One suspects that he did, especially when one looks at some of his other works, such as the altar stairs now in S. Stefano, Florence, which get narrower and narrower towards the ends and finally curl up in a way that simply mocks at function.

Michelangelo, it need hardly be said, was not this kind of architect, though for him too function definitely mattered less than form. By instinct a sculptor, he conceived buildings as compositions of solids and voids, projections and recessions, mouldings

150, 151. Mannerism frivolous and serious. Buontalenti's Porta delle Suppliche at the Uffizi, Florence (below, 1580), has a classical pediment chopped in half and reversed. Michelangelo's Medici Chapel, also in Florence (right, 1520), where many of the architectural features – aedicules squeezed between pilasters, vacant plinths and flat niches containing nothing but stone garlands – seem to have no function other than to intrigue the eye and puzzle the mind.

and planes. Not until the very end of his career did he have to concern himself with structure. His first work was the memorial chapel of the Medici family in S. Lorenzo, Florence, begun in 1520 — 151 as the setting for the famous tombs. It is a small room balancing Brunelleschi's Old Sacristy on the other side of the church. His contribution consists entirely of non-functional elements – pilasters, tabernacles, niches, window frames – all of which are designed with great care to produce effects that are not quite what is expected and which critics from Vasari onwards have found disturbing. The niches, for instance, do not quite fit the spaces between the pilasters and their pediments have to overlap the capitals. They also have odd rectangular recesses at the top, and when these touch the segmental pediments, the latter jerk forward 'as if', said John Summerson, 'they had been given an electric shock'. The same obsession with detail is what makes the vestibule of the nearby Laurentian Library, begun four years later, so exciting. As — 152 soon as one looks closely, questions arise. Why are the stairs in three parallel flights with different numbers of steps? If the paired consoles support the columns, why do they project in front of them? If the columns support the wall, why are they recessed into it? These are the archetypical questions of Mannerism.

During these same years Bramante's achievements were being developed by a group of highly gifted architects, all of whom had contacts with Rome but of whom many settled and practised in

various cities of northern Italy: Raphael, Giulio Romano, Peruzzi, the two Sangallos, Sanmicheli and Sansovino. Sharing many of the same aesthetic values and using largely the same repertoire of forms, they produced buildings that are strikingly different and intriguingly individual.

Raphael knew Bramante and may have designed the little church of S. Eligio degli Orefici in Rome with him. Unfinished but influential was the Villa Madama, just outside Rome, a work where classical inspiration and Renaissance invention met. Here, as in his Vatican frescoes, Raphael was assisted by Giulio Romano; the Villa Madama was clearly in Giulio's mind when he designed his first independent commission, the Palazzo del Tè outside — 153 Mantua. Begun in 1526, this is essentially a country villa, four single-storey blocks around a square courtyard, with a big garden court to one side. Because of its rustic connotations Giulio indulges in such oddities as irregularly placed pilasters, patchy rustication, and dropped sections of entablature as if the building were falling into ruin.

Baldassare Peruzzi also belonged to the Bramante circle. He is remembered for the Palazzo Massimo alle Colonne in Rome, begun in 1532, which broke new ground by having a curved façade. The entrance, through a wide columned opening, is flanked by pilasters. Above this, the wall lacks any classical articulation and has only oddly framed windows.

Antonio da Sangallo the Elder was Giuliano's brother. His great work is a pilgrimage church just outside the little town of Montepulciano in Tuscany, the Madonna di S. Biagio (begun in 1518). It is very much in the Bramante tradition, a Greek-cross plan with (freestanding) towers in the corners flanking the façade, and an interior of severely Roman style. Close to it, in date and location, is a more remarkable church in the same tradition, S. Maria della Consolazione at Todi (begun in 1508), for which no certain architect has been found. Leonardesque in its uncompromising geometry, this very large church consists of a cubic central space (in fact higher than a cube) opening into four equal apsidal arms. Above it rises a high dome on a drum. Another member of Bramante's circle, Antonio da Sangallo the Younger (the son of a third brother), remained in Rome and gained the commission for the grandest of all Roman palaces, Palazzo Farnese (1513 onwards). The exterior renounces the orders, relying instead on

154, 155. The centralized church of S.Maria della Consolazione at Todi (below, begun in 1508), a beautifully consistent exercise in Bramantesque logic, would be more widely admired if it were attributed to a more eminent architect than the obscure Cola da Caprarola. It is known that Peruzzi, designer of the strikingly original Palazzo Massimo alle Colonne (below right, 1532) also worked on it.

156. Palazzo Bevilacqua, Verona, by Sanmicheli (c. 1535), a complex façade that suggests but subtly avoids exact symmetry.

its large scale, its sequence of thirteen huge windows set in colonnaded aedicules, and the expanse of smooth ashlar masonry. In the courtyard, the Doric and Ionic orders support an entablature, with arches threading through, like the Colosseum. The top storey and the huge crowning cornice were finished after Sangallo's death by Michelangelo.

Michele Sanmicheli may have worked with the younger Sangallo before returning in 1527 to his native Verona, then Venetian territory. His three palaces there, each dating from the 1530s, are all variations on the two-storey elevation of the House 148 of Raphael, with rusticated ground floors and orders of columns or pilasters above. Palazzo Bevilacqua has the innovation of spiral- 156 ly fluted columns, sometimes seen as a symptom of Mannerism, but in fact imitated from an ancient Roman arch only a few hundred yards away. Sanmicheli's only excursion into ecclesiastical architecture, the circular Pellegrini Chapel (begun in 1529), also in Verona, is an interesting adaptation of the Pantheon. Much later, in the 1550s, he designed a palace in Venice, Palazzo Grimani, which relies on a more straightforwardly Bramantesque 157 monumentality.

157, 158. Two palaces that translate the traditional Venetian façade (e.g. the Ca' d'Oro, ill. 138) into Renaissance idiom: the Palazzo Grimani (c. 1556) by Sanmicheli, and the Palazzo Corner della Ca' Grande (1537) by Sansovino. Venetian architecture keeps its own instantly recognizable character throughout all changes of style.

159. Sansovino's masterpiece, the Library of St Mark's (begun 1536). Equally successful as a building in its own right and as a piece of townscape, it unites the Piazza opposite St Mark's, the Piazzetta opposite the Doges' Palace (ill. 137) and the waterfront.

Palazzo Grimani stands out in Venice as the most uncompro- 157
mising example of the High Renaissance on the Grand Canal. It
was not the first. By 1550 Venice had long been familiar with the
new style, but the city never compromised its own regional character. This is true of all the Italian city-states, but is particularly
easy to see in Venice, which had also evolved its own exclusive
brand of Gothic. Venetian palaces, fronting onto water, almost
always have a triple entrance leading to an open ground-floor hall,
above which is the main state room (*gran salone*) with three large
windows. This pattern remained standard, whether dressed in
Gothic or Renaissance: Mauro Codussi's Palazzo Vendramin-
Calergi of about 1500 had endowed it with three orders of columns
but retained Gothic-type windows; and Sansovino's Palazzo
Corner della Ca' Grande (1537) had given it a definitely more 158
Roman look, with paired columns alternating with arched windows, but the pattern is still unmistakably Venetian.

Jacopo Sansovino is the last of the Bramante circle. Born in
Florence, he went to Rome in 1505 and twenty years later to
Venice, where he became the leading architect until his death in
1570. His Library of St Mark's, one of the grandest of all 159
Renaissance buildings, forms one side of the Piazzetta, opposite
the Doges' Palace. Its two-storey elevation uses a whole range of
classical elements – Doric and Ionic orders supporting entablatures, with smaller versions of the same orders running through
supporting arches – solving all the problems with seemingly
effortless ease. Sansovino enriched every surface with carved
ornament, culminating in a huge frieze and balustrade.

While Sansovino's building was under construction it was
being watched with fascinated attention by a young architect from
nearby Vicenza, upon whom a generous patron had bestowed the
poetic pseudonym of Palladio.

A developing Renaissance
Palladio was an architect of fertile imagination, with a firm grasp
of classical principles and an ability to produce buildings that were
both convenient and enjoyable to live in. What gives him his
unique place in the history of architecture, however, is none of
these qualities, but the fact that he was able to codify his methods
in a book, *I Quattro Libri dell'Architettura* (The Four Books of
Architecture, 1570) which became a manual for the rest of Europe,
and beyond, for two hundred years.

Palladio's works consist of a major civic building, a theatre and
several town palaces in Vicenza; a large number of villas in the

160. Palladio's first commission was to surround the old Palazzo Comunale in Vicenza with a classical wrapping of columns and arches – the Basilica (1549). Taking the hint from Sansovino's Library in Venice (ill. 159), he devised a system which by concealing the different bay-widths gave the building a monumental regularity.

161. Palladio's last building, the Teatro Olimpico at Vicenza (1580), was an indoor version of a Roman theatre, built for a society of learned classicists.

162. For his Vicentine palaces Palladio invented a whole series of variations on the theme of column, loggia, frieze and aedicule. His Palazzo Chiericati (1550s) was intended as part of a 'forum', with the colonnade as public space.

surrounding countryside; and three churches in Venice. All of them use the classical vocabulary of the High Renaissance, mostly without Mannerist eccentricities and mostly adapted to the fairly modest budgets of his patrons.

The civic building is the Basilica of Vicenza; here the commis- 160 sion was to encase the old medieval hall in an up-to-date double loggia. Palladio's model was Sansovino's Library, and the chief 159 motif is a combination of column-plus-entablature with a tripar-tite arch-plus-lintel arrangement which came to be called, unjust-ly, the 'Palladian motif'. The theatre is the Teatro Olimpico, a 161 re-creation of a Roman theatre for a learned society, with perspec-tive scenery probably devised but not actually installed by Palladio. These two buildings mark the beginning and end of his career (1549 and 1580).

The town palaces present a whole array of variations on the two-storey façade: rusticated ground floor with columns or pilasters above (Palazzo Porto, Palazzo Thiene), a giant order of pilasters uniting both storeys (Palazzo Porto-Breganza, Palazzo Valmarana), two tiers of engaged columns (Palazzo Barbarano) or of free-standing columns (Palazzo Chiericati). 162

163. Palladio's country villas had to incorporate a house for the owner and accommodation for the farm and its workers. The Villa Emo is among the more modest, but dignified by a grand approach and a classical portico recessed into the body of the building.

164. The Villa Capra, known as the Villa Rotonda (c. 1550), was a rich man's summer-house, not the centre of a farm. Palladio made it completely symmetrical, with a domed circular hall in the middle.

In the villas he was freer to plan in three dimensions and to expound his proportional method most fully. Built for the patricians of Venice partly as country retreats and partly as working farms, they allowed Palladio to produce almost endlessly varied settings where the humanist owners could imagine themselves part of the world of Pliny or Cicero. His villas are in fact nothing like their classical prototypes; he had succeeded in convincing himself that the portico, a feature virtually confined in the ancient world to temples, had been used on private houses. A large number of his villas have it as a main feature (Villa Malcontenta, Villa Chiericati). One variant was to construct it in two storeys and recess it into the body of the house (Villa Cornaro, Villa Pisani). A characteristic feature of the villas is their ranges of farm buildings (*barchesse*), which can be straight (Villa Barbaro, Villa Emo) or curved (Villa Badoer). The interiors are planned according to a carefully calculated but basically fairly simple system of ratios. The Villa Rotonda is a particular *tour de force*, with a circular central hall and four identical porticoes. Impractical as such a plan might seem, it was to engender more offspring than any other Renaissance building.

The three Venetian churches, S. Giorgio Maggiore, Il Redentore and S. Francesco della Vigna, have the same merits of clarity and invention. Palladio's contribution to façade design was the combination of two pediments – a high one over a central portico (corresponding to the nave inside), flanked by the fragmentary ends of another broader, lower one (corresponding to the aisles). This was both classical and rational and he used it on all three churches. The interiors show similar logic, their parts clearly defined by giant orders resting either on pedestals or on the ground.

Palladio's legacy passed to his pupil and follower Vincenzo Scamozzi, who continued to build villas on the Venetian terra firma. After that his style was overtaken by Baroque. Palladio's day had not yet come, and when it did, it was to be on non-Italian soil.

One other building solicits attention not so much for its own merits as for the influence it was to have in another country, France. This is the Certosa (Carthusian monastery) near Pavia, in Lombardy, the façade of which was under construction in the early years of the 16th century. It is a huge screen of marble covered with every conceivable form of ornament – pediments, friezes, cornices, panels of relief-carving and statuary, much of it following the Roman arabesque patterns made popular by Raphael.

163

164

165, 166. Looking at St Peter's in Rome from the end opposite the entrance, its lines unobscured by the later nave, one can appreciate Michelangelo's vision: this is very much how it would have been seen from the Piazza, the dome drawing the eye in a way that is now impossible. The interior (right) is dominated by Bernini's huge baldacchino over the altar, but the proportions, the giant pilasters and the coffered tunnel vault go back to Michelangelo.

Finally we return to Rome and the unfinished story of St Peter's. Bramante was succeeded as architect in charge by Raphael, under whom the idea of a centralized plan, never popular with the clergy, seems to have been given up and designs for a nave prepared, though nothing much was done. After Raphael came Peruzzi and Antonio da Sangallo the Younger. Very little progress was made under them either, though both produced drawings for the building's completion. In 1547 Michelangelo took over. He returned to Bramante's Greek-cross plan but changed the proportions by thickening the piers and walls, an essential precaution to bear the weight of the dome. By the time of his death work had progressed as far as the drum.

149
166
165

The other notable late work of Michelangelo is the replanning of the Capitol, or Campidoglio, as the secular counterpart of the Vatican. Partly incorporating existing buildings, his design was for a wedge-shaped space, entered by a monumental flight of steps and centred upon the ancient Roman equestrian statue of Marcus Aurelius. On either side he placed the Palazzo dei Conservatori and the Palazzo Capitolano (not built until the 17th century), both of which have powerful façades using, for the first time, a giant order of pilasters, i.e. an order rising through two storeys.

167

167. The Campidoglio, the ancient Capitol, symbolized the prestige of the Roman Empire, and its development by Michelangelo from 1546 was a political statement. The pavement design and some details of the two palace façades were modified after Michelangelo's death, but the grandeur of his concept (seen here in an 18th-century painting) survives.

Between Michelangelo's death in 1564 and the last years of the century the leading Roman architect was Giacomo Barozzi da Vignola. His buildings include the first church with an oval plan (S. Anna dei Palafrenieri, 1565) and the mother church of the Jesuit Order, the Gesù (1568), which, by being the model for Jesuit churches everywhere, became extremely influential. It looks back to Alberti's S. Andrea at Mantua in having a wide tunnel-vaulted nave flanked not by aisles but by internal buttresses forming chapels. The façade, designed by Vignola's younger contemporary Giacomo della Porta, was equally influential, especially in its use of scroll-buttresses to hide the aisle roofs; replicas of it too are found all over the world. On the outskirts of Rome, Vignola built the Villa Giulia for Pope Julius III (1551), a continuation of the tradition begun by Raphael's Villa Madama, freely using classical elements to make varied elevations and intriguing spaces, and at Caprarola, north of Rome, he finished the Villa Farnese (1559), a fortress-like palace on a pentagonal plan with a circular courtyard.

What is called Mannerism is perhaps best seen as a necessary phase of exploration and experiment before a coherent new style could emerge. Up to Vignola's time it still made sense to expound the classical 'rules', and in fact Vignola did so in his book. After 1600 they no longer had any prescriptive force (though they would later). Doric, Ionic, and Corinthian, entablature, frieze and cornice, were tokens to be manipulated at the architect's whim. It was fitting that the man who did finally finish St Peter's by building the present nave and façade was Carlo Maderno, the last of the Italian Mannerists and the first master of the Baroque.

Before going on to follow the spread of the Renaissance, in the sense of a revival of classicism, outside Italy, we must pause to look briefly at another aspect of architecture in which Italy provided the model for the rest of Europe but which had nothing to do with ancient Rome: the science of fortification. By the 15th century the use of gunpowder and the development of cannon had rendered all medieval castles obsolete. Defences now had to consist of massive earth ramparts to absorb cannon-balls, and from which artillery could fire on an attacking force without itself being exposed. The solution to this problem was the star-bastion, the invention of which is generally credited to Sanmicheli. Whole towns, as well as isolated strongholds, had to be surrounded by earthworks designed as a series of blunt arrowheads, with gun-emplacements in the re-entrant angles, recessed so that they were protected from hostile gunfire but so sited that they could cover the flanks of the ramparts with a continuous barrage. There were generally a dozen

168. The city of Lucca, in northern Italy, has preserved its ring of Renaissance fortifications, including the star-bastions protecting gun-emplacements.

or so such bastions around a town. It was a system enormously wasteful of space, but by the 16th century almost every large town in Europe was so protected. Most Renaissance architects were called upon to design them, a task which they embraced willingly, perhaps because the bastions possessed a pure mathematical beauty unseen, and unwanted, in any other aspect of building. In the 19th century, when this system too had become militarily obsolete, they were nearly all demolished, to be replaced by spacious new roads (the word *boulevard*, originally a rampart or 'bulwark', thus gained a new meaning). But a few remain: in Italy the walls of Lucca and Palmanova, in England those of Berwick-on-Tweed, in Malta those of Valletta, and in France the numerous *places-fortes* of the great 17th-century engineer Vauban, for instance at Neuf-Brisach on the Rhine.

168

The Renaissance outside Italy: Eastern and Central Europe
In Italy, Renaissance architecture had been a natural growth. In all other countries it was an exotic import. Italy was its only source, and there were only three ways for it to become known: by Italian architects going abroad, by foreign architects or patrons coming to Italy, or by the distribution of illustrated books such as those by Serlio, Vignola and Palladio. Other countries caught

up with the Italian Renaissance, as it were, at different points, understood it in many different ways and found in it many different possibilities.

One of the surprises of history is how quickly the Renaissance was adopted in Eastern Europe. There are records of Italian architects in *Hungary* from the early 15th century onwards, but the story really begins around 1460, when an enlightened humanist, King Matthias Corvinus, assembled a whole company of Italian painters, sculptors and architects (notably Chimenti Camicia, a Florentine) to work on his palaces at Buda and Visegrád. Fragments that remain show that these must have been as sophisticated as any palaces in Italy. After his death in 1490, patronage of Renaissance architects was continued by Tamas Bakócz, archbishop of Esztergom, who visited Italy several times. His chapel in Esztergom Cathedral, begun in 1506, survives more or less intact, although in the 19th century it was actually moved bodily and incorporated into a new cathedral. The architect's name is not known, but he was presumably Italian; an Italian sculptor certainly carved the altar. The chapel is square, with tunnel-vaulted recesses and a domed ceiling; the style is wholly Florentine and the material red marble.

How the Hungarian Renaissance would have developed we shall never know. The Turkish victory at Mohács in 1526 and the subsequent occupation of Buda removed Hungary from Christendom for several centuries.

169, 170. The Bakócz Chapel of Esztergom Cathedral, Hungary (above left), is among the earliest and purest examples of Renaissance architecture outside Italy. Begun in 1506, it is fully equal to Florentine standards. In Russia, the Cathedral of St Michael in the Kremlin (above right) combines an Italianate elevation with Byzantine domes.

Had *Russia* enjoyed a humanist tsar there might have been a similar tale to tell of Moscow. But Ivan III was no Matthias Corvinus. He did, however, poach one of Matthias's architects, Aristotele Fioravanti from Bologna, in 1474, though one wonders why, since the latter was not permitted to show the Russians what the Renaissance could do but instead made to conform to Russian traditions. The Cathedral ˏof the Dormition in the Kremlin is his, but one would never know it. Twenty years later came Pietro Solari, who built the Faceted Palace, next to the Dormition, with the kind of diamond-rustication fashionable in Ferrara and elsewhere. Finally in 1504 came an architect called 'Alevis' (Alvise?), who built the Cathedral of St Michael, opposite the Dormition, where the full Renaissance style is finally allowed to appear (though with five domes on tall drums). After that, Russia turned its back on the West for two hundred years. 170

Bohemia, too, owed its earliest Renaissance architecture to the example of Hungary. In the 1490s Vladislav II, of the Jagellonian dynasty, ruler of united Bohemia and Hungary, summoned Benedikt Ried to Buda to learn the new style. We have already met Ried as the wizard of late Gothic. He seems to have been one of those architects who can never leave things alone. Having played games with Gothic, he now played games with classicism, and in the Vladislav Hall of Prague Castle (1493) he did not scruple to 171

171. In the Vladislav Hall in Prague Castle (1493) the playfully perverse Renaissance doorways were designed by the same man who built the Gothic vault (see also ill. 109) – the extraordinary Benedikt Ried.

172. Below right: the Sigismund Chapel, Cracow Cathedral (1521), by the Florentine Bartolommeo Berrecci.

mix them together. The exterior windows look fairly orthodox Florentine, but on the inside Ried placed classical columns with spiral fluting, and even fluted square piers which twist between base and Corinthian capital by 90°. This would have been extremely bold even in Mannerist Italy.

Later Renaissance buildings in Prague look old-fashioned by comparison. The Villa Belvedere, begun in 1538, is the result of a collaboration between an Italian, Paolo della Stella, who built the arcaded loggia, and a German, Bonifaz Wohlmut, who built the more sober upper storey. A similar combination of national talents produced Hvezda Castle (1555), just outside Prague, the first of the star plans that were to be a feature of Eastern European Baroque.

The trail now leads to the capital of *Poland*, Cracow, where another member of the Jagellon family, Sigismund, took up residence in 1502. During the next twenty years we find two Florentine architects working there – 'Franciscus Florentinus' and Bartolommeo Berrecci. The first had the task of modernizing the old Wawel Castle, the Polish royal residence. In the courtyard he constructed a three-storeyed loggia, the lower two storeys arcaded, and the third, double-height, given a series of very tall shafts like masts. The general impression is hardly Italianate, but it was copied at many other Polish castles.

Berrecci, an architect of much purer Florentine taste, received the commission for the Sigismund Chapel in the Cathedral on the 172 Wawel, begun in 1521. Cubic in shape, it is surmounted by a dome on an octagonal drum with circular windows and has arched recesses on three sides holding the altar and royal tombs. The tomb effigies themselves, the statues in niches flanking them, and the relief carving that covers every surface including the dome are of the highest quality. This exquisite little building is as fine as anything in Italy, and nothing else like it exists north of the Alps.

In *Germany* and in England Renaissance architecture received a guarded welcome. Two reasons are given for this. One is that after the Reformation the general hostility towards Catholicism discouraged Italians from seeking employment at Protestant courts (and architecture, unlike scholarship, cannot live by books alone). The other is that the Gothic tradition was still strong and many of its greatest glories, as we have already seen, were created after 1500. However caused, this separation marks the beginning of a split along religious lines that was to affect architecture until the late 18th century.

173. To the builder of the Ottheinrichsbau of Heidelberg Castle, orthodox Italian Renaissance architecture would have seemed boringly austere. So he added rusticated pilasters, caryatids, scrolls and ornaments – all ultimately classical in origin but applied with no thought of classical discipline.

The Fuggers of Augsburg, bankers and lovers of art, were the Medici of the north. In 1509, ten years before Luther's revolt, Jakob Fugger commissioned his family chapel in St Anna's, the first example of Renaissance architecture in the German lands. For its plain classical piers, round arches and marble decoration the architect, Sebastian Loscher, looked to Venice, but he could not bring himself to renounce a Gothic rib vault.

Thereafter, the 16th century can show only a very meagre crop of true Renaissance buildings. The Stadtresidenz or town palace of Landshut (1536) is a very respectable exercise in High Renaissance classicism, with a (rear) façade using Tuscan pilasters over a rusticated ground storey and a courtyard with a Corinthian order over a graceful Doric arcade. The interiors too are of high Italianate quality. Here the architect does seem to have been Italian – 'Meister Sigismund' from Mantua – as were his stuccoists and painters.

For the rest, up to the last twenty years of the century, it is a matter of watching the gradual infiltration of Renaissance features divorced from any sympathy with the fundamental principles of Renaissance architecture. The effect is often incongruous, as when a steep German gable is filled with rows of attached classical columns. The courtyard façade of the Ottheinrichsbau of Heidelberg Castle (1556) is a sort of anthology of bizarre Italian Mannerist motifs piled on top of one another. The best of such exercises is the two-storeyed loggia added to the Rathaus (town hall) of Cologne in 1567, probably by the Netherlander Cornelis Floris, which combines two orders of columns supporting an entablature with arches inside them.

173

174. In Flanders, for most of the 16th century, the Italian Renaissance was the source of a whole new repertoire of ornament but not a new concept of building. The centre of Cornelis Floris's Stadhuis (town hall) of Antwerp (1571) transforms the traditional Flemish gable into a tiered composition of coupled columns, niches, statues and aedicules.

By the 1580s, however, the Catholic south of Germany was ready for a full-scale demonstration of the new style. St Michael's in Munich, begun in 1583, is the first really grand classical church north of the Alps. Erected for the Jesuits, it closely follows the model of Vignola's Gesù, then nearing completion in Rome. The architect was probably Frederik Sustris, Italian-trained.

At Augsburg Elias Holl brought an up-to-date Mannerist style to his Rathaus of 1615. He was not a very inspiring architect, though the interior has one magnificent room, the Goldener Saal. The mysterious Englischebau ('English building') of Heidelberg Castle, of 1613, shows an altogether more refined touch and has been attributed to Inigo Jones. One would like to believe it.

Architecture in the *Netherlands* and *Flanders* is closely linked to that of Germany. Cornelis Floris was responsible for the pala-tial Stadhuis of Antwerp, begun in 1571, where classical columns, pediments and niches are liberally applied to a building that is essentially unclassical.

The Netherlands have a particular significance for England, partly because of the wave of immigrant craftsmen who settled in London to escape the Counter-Reformation and partly because of the number of books published there, notably those by Vredeman de Vries (1583) and Wendel Dietterlin (1593 and 1594), which were widely used as models for such things as screens, tombs and chimneypieces. These books popularized a particular type of deco-ration called 'strapwork' which derived from the French School of Fontainebleau (see below) and ultimately from the circle of Raphael. It has come to be called Mannerist, but has little in common with Mannerism as defined in the context of Italy.

156

England, France and Spain: problems of adaptation

If Germany moved only slowly in the direction of the Renaissance, *England* was virtually stationary. At the beginning of Henry VIII's reign, in 1509, one might have predicted otherwise. He invited a number of Italian painters and sculptors to London, the most notable being Pietro Torrigiano, who made the tomb of his father Henry VII, and they introduced Renaissance details into Hampton Court and Nonsuch palaces. The builder of Longleat, in 176 Wiltshire, after 1554, was sufficiently up-to-date to incorporate classical pilasters in the façade. In the reign of Henry's daughter Elizabeth, Robert Smythson certainly had access to Italian books and based the plan of Wollaton Hall, Nottinghamshire, on Poggio 175 Reale, near Naples, which he found in Serlio. In 1563 John Shute

175, 176. Two up-to-date English houses of the second half of the 16th century, Wollaton (below) and Longleat (bottom). Both use Renaissance motifs freely, probably derived from France, and both obey the laws of symmetry. But neither renounces the big quasi-Perpendicular windows.

177. The hall range of Kirby Hall, Northamptonshire (1570). Its use of Renaissance features like the long fluted Ionic pilasters is already quite sophisticated, but the windows remain very English. (The round-headed window in the porch is a later, 17th-century, addition.)

published his *First and Chief Groundes of Architecture*, the first architectural manual in English. Based entirely on Vitruvius and Serlio, and showing no awareness of any actual building, it was of little practical help. No Italian architect came to England and no English architect went to Italy.

The result is that although a large number of spectacular houses were built between 1550 and 1610, and although they break free in many respects from medieval convention, they cannot really count as part of the mainstream of Renaissance architecture. They owe their effect to their great expanses of window, an inheritance from the Perpendicular style (e.g. Hardwick Hall, Derbyshire, 1590), their naive use of Italianate ornament (e.g. the huge obelisk at Burghley House, Northamptonshire, of 1577) and their atmospheric interiors, including that specifically English feature, the long gallery. There was also a quite conscious nostalgia for the Middle Ages (the architectural equivalent of Spenser's *Faerie Queen*), encouraged by the Tudors as part of their political ideology. Only two buildings showed any real awareness of what classicism meant. One was Old Somerset House, in London (1547), which had a frontispiece making use of the three orders with a triumphal arch motif as the base (long destroyed). The other is Kirby Hall, Northamptonshire, begun in 1570, which features an order of giant pilasters, though without any attempt at an entablature and combined with traditional Tudor grid-windows and details copied from Serlio.

177

All this changed dramatically with the advent of Inigo Jones, who (it is not too much to say) single-handedly dragged England to the forefront of architectural fashion.

Jones began as a designer of sets and costumes for court masques. He visited Italy twice, the second time staying for over a year as part of the household of the Earl of Arundel. He saw Milan, Padua, Rome, Naples and, most importantly, Vicenza and Venice. The works of Palladio made the greatest impression on him; he met Scamozzi and made detailed notes in his copy of the *Quattro Libri*. Back home, in 1615, he was appointed Surveyor of the King's Works and was therefore the unrivalled leader of his profession.

Jones's dependence on Palladio is very direct but never slavish. His works are totally original essays in the Palladian manner, in every way worthy of their models. The Banqueting House in Whitehall, London (1619) – all that was built of an intended huge new palace – is a formal composition with superimposed Ionic and Corinthian orders, columns for the four centre bays, pilasters for

178

178. With Inigo Jones's Banqueting House, London (1619), the Renaissance appears in England fully formed. The building's proportions, its use of attached columns in the centre and pilasters at the sides (doubled at the ends), its alternation of triangular and segmental pediments and its garlanded frieze all show a confident familiarity with Italian models.

179. The Queen's House, Greenwich (begun 1616), Inigo Jones's version of a Palladian villa, was long in building. The left-hand side was originally open in the middle with a road running between the two halves; the gap was filled by Jones's successor John Webb as late as 1662.

180. The châteaux of François I's reign along the Loire betray an innate romanticism quite remote from classical values. At Chambord Italianate elements cluster into a northern fairy-tale skyline.

the slightly recessed sides, and an ornate frieze of garlands, crowned by a balustrade. In the London of the 1620s it must have stood out from its neighbours like a visitor from another world. At Greenwich, the Queen's House (begun in 1616 but not finished, to a modified design, until shortly before the Civil War in 1635) is a neat Palladian villa with a first-floor loggia of Ionic columns and a cubic hall with a gallery. Three other highly influential London works are the Queen's Chapel at St James's, the 'Piazza' of Covent Garden (the first London square), with its barn-like church of St Paul's, and the additions to Old St Paul's Cathedral – destroyed in the Great Fire – which included a portico of giant Corinthian columns. His commissions outside London are harder to document, but they probably included Wilton House, Wiltshire. Inigo Jones is one of the truly crucial figures in the history of architecture. It was through him that Palladianism found a new home in England, and from England that it set out to conquer the world. 179

In *France* contacts with Italy were far closer than they were in England. Between 1494 and 1525 three French kings – Charles VIII, Louis XII and François I – actually invaded Italy. They were successful to the extent of conquering the Duchy of Milan and holding it for twenty-five years, but came to a disastrous end at the Battle of Pavia. During those years, however, Frenchmen had become familiar with the architecture of the region, and especially with the Certosa of Pavia, a familiarity that bore fruit in the lavish palaces erected by François I – the Château de Madrid outside Paris, Chambord, and parts of Blois and Fontainebleau – where Italianate ornament is applied to buildings that otherwise remain in the medieval French tradition. Similarly hybrid forms can be seen in ecclesiastical architecture. At Caen, the choir of the late Gothic church of St Pierre (finished in 1528) is covered inside and out with rich Italianate ornament. In Paris, a few years later, the church of St Eustache seems at first sight purely Gothic, and it is only when one looks closely that one sees that the piers are fluted pilasters and have Corinthian capitals, the arches round, and the string-courses classical cornices, a bizarre re-creation of one style in the idiom of another. 180 181

A much more decisive impact came from the influx of artists from Italy into France. In 1530 Rosso Fiorentino arrived; in 1532 Francesco Primaticcio; in 1536 the French architect Philibert Delorme returned from three years' intensive architectural study in Rome; and in 1541 came Sebastiano Serlio. These men brought a degree of professional expertise that was not available elsewhere

181. The church of St Eustache in Paris was begun in 1532 clearly by a Frenchman used to the Gothic tradition, but reputedly with the advice of an Italian woodcarver turned architect, Domenico da Cortona, who also worked at Chambord. The result is a strange hybrid in which classical pilasters, capitals and entablatures seems to be taking part in a medieval charade.

in northern Europe. Rosso and Primaticcio were set to work by François I on his château at Fontainebleau, where Gilles Le Breton had just previously made the first attempt to translate the Italian Renaissance into French. Here they decorated the Galerie François I (1533–40), combining life-size stucco figures and painted panels, thereby creating the French equivalent of Mannerism, the School of Fontainebleau. Primaticcio went on to design a whole new wing of the palace in 1568, and a remarkable circular mausoleum at St Denis, never finished and later demolished. Serlio, whom we have met as the author of an influential book, designed a château, Ancy-le-Franc (1546), with a courtyard that looks back, distantly, to Bramante's Belvedere.

Philibert Delorme was in a sense the French Inigo Jones, though considerably less lucky in the survival of his buildings. His first work, the château of St Maur, has been demolished. So has the château of Anet (1550) except for its entrance, its chapel – an interesting experiment in centralized planning – and its frontispiece, a composition using three orders superimposed, now re-erected in Paris. In 1564 Catherine de Médicis commissioned the palace of the Tuileries from him and he built a central domed pavilion flanked by wings, all demolished after 1870. Delorme made a conscious effort to naturalize the Renaissance and make it French, an ambition expressed in his book, *L'Architecture* (1561), in which he advocated a new 'French order' to be added to the classical ones, and which he actually used at the Tuileries.

The most important commission of all was given to a less interesting architect than Delorme, Pierre Lescot. The Paris Louvre was a medieval fortress. François I decided to pull it down and replace it, a project which grew until it encompassed something four times the size of the old Louvre. Lescot's part of the courtyard (begun in 1546) is roughly one-eighth of the present Cour Carrée but it set the style for all the rest, and continued to be a model even into the 19th century. Horizontally it consists of an arcaded ground storey, a middle storey of large classically framed windows, and an attic (all three with Corinthian and Composite pilasters), crowned by a high French roof. Vertically it is articulated by three pavilions using the triumphal arch motif with freestanding columns and big segmental pediments. Sculpture, by the greatest of French Renaissance sculptors, Jean Goujon, is used lavishly and the whole effect is extremely rich.

182

Under Henri IV (who died in 1610) the emphasis turned to urban planning on a grand scale. In Paris he began the Place Dauphine and the Place Royale (now Place des Vosges, the inspiration for Jones's Covent Garden) and planned the even more ambitious semicircular Place de France, never realized.

182. With Philibert Delorme and Pierre Lescot French architects began to design confidently in an authentic Renaissance style, though Lescot's main work, the first wing of the new Louvre (1546), is recognizably French in its sculptural decoration and pitched roof.

If a dynamic and healthy Gothic tradition were a barrier to the acceptance of the Renaissance style, then it is surprising that it ever took root in *Spain* at all. Two of the largest Gothic cathedrals, Salamanca and Segovia, were begun in 1512 and 1522 respectively and not finished until the end of the century. The central tower of Burgos was completed only in 1568. These are not the last, wilting flowers of an exhausted style, but as proud and inventive as anything that had gone before.

Nevertheless, the situation in Spain was not a simple or confident one. In fact it was more confused than in any other European country. Architects found themselves faced with the choice of a number of styles, and could submit designs for the same project in Gothic, classical or Plateresque.

'Plateresque' is the term used for the style current between about 1475 and 1550. Literally it means 'in the manner of silversmiths' work', and refers to the ornate altars, crosses, reliquaries and shrines made from the abundant silver now arriving from the New World. These objects, created by virtuoso silversmiths, were loaded with decoration combining Gothic, Mudéjar (Moorish) and classical motifs in a sort of frenzied *horror vacui*, and the fashion soon passed into architecture. To come across really extravagant Plateresque in the streets of Spanish towns is a mild shock to the aesthetic system. Crockets, finials, shields, cherubs,

183, 184. Spain, land of extremes. Salamanca University (above, 1516) displays the earliest phase of the Renaissance, the Plateresque, essentially a decorative style, where classical elements jostle wildly with Gothic and Moorish. This was followed by its complete opposite, the austere classicism of Charles V's palace at Granada (above right, 1526).

164

candelabra and horseshoe arches may be spread across a whole façade like one of the huge altars (*retablos*) of a Spanish church. Look, for instance, at the College of San Gregorio at Valladolid (1492) or the front of Salamanca University (1516). ¹⁸³

Suddenly all this clamour falls silent. In 1526 the Emperor Charles V decided to build a palace in the precincts of the newly conquered Alhambra, the Moorish palace at Granada. His architect, Pedro Machuca, had studied in Rome as a painter under Raphael, but must also have come into contact with Bramante. His palace is square in plan, and its main façade has a three-bay two-storeyed centre marked by coupled Doric and Ionic columns on pedestals. The sides have rusticated masonry below and Ionic pilasters above, with round windows lighting mezzanines at both levels. The courtyard is also square, but built into it is a two-storeyed circular open colonnade of Doric and Ionic columns.

Simultaneously, a few hundred yards away, the new Granada Cathedral was being built. Begun in 1523 to a Gothic design, it was taken over in 1528 by Diego de Siloé and continued in Renaissance style. At the east end Siloé completely transformed the design he had inherited by building a ten-sided chancel entered through massive coffered arches and crowned by a dome. The example of Granada was quickly followed at Málaga and Jaén.

185, 186. Mature Renaissance of Spain and Portugal. Below: the east end of Granada Cathedral (1528), a ten-sided rotunda resting on deep coffered arches. Below right: the new cloister of the Cristo Monastery, Tomar (1554), barely behind the latest Italian developments.

The trend towards sobriety was reinforced by the personality of Charles's successor, Philip II. In 1562 he initiated the great work of his reign, the Escorial, a few miles outside Madrid. Conceived on a vast scale (a rectangle 670 feet by 530), this was to be at once palace, monastery and mausoleum, the symbol of the Spanish monarchy as champion of Catholic Europe – and of much else, including the Temple of Jerusalem and the gridiron of St Lawrence, which is suggested by its plan of rectangular court-yards. As his architect Philip chose Juan Bautista de Toledo, a Spaniard with experience in Naples. He drew up the plans and began the building, but died in 1567, to be succeeded by Juan de Herrera. Herrera was responsible for the interior elevations and for the church, but the general character of the Escorial, and in particular its grim, monotonous, overpowering façade, had already been fixed by Toledo. It was, however, clearly what Philip wanted. In a letter to Herrera he said: 'Above all, do not forget what I have told you – simplicity of form, severity in the whole, nobility without arrogance, majesty without ostentation.'

From a distance, it is the dome and twin towers of the church, the last part to be built, that impress. Basically a square, this is divided internally into nine bays with a dome in the middle, a vestibule on the entrance side and a choir for the friars opposite.

187. The Escorial, Philip II's huge palace-monastery not far from Madrid (begun in 1562), stamped the seal of austerity upon decades of Spanish architecture. This schematized bird's-eye view shows its division into courtyards and the great domed church that broods over the centre.

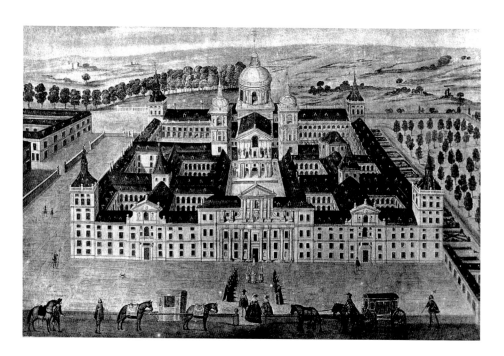

An upper gallery or tribune communicates with the king's apartments in the palace. In the crypt is the spacious mausoleum, burial place of the Spanish kings. The Escorial was the first of the royal palaces of Europe to be built as a grand architectural statement, ancestor of Caserta, Versailles, the Winter Palace in St Petersburg and countless others, replacing the rambling collections of buildings, like Whitehall Palace or the Kremlin, which had previously served as centres of government.

For many decades Spanish architecture lay in the Escorial's gloomy shadow. Of Herrera's later buildings the most interesting was his design for Valladolid Cathedral which was never carried through but which later influenced the strange rectangular, multi-domed church of the Pilar at Zaragoza.

In *Portugal* a similar revolution in taste was overthrowing Manueline and replacing it with its complete opposite, the 'Plain Style' as it has been christened. Gone is every vestige of fun and fantasy; Roman austerity rules. Paradoxically (or perhaps understandably) the new manner was first seen at Tomar, where the chapter-house window had taken Manueline about as far as it 125 would go. The little Conceição Chapel by João de Castilho, built in the 1530s, consists of two bare colonnades with flat entablature supporting a tunnel vault. And in the Cristo Monastery itself a new cloister was added in 1554 by Diogo de Torralva consisting of 186 a two-storeyed loggia with the 'Palladian motif' straight from Sansovino's Library in Venice. 159

It is in the context of Spanish and Portuguese architecture that we must look for the first time across the Atlantic. Mexico and the Caribbean islands had been conquered by the Spaniards at a time when the Renaissance had hardly made an impact, and the first churches there are Gothic, e.g. the cathedral of Santo Domingo (1512). By the 1560s classical columns, coffered vaults and domes had reached the New World at Mérida in Yucatán. Around the same time ambitious cathedrals were begun in several Mexican cities – Guadalajara, Mexico City and Puebla, the latter another offspring of Herrera's Valladolid. In Peru during the 1580s the cathedrals of Lima and Cuzco also show awareness of the latest innovations of Diego de Siloé and Herrera.

In tracing the story of Renaissance architecture in Spain and the north, we have been watching a speeded-up version of events in Italy. What had taken two hundred years to develop there was compressed into one hundred or less. But by 1600 the attention of Western Europe was firmly fixed upon Italy and was ready almost at once to receive a new gospel: the Baroque.

Chapter 6:   Baroque and Anti-Baroque

By the end of the 16th century the Catholic Church was recovering from the damage inflicted on it by Luther and the defection of many parts of northern Europe, and was beginning to regain the initiative. The Council of Trent (1545–63) had clarified doctrine and reformed abuses. New, aggressive religious orders, notably the Jesuits, set out to win back what had been lost and to evangelize America and Asia, and in this cause all the arts were conscripted. The message was one of rejoicing – the miracle of salvation, the benevolent intercession of the Virgin and saints, and the ultimate ecstasy of heaven. Baroque (a word originally applied pejoratively, meaning 'a misshapen pearl') evolved to meet the needs of this movement. It is essentially the style of the Counter-Reformation.

The Protestant countries had no such motivation. Rejecting much of the supernatural side of worship (the cult of the Virgin, the invocation of saints, the veneration of relics and the use of images), they stressed moral purity, faith and good works, and had a puritanical hatred of 'idolatry'. Can a style that reflects these values ever be genuinely Baroque? In a sense this is merely a question of terminology. But not entirely. The difference between a Catholic church in Bavaria of the 1740s (say Vierzehnheiligen) and 188 a Protestant church in New England of exactly the same date (say the King's Chapel, Boston) is very obvious. One factor is certainly 189 the absence in the latter of painting and sculpture. But even without that, the architecture itself expresses a sobriety and austerity totally at odds with the heightened emotion of the Catholic example. Is it unfair to call this 'anti-Baroque', as it was certainly anti-Catholic? On the other hand, we must be careful not to confuse aesthetic feeling with religious. The Baroque style was powerfully attractive to many architects of an undoubtedly anti-Catholic persuasion, for instance Georg Bähr, builder of the Frauenkirche in 212 Dresden. Even Wren and Hawksmoor had a Baroque side which perhaps they would have liked to indulge more than they did. What is interesting is that hostility to Baroque, outliving any overtly religious prejudice, persisted among Anglo-Saxon Protestant historians and art critics until well into the 20th century.

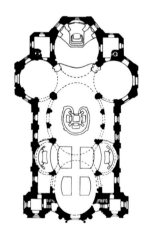

188, 189. A Catholic and a Protestant church under construction at the same time, the 1740s. Above and opposite, above: Vierzehnheiligen in Bavaria by Balthasar Neumann. Opposite, below: the King's Chapel, Boston, USA, by Peter Harrison. Doctrinal division leads to architectural division. Does it make sense to call both Baroque?

190. S. Giorgio Maggiore, Venice, begun 1565 by Palladio but completed as late as 1610, retains High Renaissance values embodied in a logical hierarchy of elements. Full columns on pedestals support a main pediment reflecting the nave, pilasters on the ground support the half-pediments reflecting the aisles.

Baroque in Italy: the seed-bed

The transition from Mannerism to Baroque is not immediately obvious. The same forms are used, grouped in roughly the same way. The difference lies in emphasis and overall effect. Compare three church façades. The High Renaissance façade of Palladio's S. Giorgio Maggiore in Venice (designed in 1565) speaks of repose 190 and stability; each part is clearly defined and each has its function. In Giacomo della Porta's Mannerist façade of the Gesù in Rome 191 (1571) those qualities are dissipated and, to an extent, negated; the parts are distinct, but their roles are duplicated, their identities blurred. The Baroque façade of Longhi's SS. Vincenzo ed Anas- 192 tasio in Rome (1645) regains clarity of purpose, but now allied to a dynamism that overrides logic. How is this done? By subordinat- ing the whole classical system to the single-minded expression of energy and movement. The columns no longer pretend to support a load, but hammer out their *sforzandi* like repeated chords in an orchestra; the entablature responds to the same insistent rhythm; while in the grand climax of the triple pediment, cherubs and angels lift a cardinal's hat to heaven. Is this architecture, sculpture or opera? Vitruvius would have fled in horror.

191. In Giacomo della Porta's façade of the Gesù, Rome (opposite below, 1571), Renaissance values are challenged and logic defied. One pilaster hides behind another, and in the central bay two complete ensembles – one with pilasters and segmental pediment, the other with demi-columns and triangular pediment – are squeezed together.

192. By the time of Martino Longhi's SS. Vincenzo ed Anastasio, Rome (right, 1645), a new logic has emerged, in which drama overrides function.

193. Carlo Maderno's façade of S. Susanna, Rome (1597) is worth a careful comparison with the Gesù. The same elements are present, but organized with clarity and a sense of purpose. The whole ground storey, except for the flanking aisles, is given full columns, the upper storey pilasters. A segmented pediment covers the door, and a triangular one the frame in which it is placed.

The first clear statement of the Baroque in architecture is Carlo Maderno's façade of S. Susanna in Rome (1597), where he took the conventional Gesù-type format and gave it depth and emphasis by bringing the centre forward and modulating from pilasters to full columns. In the year that this was finished Maderno was appointed architect to St Peter's with the task of building the nave and the façade. This was the most prestigious architectural post in the world, but it was a distinctly unenviable one. Whatever was done would contradict Michelangelo's intentions and obscure the view of his dome, yet it had to be conditioned by what he had already built. In the event Maderno neither succeeded nor wholly failed. His nave preserves the scale and main elements of Michelangelo's crossing and transepts. For the façade he used a giant order of Corinthian columns, though its grandeur is marred by two papal requirements. One was to incorporate the Benediction Loggia in the centre, the other to add two towers at the sides, which were begun but for structural reasons abandoned, so that their lower storeys merely prolong the façade to the detriment of the proportions.

The generation after Maderno produced three architects of genius, born within three years of each other and all working in Rome: Pietro da Cortona (born 1596), Gianlorenzo Bernini (born 1598) and Francesco Borromini (born 1599).

Pietro da Cortona, equally renowned as a painter and an architect, designed one complete church and the façades of two more. The first, SS. Martina e Luca, has a Greek-cross plan with apsidal arms, strongly articulated internally by clusters of Ionic columns and pilasters. Its façade, in two storeys, is anchored left and right by double pilasters, but between them the wall swells out in a shallow curve, as if responding to pressure from within. Even more three-dimensional is the façade of S. Maria della Pace. Against a concave wall, the porch projects in a strong half-circle of columns, while above it a composition similar to that of SS. Martina e Luca contains a window and a big segmental pediment which (like comparable forms in Michelangelo's Medici Chapel) seems too big for the space into which it has to fit. At S. Maria in Via Lata, Cortona renounces this effect of contained pressure and builds a monumental front that looks back to Late Antique. 194

Longer-lived and even more versatile was Gianlorenzo Bernini. Success came easily to Bernini. He became architect to St Peter's in 1629 at the age of thirty-one. His first talent was sculpture, and his architecture remained strongly sculptural. Works such as the baldacchino over the high altar of St Peter's 166 and the Cathedra Petri beyond belong equally to both arts. His church of S. Andrea al Quirinale uses a favourite Baroque plan, 195 the oval (a circle with direction), which is exposed on the exterior

194, 195. Roman Baroque at its most fertile. Below left: S. Maria della Pace (1650) by Pietro da Cortona, a complex play of convex and concave, the upper wall swelling in a tense curve new to architectural form which Cortona seems to have invented. Below right: Bernini's S. Andrea al Quirinale (1658); the oval nave is expressed on the outside behind the monumental porch.

196. Maderno's façade to St Peter's created a problem that was brilliantly solved by Bernini's Piazza, which masterfully moulds the open space by two ovoid colonnades and then funnels it between two angled lines which seem to make the church both closer and narrower.

197. Bernini's first design for the east front of the Louvre (1665). A wonderfully theatrical concept playing off convex against concave curves, it was sabotaged by Louis XIV's minister Colbert over such mundane objections as the fact that the king's apartments would be too noisy.

and from which the heavy rectilinear porch with its semicircular 'porchlet' seems somehow propelled. The interior, luminous with coloured marble, is peopled with angels, putti and saints, whose gestures reinforce the impression of movement. Bernini's instinct for the drama of architecture is perhaps most fully realized in the huge elliptical colonnade he built in front of St Peter's. If anything can save Maderno's façade, this does. The massiveness and strength of the four-deep Doric colonnade, combined with the oval shape that it encloses, create an unforgettable impression of power. In 1665, Louis XIV invited Bernini to Paris to design the east front of the Louvre (the side facing the city). Bernini made three designs, none of which was built. The first involved a combination of convex and concave forms. It was to have its influence elsewhere.

196

197

Francesco Borromini made his architectural debut with S. Carlo alle Quattro Fontane (1638). It immediately manifests two aspects of his artistic personality – his fascination with geometry and his endless inventiveness of detail. The plan is based on two equilateral triangles joined to form a diamond or lozenge shape, of which only the central sections of each side survive as straight lines. The two acute and two obtuse angles of the lozenge are rounded into curves, producing a wavy motion that combines logic and caprice, and is strongly expressed by applied Composite

198

199

198, 199. Borromini's church of S. Carlo alle Quattro Fontane (1638, façade 1665) compresses all his inventive genius into a tiny compass. In the interior the straight sections of entablature represent the basic double triangle of the plan. The altar stands in a semicircular apse, with segmental curves left and right. The façade is again based on a play of curves, producing an undulating line imbued with energy.

200. Borromini's S. Ivo della Sapienza (1648) is as small as S. Carlo (ills 198, 199) but equally rich in spatial ideas. Here we are looking up into the vault, where the way in which the six points of two interlocking triangles are smoothed into alternating convex and concave curves is made effortlessly clear.

columns and an architrave that breaks at each crucial point. Pendentive-like shapes rise from the straight sections to support an oval dome, patterned with crosses and octagons copied from a Roman pavement and ending in a lantern with, at the apex, the triangle of the Trinity where all conflicts are resolved.

The church of S. Ivo della Sapienza, the university church of Rome, again bases its plan on two equilateral triangles, this time superimposed to form a six-pointed star. Three of its points are chopped off with concave curves, the other three rounded into convex semicircles. The resulting shape is articulated by the orders (Corinthian pilasters) and a strong entablature, resolved into a circle in the vault.

Borromini's exteriors reflect the complexity within. The façade of S. Carlo undulates with a concave–convex–concave rhythm. His oratory of S. Filippo Neri is a long, shallow concave curve. Above the dome of S. Ivo rises the most extraordinary

20(

steeple in Rome, a spiral that looks back to the medieval allegory of the Hill of Knowledge. But perhaps the most influential aspect of Borromini's work is his detailing. Following in the direct line of Michelangelo he invents endless versions of window-surround, door-frame, baluster-shape, pediment, niche, cornice and garland. Circulating as drawings and eventually published, these forms swept through Europe in the early 18th century and can be found everywhere from Poland to Portugal.

Francesco Borromini, lonely, obsessive and neurotic, who lived under the shadow of Bernini and who eventually committed suicide, was one of those key figures who seem to sum up the past from long before they were born and to determine the future long after they are dead. A Borromini building is inexhaustible, an imaginative adventure which never palls with repetition and which can never be completely known.

In Rome, during the later 17th and early 18th centuries, interest shifted from the individual building to its effect in the larger urban ensemble. Grand projects included the Piazza del Popolo (1662–79) with its twin churches, the Spanish Steps (1723), the Piazza S. Ignazio (1727) and the Trevi Fountain (1732). This

201. The Spanish Steps in Rome (1723), by Alessandro Specchi and Francesco de Sanctis, connect the Piazza di Spagna, with its Bernini fountain, to the church of S. Trinità dei Monti – a typical piece of Baroque city planning.

201

ambition, to transform a whole city into Baroque drama, was taken up even more keenly in other parts of Italy. In Sicily, an island prone to earthquakes and volcanic eruptions, Messina, Catania and Noto were rebuilt as Baroque showpieces. In the capital Palermo and the villas in its neighbourhood, Baroque reaches some of its most bizarre extremes. Naples, politically linked with Sicily, boasts an architect with an unusual speciality, Ferdinando Sanfelice, builder of staircases. The staircase is a feature particularly congenial to the Baroque spirit, with its complexity (many of Sanfelice's are double or triple staircases), its sense of movement, and its infinite number of possibilities for spaces flowing into each other. Perhaps the grandest Baroque gesture of all is the church of S. Maria della Salute at the entrance to the Grand Canal, in Venice, commissioned from Baldassare Longhena in 1631, which is essentially a huge dome, supported by scroll-buttresses on an octagonal base.

20

202. Longhena's S. Maria della Salute, Venice (1631) is the dominant accent at the entrance to the Grand Canal. Here is Baroque drama at its most rhetorical – eight sides, sixteen scroll-buttresses and a single dome, visible from every angle.

203, 204. Guarini's two Turinese domes of 1667 and 1668, the Chapel of the Holy Shroud and the church of S. Lorenzo, explored new realms of spatial imagination. The first rests on a triangular base and rises into a network of segmental arches. The second must have been inspired by Islamic vaulting (compare an example from Romanesque Spain, ill. 70).

Finally the legacy of Borromini passed to an area hitherto an architectural backwater, the north-western province of Piedmont. Here Turin had become the capital of a new dynasty and during the early 17th century began to be developed in a vigorously up-to-date style. In the hundred years from 1666 to 1770, it was the setting for the careers of three very remarkable men – Guarini, Juvarra and Vittone.

Guarino Guarini's domes over the Chapel of the Holy Shroud 203 and the church of S. Lorenzo are like nothing seen before or since. 204 The chapel (1667), which is circular in plan, is turned into a triangle by three arches, upon which sits a circular drum articulated by six arches and six niches. On the crowns of each pair of adjacent arches rests a shallow segmental arch, six in all; on the crown of those six another six, and so on, getting smaller and higher each time until the whole ends in a circle. By turning a hemisphere into a series of steps in this way, Guarini is able to admit light through small, invisible windows at every stage. S. Lorenzo (1668) is equally extraordinary. Here the dome is spanned by eight ribs, which, however, do not cross at the centre but are deflected, leaving an open octagonal space which rises into a lantern. Here too, between the ribs, are opportunities for the admission of light. Guarini was a student of both geometry and Gothic architecture (and, it seems, Islamic) and he brings to the Baroque something of the tension and linear complexity of that style. His major secular work, the Palazzo Carignano in Turin, shows that he must have known Bernini's design for the Louvre.

Filippo Juvarra's imagination also had its theatrical side; this comes out strongly in his designs for stage sets, which focus especially on diagonal views, but it submits to a classical restraint in his actual architecture, notably the Queen's palace in Turin, the Palazzo Madama (1718). His country castle, Stupinigi (1729), centres upon a high domed hall from which four diagonally set wings diverge. And on a hill overlooking Turin rises the dome of his great monastic church, the Superga (1717), with its circular nave and thrusting Corinthian portico. Juvarra was a very prolific architect, highly accomplished in several styles, working in and absorbing influences from France, Germany and elsewhere.

The last of the trio, Bernardo Vittone, is in some ways the most intriguing because he points forward most clearly to the way Baroque was developing in Central Europe. Working only in Piedmont, and mostly in small country towns and villages, he produced a series of dazzling variations on the theme of the dome, making the manipulation of light the governing principle of the whole design. In the sanctuary of Vallinotto (1738), S. Bernardino at Chieri (1740), S. Chiara at Brà (1742) and S. Croce at Villanova di Mondovì (1755), the spectator, gazing upwards, sees domes within domes, receding vistas of space, lit through apertures in unexpected places that seem to have no structural explanation, so that the parts of the building are no longer distinct but merge into one another. More flamboyant than Borromini's, more playful than Guarini's, Vittone's churches radiate a quality of sheer virtuosity that has few parallels in the whole history of architecture.

205. Filippo Juvarra combined a vigorous Baroque energy with an instinct for discipline that has to be called Neoclassical. His circular church of the Superga (1717), poised on a hilltop outside Turin, makes a calmly monumental statement, though the details, especially of the side pavilions terminating the monastery wings, are unrestrainedly Baroque. The tall dome, widely set towers, and unusually deep portico ensure its legibility from a distance.

206. 'The interior consists of one single storey surmounted by three vaults, one above the other, all perforated and open; thus the eye of the visitor roams freely from space to space...' – Bernardo Vittone on his church at Vallinotto (1738). In the vaulting he is clearly developing ideas that originated with Guarini (cf. ill. 204).

Central and Eastern Europe: the flowering

For the architects of Central Europe, Baroque was Gothic reborn. All the mystery and movement, the fluidity and freedom, the dynamic lyrical energy that the Renaissance had banished could now return in a new guise.

The first phase of Central European Baroque, up to 1700, is marked by exchanges between Italy and the north. Some northern architects went south (Fischer von Erlach and Hildebrandt). More often Italian architects travelled north – Santino Solari to build Salzburg Cathedral, Carlo Lurago that of Passau, Carlo Antonio Carlone the monastery of St Florian. A large proportion came from the Swiss cantons of the Ticino, Grisons and Vorarlberg, which had hardly experienced the Renaissance, and where north and south could mingle. In these years we can see a

207. Fischer von Erlach's Karlskirche, Vienna (1716) is a strange, not altogether successful, amalgam of Baroque imagination and classical scholarship. The two columns (replicas of Trajan's Column in Rome) stand for the Habsburg emblem of the Pillars of Hercules, the ancient world's image for the Straits of Gibraltar, limits of the known world.

distinctive new type of Baroque emerging, at first more in the stucco decoration than in the structure itself. Then the stucco element seems, as it were, to take over, and the whole building is conceived in terms of moulded volumes and spaces. Stucco, in fact, becomes the universal material. Inside, and often outside too, we see nothing but stucco, scagliola (imitation marble), paint and gilding.

From the first half of the 18th century there is a very large number of outstandingly beautiful Baroque churches, palaces and houses all over Bavaria, Franconia, Bohemia, Austria and Poland, many of them on a small scale and serving small communities, often built by local architects or by one of the families of mason-architects – the Thumbs, the Beers, the Dientzenhofers, the Zimmermanns and the Asams – who came to dominate the scene as such dynasties had done in the Middle Ages.

At the beginning of the story of Austrian Baroque stands the commanding figure of Johann Bernhard Fischer von Erlach, imperial architect to the court of Vienna. Fischer had spent several formative years in Italy and he remained something of a Roman – in both senses, the Rome of the Caesars and that of the popes – all his life. His knowledge of classical buildings was profound (he wrote the first history of architecture). In his most scholarly work, the Karlskirche in Vienna (1716), he employed Trajan's Column, doubled, to symbolize the emperor's power, and the portico of the

Pantheon combined with a dome that looks to Michelangelo or Cortona. What he learned from Bernini and Borromini was put to imaginative use in the great hall of Vranov Castle, Bohemia (1690), the elector's chapel in Wroclaw Cathedral (1715) and the Karlskirche, all based on the oval, and in his two Salzburg churches with convex-and-concave façades. Nor did scale daunt him. His original design for the imperial palace of Schönbrunn outside Vienna would have out-Versailled Versailles; even the reduced and altered version is impressively grand. Perhaps his most perfect work is the Imperial Library in Vienna (1722), a high, light room, divided into three sections by arches and columns and into two storeys by a gallery that advances and recedes around a series of bays. Lined with finely carved cases, it is as much a celebration of learning as a repository for books, and inspired imitations as far away as Coimbra in Portugal.

208

208. The firm structural rhythm and opulent decoration of Fischer von Erlach's Imperial Library, Vienna (1722), place it in the category of Baroque. The tripartite division is richly decorated but clearly defined.

Both Vienna and the second Habsburg capital, Prague, are cities of palaces built for the Austro-Hungarian nobility by Fischer, his successor Lukas von Hildebrandt and others; they include the Clam-Galas Palace in Prague, and the palace of Prince Eugene and the Upper and Lower Belvedere in Vienna. In the German lands outside Austria there was even greater demand; political division is often good for architects. Every prince and prince-bishop needed a princely residence; these can still astonish by their scale, verve and vitality – Schloss Pommersfelden in Bavaria (Hildebrandt, 1711), Mirabell at Salzburg (also Hildebrandt, 1715), or the Würzburg Residenz (Neumann, 1737). The components of palaces became fairly standardized. They had to include state apartments for resident

209. For Baroque architects the staircase was an art form, offering limitless opportunities for the manipulation of space. At Pommersfelden, Bavaria, by Lukas von Hildebrandt (1711), the staircase is allotted a whole galleried hall.

210. Bruchsal, by Balthasar Neumann (1731), has a double flight of curved steps leading to an open platform, glimpsed top right in this photograph, which is unexpectedly flooded with light. It has been miraculously restored after destruction in the war.

nobility, including an audience chamber and perhaps a throne room; the approach to these rooms was via monumental halls and staircases. The staircase is indeed the Baroque structure *par excellence*. Those by Neumann at Brühl (1728) or Bruchsal (1731), enriched with sculpture and painting, and carefully lit to increase in brightness as one ascends, offer a sequential unfolding of intriguing possibilities, like a Bach slow movement.

By now we have reached the latest stage of the Baroque, which has come to be known as Rococo. To call Rococo essentially a decorative style implies a distinction between architecture and decoration. As an assumption this is clearly false; as a fact it is very often true. In France, where the style originated, it was largely in the hands of men who did not build the rooms they decorated. In Germany and Central Europe, structure and decoration were usually conceived as a unity, though in fact most of the elements by which we define Rococo are decorative ones: lively, asymmetrical, completely unclassical forms based on fantastic rockwork (*rocaille* means rockery), shells, foliage, feathers, spiders' webs and insects. The Rococo line is thin, airy, curling, meandering; colours are light, blues, greens and yellows being favourites against a background of brilliant white; delicate stucco ornament invades every surface, obscuring structure and defying logic. There is something irresistibly light-hearted, even frivolous, about Rococo, so that one is surprised, almost shocked, to find it in the palaces of archbishops and on the altars of churches. (What can one say, for instance, to a pulpit in the form of a fully-rigged ship, complete with mast, sails and anchor, or a cherub creeping away with St Augustine's hat?) But it completely dominated Catholic Central Europe and even the strictly Protestant courts of Prussia and Saxony. Four outstanding masterpieces which illustrate both the range and the achievement of Rococo are the Amalienburg at 21

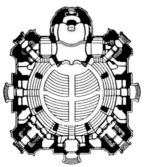

212. Dresden was a Protestant capital but its art and architecture were wholeheartedly Baroque. The Frauenkirche, by Georg Bähr, begun in 1726, is Protestant only in its emphasis on preaching rather than the administration of the sacraments; indeed its interior, with its tiers of galleries, was more like a theatre than a church. Completely destroyed in 1945, it was reconstructed from 1997 onwards.

Munich built for the Elector of Bavaria by François Cuvilliés (1734), a series of small rooms decorated with the lightest of touches; the Kaisersaal in the Residenz of the Bishop of Würzburg by Balthasar Neumann (1744), with almost neurotically detailed stuccowork by Antonio Bossi and ceiling frescoes by Giambattista Tiepolo; and, across the religious divide, the palace of Sans Souci at Potsdam (1745), built for the notably unfrivolous Protestant King of Prussia, Frederick the Great, by Georg Wenceslaus von Knöbelsdorff; and the Zwinger, a ceremonial parade-ground for the Elector of Saxony at Dresden designed by Daniel Mathaeus Pöppelmann (1711), a layout of pavilions and enclosing walls full of sculpture, graceful or grotesque, by Balthasar Permoser. None can be judged by purely architectural criteria, and that is perhaps the key to Rococo; it dissolves categories at every level.

Two new building types proved particularly responsive to Baroque and Rococo magic: theatres and monastic libraries. The first was predictable. The modern proscenium theatre originated in Venice in the 17th century, and soon began to be a feature of German court life. Two of the most spectacular are those at

213. The Zwinger in Dresden, begun in 1711, is the parade-ground of an unbuilt palace with pavilions at the ends serving as orangeries. Its architect, Daniel Mathaeus Pöppelmann, had studied the palaces and gardens of Rome and Vienna. (The far side, formerly open, was closed in the 19th century by Gottfried Semper's ponderous museum.)

214. The Margrave of Bayreuth's
court theatre (1748), an exquisite
building with a surprisingly large
stage, was designed by Giuseppe
Galli-Bibiena, one of a famous
Italian theatrical dynasty. We are
looking from the stage towards
the Margrave's box.

215. Libraries, both secular and
monastic, were transformed into
temples of learning by a profusion
of painting and sculpture.
That of Admont abbey, Austria,
was begun in 1742 by Gotthard
Hayberger. A series of domed
spaces with the books in curved
recesses, it follows the tripartite
scheme of Fischer von Erlach's
Vienna library (ill. 208).

216. Jakob Prandtauer's
monastery of Melk (1702) takes
dramatic advantage of its site
overlooking the Danube, the front
of its courtyard left open to expose
the towered façade of the church.
The two arms hold the Marble
Hall and the Library, while behind
stretch the monastic buildings,
larger than many palaces.

Bayreuth (designed by Italians, Giuseppe and Carlo Galli-Bibiena, in 1748) and the Residenztheater in Munich by Cuvilliés (1751). With its promise of warmth and gaiety, Baroque remained the style for theatres until well into the 20th century. Monastic libraries suggest a rather different image, but they are if anything even gayer than theatres. At Waldsassen in Saxony, St Gall in Switzerland and Admont in Austria, ecstatic putti holding up balustrades, celestial visions in the painted ceilings, and the ceaseless undulation of panelling and woodwork seduced the eye more (surely) than they concentrated the mind.

215

But it is the churches that are the real glory of Central European Baroque, a creative flowering paralleled only by the late Middle Ages and never to be paralleled again. The sheer scale of building is extraordinary. The Austrian monasteries of Melk, by Jakob Prandtauer (1702), and Göttweig, by Hildebrandt and others (1719), to choose two out of dozens, are as large as small towns, so that today it is difficult to find uses for them. Clergy and architects seemed to be united in the search for originality and impressive effect, producing endless subtle and complex spaces, as if each commission were a challenge to build something that had never been seen before.

216

217

217. Austria and southern Germany, which remained fervently Catholic, saw the building or rebuilding of large numbers of monasteries, many on an enormous scale. Lukas von Hildebrandt's design for Göttweig (1719) represents an ideal, never realized in this form but not an exaggeration.

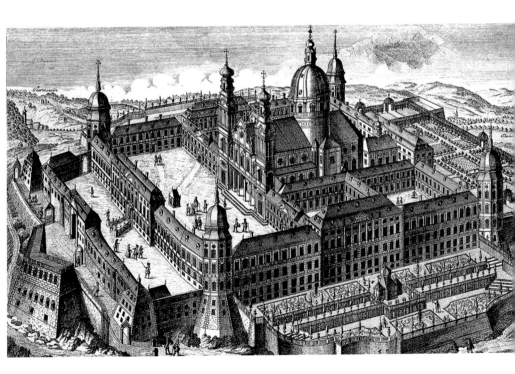

218. The church of Stadl Paura, Austria, dedicated to the Holy Trinity, has three sides, three towers (one is in the foreground here), and three apses. The date is 1714, the architect Johann Michael Prunner.

Sometimes special requirements gave opportunities for an unusual plan – triangular, for instance, to symbolize the Trinity, as at the Kappel, Waldsassen, in Germany by Georg Dientzenhofer (1685), or Stadl Paura in Austria by Johann Michael Prunner (1714). At Einsiedeln, in Switzerland, by Hans Georg Kuen and Caspar Moosbrugger (1703), an existing shrine had to be accommodated right inside the entrance so that the first bay of the nave became a circle. At Vierzehnheiligen ('Fourteen Saints') of 1743, the church had to accommodate a pilgrimage altar on the spot, so Neumann made the centre into an oval, opening into another oval, with smaller circles in between. Here, as at his church of Neresheim (1747), also in Germany, these ovals are defined (in a straight-sided building) by rows of columns behind which are aisles. Often the aisles are so narrow as to be little more than passageways, but they enable the interior to be divided and composed in ways that cannot be guessed from outside. Two churches by Dominikus Zimmermann (Steinhausen, 1728, and Die Wies, 1746) do express the oval on the exterior, but here too, columns, single or coupled, circumscribe narrow aisles, so that the interior space is made complex.

But the plan is merely the beginning. Our actual experience of these churches depends on the way the elevations are handled, the details of the stucco, the balance of colours, the figurative sculpture, and the capricious variety of window shapes. If one looks for sources, many can be found in Borromini and Guarini, but the total effect is quite different. This is above all an architecture of movement, leading the eye on in unbroken sequences, so that columns, capitals, arches, vaults and windows merge into one another without distinction. Somewhere in the remote background is the classical vocabulary of the orders, but now uninhibitedly swaying and dancing as if intoxicated with the divine spirit.

With the Asam brothers, Cosmas Damian and Egid Quirin, dramatic effect is taken more literally and becomes a form of sacred theatre. The altars of their two major churches, Rohr and 220 Weltenburg, Germany, are back-lit illusionistic tableaux of the Assumption of the Virgin and St George and the Dragon. The tiny church of St John Nepomuk which they built at their own expense 221

219. The pilgrimage church of Die Wies ('the meadow') by Dominikus and Johann Baptist Zimmermann (1746). An oval nave, defined by coupled columns, opens onto an elongated chancel. Coloured scagliola (false marble), stucco, gilding, statuary and light proclaim the symbolic message and induce heightened emotion.

220, 221. The Asam brothers, Cosmas Damian and Egid Quirin, both practised architecture as well as being respectively a painter and a sculptor. At Weltenburg (top, 1718), St George strides forward at the far end in a blaze of light to strike down the Dragon. At St John Nepomuk (right, 1733), a tiny church built next to the brothers' house in Munich, the Trinity hovers over the altar.

222. In Bohemia, Johann Santini produced not only Baroque churches and palaces of amazing variety and brilliance, but also a kind of 'Gothic Baroque' for his restorations of medieval churches. This is part of his vault for Kladruby, a Cistercian abbey (1712).

in Munich (1733) combines restless architectural elements with a vision of the Trinity hovering miraculously over the altar lit by concealed coloured light.

The genius of Bohemian Baroque is Johann Santini (or Santini-Aichel). He represents not only one of the supreme peaks of the style but also its innate affinity with Gothic. Two of his major commissions were restorations of large Gothic churches, Sedlec and Kladruby. Santini made no attempt at historical imita- 222 tion but instead created a fantasy of Gothic vaulting in stucco. In his own original churches he uses all the devices of Baroque planning with extraordinary ingenuity – Rajhrad (1722) consists of interpenetrating oval, octagon and rectangle – often incorporating Gothic elements with no sense of strain. His most famous work is the little pilgrimage chapel near Žďár (1719), a centralized 223 building based on the star symbolic of St John Nepomuk, distantly 224 comparable to Borromini's S. Ivo but with a star vault. 200

National boundaries have never had much relevance to the arts in Central Europe, and the same styles, even the same architects, turn up over a wide area. The numerous Dientzenhofer brothers – particularly Georg, Johann and Christoph, and the latter's son Kilian Ignàz – practised in Germany, Austria, Bohemia and Poland. Their favourite stylistic trick was a plan that involves transverse ovals which merge together and in the vault intersect (Břevnov, near Prague, 1708; Banz in Bavaria, 1710). 225

223, 224. The most original of all Santini's works is the chapel of St John Nepomuk near Žďár (1719), which stands in a ten-sided enclosure with chapels and protective arcades for pilgrims. Its pentagonal star plan, which produces the most intriguing shapes both within and without, is based on the symbol of the martyred saint, much venerated during the Counter-Reformation.

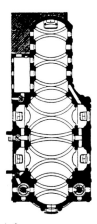

225. Johann Dientzenhofer belonged to a family of architects who worked all over central Europe. His church at Banz, Germany (1710), grows from three intersecting ovals which determine both the wall elevation and the vaulting.

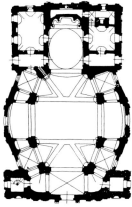

226. Poland in the 18th century was an integral part of Catholic Europe and a country where architects from Germany and Italy could look for patronage. St Anne at Lubartów (1738) by Paolo Antonio Fontana has a plan as ingenious as anywhere further west. In the photograph we are looking north-east, with a 'transept' on the left and the domed chancel on the right.

In Poland the lead of both Italy and Central Europe was being followed by the middle of the 17th century. The oval – hallmark of the Baroque – is used over and over again, from Klimontów by Laurentius Muretto de Sent (1643) to Tarnopól by Augustus, Count Moszynski (1770), with many variants. St Anne at Lubartów by Paolo Antonio Fontana (1738) is an imaginative compound of oval and Greek cross, leaving diagonal chapels in the arms.

226

Further east still, in Russia, Baroque produced yet different progeny by marrying into the Byzantine tradition. Peter the Great had founded St Petersburg in 1700 but it was not until the reign of his daughter, the Empress Elizabeth, that the city could boast architecture of a European standard. Bartolommeo Rastrelli had been brought to Russia from Italy as a small child. For the Empress he built the country palace of Tsarskoe Selo (1749) and the Winter Palace in town (1754), both in a graceful Rococo style using external colour and plentiful gold leaf. His most imaginative work is the Smolny Convent (1748), consisting of a domed church that evokes both Catholic Italy and Orthodox Russia, rising from a courtyard enclosed by low symmetrical curving wings. In the same hybrid style is the very appealing church of St Nicholas, blue, white and gold, with five cupolas, by his pupil S. I. Chevakinski (1753).

227
228

227. In the long façade of the
Winter Palace, St Petersburg
(1754), Rastrelli avoided
monotony by dividing the
composition into a series of
projections and recessions, by
articulating it with columns and
pretty Rococo ornament and by
providing an animated skyline of
statuary. In the distance is the
Admiralty (ill. 257).

228. Rastrelli's Smolny Convent
in St Petersburg (1748) is a
Baroque version of the Byzantine
and Orthodox arrangement,
in which a free-standing church
is surrounded by ranges of
monastic buildings. Here they
weave around it echoing its own
Greek-cross plan.

229. The Sanctuary, Ocotlán, Mexico (c. 1745) looks to the Churrigueresque style of Spain, taken if possible to even more disconcerting extremes. The rose-window over the door seems to be exploding.

Spain, Portugal and Latin America: the exotic harvest

Reading discussions of Spanish Baroque by non-Spaniards, one soon comes across words like 'frenetic', 'tortured', even 'neurotic'. Much Spanish religious art does indeed express pain. Are we justified in finding the same quality in the architecture that goes with it? Certainly it is not soothing, it is not joyful, it is not – as Central European Baroque is – *legato*. It is disturbing, sharp-edged, *staccato*. But beneath the differences runs the same underlying connection with Gothic. The most extreme phase of Spanish Baroque, Churrigueresque, joins hands across the Renaissance divide with Plateresque (and is in fact partly a deliberate revival of it).

Austerity was already relaxing in the early 17th century; Sebastián de la Plaza's Bernardas church at Alcalá (1617) has an oval nave and oval chapels. Façades also become more exuberant, often (as previously in Gothic) with a lavishly decorated centre between two plain towers, so-called *retablos* façades, which reach their apogee in Spanish America, e.g. Ocotlán in Mexico (mid- 18th century). The most splendid Baroque façade in Spain is that added by Fernando de Casas in 1738 to the old Romanesque cathedral of Santiago de Compostela.

229

230

Identifiably Italian forms were slowly adopted in the peninsula. Both Borromini and Guarini were influential (the latter designed a church in Lisbon, though he seems not to have gone there). Two pupils of Bernini, Giovanni Battista Contini and Carlo Fontana, worked in Spain, but a specifically Spanish Baroque appears in the work of Leonardo de Figueroa, Francisco Hurtado and the Churriguera family, who gave their name to the style.

Spanish Baroque churches are rich in spatial effects, often of a quite dramatic kind – such as the view through from the nave to a raised compartment behind the high altar known as the *camarín*, where the sacrament, a relic, or a specially holy statue was kept, usually reached by double flights of steps; or Narciso Tomé's 'Transparente' at Toledo, a theatrical *tableau* involving the insertion of a window in the vault of a Gothic cathedral. But generally speaking, plans are not as varied as in Central Europe. The impact, which can be overwhelming, comes from the stone or stucco decoration, which is immediately recognizable and uniquely Spanish.

The most famous proponents of the style were the Churriguera brothers, José Benito, Joaquín and Alberto, who

230. In 1738 the old cathedral of Santiago de Compostela (ill. 36) was given a richly Baroque façade by Fernando de Casas y Navoa. The two towers are still the original Romanesque but disguised out of recognition by their exuberant upper storeys.

practised between 1690 and 1750. Their work includes the planning of Nuevo Bastán, a new town which broke with the Renaissance gridiron tradition (*c.* 1709–13), the Plaza Mayor at Salamanca (1729 onwards), the façade of Valladolid Cathedral (1729), S. Sebastián at Salamanca (1731) and churches at Orgaz and Rueda. Ironically, none of these is what would immediately be called 'Churrigueresque'. That name is now applied to more extreme works built by architects who were the brothers' rivals, for instance Pedro de Ribera, whose portal of the Hospicio de S. Fernando in Madrid (1722) is typical: the doorway almost disappears beneath writhing curves, niches, stone drapery and *estípites* – column shafts which diminish towards the bottom like terms, their outline dissolved by ornament.

The ultimate example of this style is the sacristy of the Charterhouse in Granada (mid-18th century), for which no architect's name can with any confidence be given. Architecturally this is a normal room with arches and clearstorey. The capitals bear a remote resemblance to classical capitals, but the piers are totally

231. The Churrigueresque style could be carried no further than the Sacristy of the Charterhouse of Granada. In spite of its initial impact, this is by no means an undisciplined style. The gradations of complexity are carefully calculated, as is the telling use of totally plain surfaces.

232. Baroque 'scenographia' achieves dramatic effects in certain Portuguese hill-top sanctuaries, reached by monumental flights of stairs, such as the Bom Jesus at Braga (above, 1723).

233. Above right: Churrigueresque in a small Spanish church at Priego de Córdoba. Particularly typical are the multiple mouldings separated by a deep, calligraphic groove, and the jagged shapes suggestive of electric shocks.

encased in white stucco which seems to defy the eye to rest on it. Sharp, zig-zag lines; volutes that look like compressed springs; deep, shadowy mouldings separating part from part; jutting cornices that float above voids – everything conveys a sense of hectic, heightened emotion, yet everything is subjected to the iron laws of symmetry and repetition. This mesmerizing, technically demanding style became highly popular in Andalusia, and can be found in dozens of village churches that barely merit a mention in the guidebooks. The small town of Priego de Córdoba has six of them, 233 tiny masterpieces of febrile precision.

One of the most uncanny conjunctions in architectural history is the meeting of Spanish Baroque and the Aztecs. Many of the adjectives that have been used for Churrigueresque Spain apply with even greater force to Montezuma's Mexico, with an added dimension (to Western eyes, at least) of barbaric and blood-curdling violence. It is highly unlikely that the Spanish architects noticed any affinity with what they found in Mexico. But did none of the converts feel faintly at home in their new surroundings, which were often the work of native craftsmen?

Spanish-American architecture soon started to stray from its European models. The façade of Zacatecas Cathedral in Mexico (finished in 1752), for instance, is hard to imagine in Spain. It is a three-storeyed elevation, with triple columns flanking a doorway on the ground floor and a rose-window above. Above this is a solid attic-cum-pediment with a row of statues in niches. Every square inch of the surface – not only the decorative elements but the flat wall surfaces – is covered with tightly compressed foliage ornament. The façade of the Sagrario Metropolitano in Mexico City (1749), by Lorenzo Rodriguez, makes a similar impression, though this time the forms are candelabrum shapes and *estípites*, swelling, climbing and reproducing themselves in a proliferation of mouldings that has been aptly christened 'ultrabaroque'.

Architecture in South America was even less subject to European authority, producing a number of regional variations, especially in the façades, towers and domes of both churches and secular buildings, that must have looked distinctly bizarre to visitors from the homeland; for instance the massive cathedral of Córdoba, Argentina (begun in 1687 by Merguete and Blanqui), a huge mountain of stone whose dome seems to crush everything beneath it.

Portuguese Baroque is recognizably distinct from Spanish, and was bequeathed to the Portuguese colony of Brazil. Oval and octagonal plans are not uncommon (the Clerigos church in Porto, 1732, by Niccolò Nasoni, or the Bom Jesus at Barcelos, 1701, by João Antuñes) and became even more widespread in Brazil (Rosano Chapel, Ouro Preto, 1784, by José Araujo).

A new feature of Counter-Reformation religion was the *sacro monte*, a processional way up a steep slope marked by sculptured representations of episodes in Christ's Passion. The most realistic tableaux are Italian, but the most architecturally remarkable ensembles are in Portugal, at Braga and Lamego, where staircases on a Cecil B. de Mille scale lead up to the hilltop sanctuaries.

The vast monastery-palace of Mafra (begun in 1717 by J. F. Ludovice) is Portugal's Baroque answer to Spain's Renaissance Escorial, but its Baroque qualities are restrained, and it differs from its model mainly in bringing the church forward and incorporating its two-towered façade into the very long main front of the building, the high dome rising behind it. More Rococo and much more relaxed is the palace of Queluz (begun in 1747, by a pupil of Ludovice), sheathed in the characteristic blue-and-white Portuguese tiles.

232

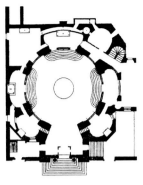

234. Among François Mansart's early buildings is Ste Marie-de-la-Visitation in Paris (plan above, 1632). In the photograph (below) we look up into the domes of the nave and one of the oval chapels.

235. Below right: a later work by Mansart, the Val-de-Grâce in Paris (1645). A difficult man, Mansart was dismissed when it was half built, and the upper parts are due to Lemercier and Le Muet.

France: a special case

French Baroque notoriously evades definition. Its very existence has been seriously questioned. One reason is that however intrigued French architects may have been by such features as domes, curved walls and the massing of columns for dramatic effect, there was always an element of ambivalence and divided loyalties. In Paris, for instance, the traditional form of the large town house, a courtyard with frontispiece to the street and *corps de logis* (main dwelling) behind, remained unchanged, though very occasionally the courtyard walls curved. The high-pitched French roof, which had survived the Renaissance, was still only rarely displaced by the flat top and balustrade. The orders, too, retained their hierarchy and formal roles: the façades of St Gervais (1616) and St Paul-St Louis (1627) are Baroque only in their sense of mass, not in their movement.

In 1624 Lescot's fragmentary Cour Carrée of the Louvre was continued by Jacques Lemercier in a way that aptly embodies French architectural attitudes. He matched Lescot's wing with an identical one, and between the two built a tall pavilion, the Pavillon de l'Horloge, the top storey of which is crowned by

236. The Collège des Quatre Nations, now the Institut de France (1662), by Louis Le Vau is the most Roman of all Parisian Baroque buildings, with its central domed chapel and concave wings.

a double pediment – segmental inside triangular. Virtually the same design was later carried around the other three sides by Le Vau (the top storey altered under Napoleon). Given an entirely free hand, Lemercier, who had studied in Rome, could be more overtly Baroque. His church of the Sorbonne (1635) has a façade and dome both strongly Italianate in style and meant to be seen together.

Arguably the purest Baroque building in France is François Mansart's Ste Marie-de-la-Visitation in Paris (1632), with its high dome (the first in France), its dynamic curving lines, and the interpenetrating spaces of the circular nave and oval chapels. His church of the Val-de-Grâce (begun in 1645, soon taken over by Lemercier) is also clearly aware of the Italian precedent; its façade has the scrolls of the Gesù, and multiplies them as real buttresses all down the nave, and its dome (due largely to Pierre Le Muet) is one of the few that can successfully challenge that of St Peter's. Mansart's proposed Bourbon mausoleum at St Denis (1665) would have surpassed both these. His secular buildings are less flamboyant but full of tense detail. The Orléans wing of Blois (1635) and the château of Maisons (1642) show him at his fastidious best, the classical elements freely but never wilfully handled.

Louis Le Vau, who has been mentioned in connection with the Louvre, was a less gifted but more diplomatic (and more showy) architect than Mansart and consequently more successful. His Collège des Quatre Nations (1662), opposite the Louvre, with an oval chapel crowned by a high dome between two projecting segmental wings, is something that Bernini would not have been ashamed of. (When Bernini came to Paris three years later, Le Vau was one of those who made him feel unwelcome.)

Le Vau's career had taken off in 1657 when he was commissioned to design the showpiece château of Vaux-le-Vicomte for Fouquet, Louis XIV's first minister. This is a splendidly confident building, unmistakably Baroque and unmistakably French. Its large oval salon is expressed on the curved garden front and in a high oval dome, flanked by wings with giant Ionic pilasters. When Fouquet fell, the Sun-King took over not only Le Vau but the painter Charles Le Brun and the garden designer André Le Nôtre. Transferred to Versailles, this team constructed a palace that was to influence every monarchy in Europe for over a hundred years.

234

235

191

165

236

237

237. Nicolas Fouquet's mansion of Vaux-le-Vicomte (1657) was calculated, all too successfully, to make a king jealous. With its two-storeyed oval salon in the centre and high slate roofs, it combines Italian and French elements to create an archetypically French effect.

Le Vau's Versailles still exists, though partly disguised by later building. The garden front had a recessed centre between two projecting wings; the wings survive but the centre is now occupied by the Galerie des Glaces. The elevation is not so very different from Vaux-le-Vicomte but the flat roof and balustrade bring it into the mainstream of classicism. In the interior Le Vau's most spectacular room, the Escalier des Ambassadeurs, has been destroyed. In its grandeur and in its confident management of scale, Le Vau's Versailles determined the future extensions of the palace itself and anticipated the way Baroque would develop towards classicism. When Mansart's great-nephew, Jules Hardouin-Mansart, came to take over in 1678, he was not so successful in avoiding monotony.

Hardouin-Mansart was, however, responsible for the last great monument of the Baroque in Paris, the church of the Invalides (1680). Here he found a panache that eluded him elsewhere – a vast, wonderfully inventive dome rivalling that of the Val-de-Grâce, and an interior which, even disfigured by the excavation of Napoleon's tomb in the 19th century, is an experience to remember with free-standing columns leading into openings on the diagonal. On a much smaller scale, but equally ingenious geometrically, is the chapel that Libéral Bruant designed in 1669 for the hospital of the Salpêtrière. For practical reasons this had to be divided into eight discrete sections; Bruant's solution is essentially Baroque, using a Greek-cross plan with square spaces in the corners, all opening onto a central octagon.

A further indicator of the classicism that was to dominate the 18th century is the east front of the Louvre, which was finally built in 1667–70 to the design of Claude Perrault, a gentleman architect

238. The garden front of Le Vau's Versailles (1669) had projecting pavilions at the ends and a recessed centre, which Jules Hardouin-Mansart filled in with his Galerie des Glaces (1678), carefully matching the earlier elevations. The long wings at the sides are also by him.

239. Jules Hardouin-Mansart's church of the Invalides, in Paris (1680), dependent as it is on ideas of his great-uncle François Mansart, is close to Roman Baroque, the dome a clever adaptation of St Peter's (ill. 165).

240. The east front of the Louvre, for which Bernini had been summoned from Italy (ill. 197), was finally begun in 1667 to designs by Claude Perrault, or a committee of which he was the chair. It has distinctly Baroque qualities, e.g. the rhythm of the coupled columns, but the overall effect is classical, pointing forward to the future.

who was possibly aided by Le Vau. It is a brilliant concept. Grandeur is achieved by the long row of giant Corinthian columns, while on the skyline the high roof is abandoned for the straight balustrade. Although it lacks the excitement of Bernini's play of concave and convex, dramatic movement (the Baroque element) is retained in the coupling of the columns and the recession into depth behind them to a wall articulated originally only by niches (later changed to windows). The centre and end pavilions are the most classical part and the most imitated in the years to come.

Outside Paris, Baroque continued to find favour well into the 18th century. The decade of 1680–90 saw the creation of the highly eccentric, indeed unique, church of St Didier at Asfeld in Champagne. Its plan has been compared to a hand-mirror. Entered via the 'handle', it opens out into a large central space which seems to be circular but is in fact pentagonal. From the outside one sees five concave curves through which five convex chapels protrude. Who designed it? The name of Guarini has been mooted, and he was certainly in Paris in 1662 building the now-destroyed church of Ste-Anne-la-Royale.

Provincial France is rich in buildings of this period whose elements have to be called Baroque and which still give pleasure as they were intended to: window-surrounds like the title-pages of books inhabited by mermaids and fat angels, rusticated doorways guarded by giants with clubs, façades loaded – overloaded – with huge sculptured garlands, official buildings proclaiming fantastic stone heraldry, like the six-foot-high griffins on the Hôtel des Monnaies in Avignon. Only rarely, however, is the plan, the management of space, as adventurous as in Italy or Central Europe. In the south of France, close to the Italian orbit, the oval plan kept its

241. The church of St Didier at Asfeld in France (1680) is a mystery. The strange rotunda on the right is the choir with the much narrower domed nave on the left. Unlike other churches in the region, it is built of brick.

devotees – as at the chapel in the middle of the Vieille Charité at Marseilles (1679, by Pierre Puget), St Pons at Nice (1705), or the chapel of the Oratoire at Avignon (1730). At Lyons, amid the rising classical tide, the church of St Bruno by Ferdinand Delamonce (1735) has a crossing that is pure Baroque, with transepts seen through open apsidal walls.

Rococo, which has been defined in a German context, actually originated in France in the 1720s, but in that country remained most characteristically a style for secular interior decoration. Only rarely did it escape from these limitations to assert itself as fully-fledged architecture. French fidelity to classicism did not waver but grew steadily stronger as the 18th century progressed. Rococo acts as a muted counterpoint to classicism, all the more appealing because of the contrast, appearing in the form of isolated accents, subtle touches which soften, but do not transform, the prevailing austerity. In Ange-Jacques Gabriel's Pavillon Français at Versailles (1749), for instance, an otherwise classically correct façade has little Rococo flourishes over the windows and doors.

The most consistent example of French Rococo is found in Lorraine, which had been made into a small client kingdom for Stanislas Leszczynski, the father of Louis XV's queen, to console him for losing the throne of Poland. Between 1735 and his death in 1766, he and his architect Emmanuel Héré turned his capital Nancy into an architectural ensemble of great finesse. At its centre are three monumental spaces. The Place Royale (now Place Stanislas), its corners closed by gates of the most sophisticated Rococo wrought ironwork, leads via a triumphal arch into a long tree-lined space, the Place de la Carrière, an old tilting-yard, which in turn opens out into another *place* closed to left and right by curved colonnades, the Hémicycle. The surrounding palatial buildings belonged to the court and administration. In Stanislas's second city, Lunéville, Héré built one of the few French churches that can truly be called Rococo, the Abbaye de St Jacques, with two flamboyant round towers topped by saints and a sculptured centrepiece with floating figures surrounding a huge clock.

But it is as a style for interiors and furniture – also known as the *style Louis XV* – that French Rococo comes into its own. This is a subject that cannot be pursued here, but a visit to the state rooms at Versailles (1737, by Jacques Verberckt) or to the Hôtel de Soubise in Paris (1736, by Germain Boffrand) is enough to show why it conquered the whole of Europe.

Flanders and the Netherlands

Nothing better illustrates the effect of religious division upon architectural style than the contrast between Catholic Flanders and the Protestant Netherlands in the early 17th century. Generally speaking, architecture continued to be led by church building in Catholic countries but lost that role in Protestant ones. (This fact is obscured in England by the large number of churches rebuilt in London after the Great Fire and the subsequent growth of the city – relatively few were built outside London – and in America by the need to provide churches where none existed.)

In Flanders the Jesuit plan (see p. 150) and façade found widespread favour, and occasionally an architect would attempt something more ambitious in the management of space. St Peter's at Ghent (begun in 1629, architect unknown) embodies Jesuit elements but brings the dome forward to cover the western bays of the nave so that it reads with the façade. The first dome north of the Alps was that of Scherpenheuvel, in Belgium (begun in 1609 by Wenceslas Cobergher), a highly unusual church with a seven-sided plan symbolizing the Seven Sorrows and Seven Joys of Mary. Two interesting churches from the spatial point of view are Notre Dame-du-Bon-Secours in Brussels (begun in 1664 by Jan Courtvriendt) and Our Lady of Hanswijk in Mechelen (begun in 1663 by Lucas Faydherbe). The first has a six-sided plan producing complex relationships between nave, choir and chapels; the second combines the centralized and longitudinal plan by making the centre swell out into a circle of ten piers below a high dome.

Far more frequently, however, Baroque in Flanders depends for its effect on profusion of ornament and richness of materials. The result is a combination of architecture and sculpture in which each reinforces the other but which can be almost claustrophobic in the way every element clamours for attention at the same time. The façade of St Michael at Leuven (Louvain) of 1650 shows this on an exterior; the Premonstratensian abbey of Averbode (1664, by Jean van der Eyndes) in an interior. By its very nature, the style is at its most intense in small spaces. The Lady Chapel in the church of St Charles Borromeo in Antwerp (begun in 1615 by the Jesuit architect Pieter Huyssens) is a modest-sized room with a coffered tunnel vault. It is lined with pale marble, the cornice and picture frames outlined in black. Into these are set paintings and between them panels of red and yellow marble. Finely detailed life-size statues of saints and virtues line the walls, standing on elaborately sculpted brackets. The altar rail is a network of foliage and fruit in white stone. There are three confessionals in polished

242. Notre Dame-du-Bon-Secours, Brussels (1664), by Jan Courtvriendt, looking up into the six-sided dome of the nave with chapels and choir opening off it.

243. Baroque space is not a matter of architecture only. Richness of texture, variety of materials, profusion of painting and sculpture, all produce a charged and heightened atmosphere, as in the Lady Chapel of St Charles Borromeo, Antwerp (1615), by Pieter Huyssens, which still owes a lot to Flemish Mannerism.

244. Protestant Netherlands: the Mauritshuis, The Hague (1633, probably by Jacob van Campen), a forward-looking palace for Prince Maurice of Nassau, expressive of dignity and restraint.

wood, the partitions shaped into winged seraphim. Abstract and figural, flat and three-dimensional, static and climactic, this kind of space is archetypically Baroque. Not by chance is this the age of magnificent tombs and fantastic pulpits.

To the traveller, Flemish Baroque is more immediately apparent in urban façades. It became fashionable to elaborate the gable-ends of houses with scrolls, niches, pediments, obelisks and heraldic devices, which still make walking through towns like Antwerp and Bruges an absorbing experience. Most splendid of all is the Grand' Place in Brussels, rebuilt after a bombardment in 1695, where each house seeks to outdo its neighbour in richness (many have gilded details) and invention.

The Protestant Netherlands saw no such boom in church building. Existing Gothic churches were stripped of their images and much of their furnishings and turned into the bare white-washed rooms that they remain today. New churches were simple brick boxes that became the model for Nonconformist meeting-houses in Britain and America. The Nieuwe Kirk in Haarlem (1645, by Jacob van Campen) is a typical example. One of the best buildings in this style is not a church but the Spanish and Portuguese Synagogue in Amsterdam (1670, by Daniel Stalpaert), copied a few years later for the same community in London. The most Baroque features in Dutch churches are the tombs, which followed those of Flanders in their lavish use of black and white marble and expressive sculpture.

Secular architecture is equally sober – for instance, the Huis ten Bosch (1650, by Pieter Post) or the Mauritshuis (1633, probably by Van Campen), both in The Hague. Even the royal palace of Het Loo (1685, by Jacob Roman and Daniel Marot) keeps to this style, which appealed to William of Orange and was followed in his English palaces when he became King William III. Only in the gables did Baroque bravura fly free, and the skylines of Leiden or Amsterdam are nearly as spectacular as anything in Flanders.

245. Catholic Flanders: the Grand' Place, Brussels, lined with the houses of the guilds and rich burghers, mostly built after war damage in 1695, in a style by then nearly out of date.

England and North America

English architecture after Jones went through a phase that is conventionally called Baroque, but has so little in common with what has been described hitherto that the term is perhaps more misleading than helpful. Apart from garden buildings, how many English domes are there? Three. How many oval churches? None. How many convex or concave façades? None. English Baroque is a style not of movement but of eccentric solidity.

The only exception – a major, unequivocally Baroque English building – is one that was never built: Wren's 'Great Model' for St Paul's. This superb design, a Greek cross surmounted by a dome, the arms connected by concave walls, would have put England in the mainstream of European architecture and possibly changed the course of English architectural history. In the event, Wren was forced by the clergy to conform to the normal Latin-cross plan. The dome remained dominant, though its dramatic impact was weakened by being deprived of the contrasting curve of the sustaining walls. To light the redesigned nave and choir Wren had to resort to clearstoreys which, in order to provide the right visual base for the dome, are concealed behind screen walls articulated by giant niches. The effect is successful and the charge of 'dishonesty' levelled against Wren in the 19th century is not worth considering. Inside, the opening out of the space under the dome, achieved by cutting off the last bays of the adjoining aisles diagonally (just as at the Ely octagon centuries before) is a calculatedly thrilling experience.

Wren is the perfect example of the gentleman architect. He was by profession a university mathematician. The geometrical play that had been frustrated at St Paul's could be indulged on a smaller scale in the fifty-two City churches that had to be rebuilt after the Great Fire of London in 1666. At St Stephen, Walbrook, Wren inscribed a circle inside a Greek cross, prolonged by one bay at the west end, thus ingeniously combining the centralized and longitudinal plan. In other cases (St Mary, Abchurch, or St Swithin, Cannon Street), he managed to fit a circular ceiling into a square. One of the most interesting was demolished in the 19th century, St Benet Fink, whose plan was an elongated decagon approximating to an oval. The rest are rectangles of differing shapes and sizes divided internally into basilican or square spaces by arcades, often with galleries. Within the constraints imposed by the sites they show remarkable variety and with their original fittings were buildings of considerable charm.

Nearly all the City churches have steeples, ingenious adaptations of a Renaissance vocabulary to a medieval feature. Wren's steeples form an intriguing array of possibilities, and when seen together, clustering around the bulk of St Paul's and its dome, the effect must have been unmatched in the whole of Europe. Wren's details often show familiarity with Italian sources, though he never went there. Are they due to his younger assistants? The transept ends of St Paul's recall S. Maria della Pace, and the steeple of St Vedast, Foster Lane, even has a look of Borromini.

246, 247. Wren's plans for St Paul's evolved, with many changes, over a long period, starting before the old cathedral was destroyed in the Great Fire of 1666 and continuing even after the foundations of the present one had been laid. His favourite design is known to have been the Great Model (above), an inspired, uncompromisingly Baroque scheme based on a Greek cross, the arms connected by concave walls.

The final building is still dominated by its magnificent dome, which covers not only the crossing area but the adjacent bays of the nave, choir and transepts. Structurally it consists of an outer dome, seen here, a much lower inner dome seen from inside, and an invisible brick cone between them which supports the lantern. The cathedral's exterior also involves a degree of illusionism; the nave and choir are lit by clearstorey windows concealed behind high screen walls.

248. Wren's St Stephen, Walbrook (1672), is probably the most perfect of the fifty city churches that he, or his office, designed. In a sense it is a miniature St Paul's with a Greek-cross plan supporting a circular dome on eight equal arches.

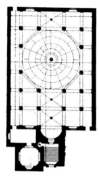

249. The two completed ranges of Wren's intended rebuilding of Hampton Court Palace (1689) look to Holland, the home of his patron William III, in their mixture of stone and red brick.

Wren was equally productive with important official commissions. He contributed largely to the only two complexes of English buildings that can compare with the palaces of continental royalty. At Hampton Court (1689) he built two imposing ranges of brick and stone, owing something to Dutch models, grafted onto the old Tudor palace. And at Greenwich (1696) he gave the Naval Hospital two pavilions with ornamental domes and porticoes for the hall and chapel, the whole composition, viewed from the river, being the closest England was to come to the Escorial. Wren was an eminently rational architect, willing to adapt to whatever was required. Exceptionally for his time, he appreciated Gothic and designed Tom Tower at Christ Church, Oxford (1682), to harmonize with the older buildings. Trinity College Library, in Cambridge (1676), by contrast, is self-consciously up-to-date; it takes ideas (e.g. disguising the unequal storey heights by a misleading exterior elevation) from Le Vau's Collège des Quatre Nations in Paris, which Wren saw under construction during his only trip outside England.

249

250

236

Wren's four most notable successors illustrate both England's links with the continent and her independence from it. Hawksmoor never went abroad; Vanbrugh experienced Paris (mainly from inside the Bastille); Archer travelled in Germany and lived in Italy; Gibbs worked in the office of Carlo Fontana in Rome.

250. The Library of Trinity College, Cambridge (1676), is Wren's tribute to Parisian architecture, which he had seen on his only foreign trip in 1665. By another neat piece of artifice he suggests that the floor level of the library corresponds to the cornice above the lower columns; in fact, it is to the lintels within the arches.

Nicholas Hawksmoor, by training a mason, began as Wren's assistant, working on practically all his major commissions. In his thirties he began to assist Vanbrugh in the same capacity. Not until 1707, when he was in his mid-forties, did he undertake commissions of his own. His share in Wren's and Vanbrugh's work is difficult to disentangle and his reputation rests on the six London churches he built in the second and third decades of the 18th century. They are all highly individual – it is not too much to say eccentric – fitting into no definable tradition. They are strong, serious and classical, seemingly descended from late Roman buildings (which he knew only from books) rather than from anything more recent, except possibly Michelangelo. Plans are conventional, but details such as door- and window-surrounds are designed with marked originality, e.g. using triglyphs instead of capitals. The exteriors, especially the steeples, are the most original of all. That of St George's, Bloomsbury, is a fanciful reconstruction of the Mausoleum at Halicarnassus, that of Christt Church, Spitalfields, an Early English spire grafted onto a triumphal arch.

251, 252. Hawksmoor and Archer are two of the 'Baroque generation' which succeeded that of Wren. Hawksmoor's London churches are all disturbingly idiosyncratic. His Christ Church, Spitalfields (below, 1714) is a powerful combination of classical portico and triumphal arch with a medieval spire. Archer's St Paul's, Deptford (below right, 1712), with its curved porch, is closer to Italian models.

John Vanbrugh, Hawksmoor's complete opposite temperamentally and professionally, had no architectural training and designed Castle Howard in Yorkshire (1699) as a gentleman amateur, making his way by patronage, adroit diplomacy and sheer brilliance. In 1705 he landed the commission to build

Blenheim Palace for the Duke of Marlborough. Everything that Vanbrugh did is marked by an originality that equals Hawksmoor's (and must owe much to him). He excelled in the handling of mass, which gives his buildings an immediate impact from a distance, reinforced by the clear bold motifs that articulate them. At Castle Howard he used a long elevation with a giant order over a rusticated basement, and built the second dome of English Baroque, covering an entrance hall that is as exciting as a stage set (Vanbrugh was a dramatist and theatre designer too). At Blenheim he organized a monumental central block, flanked by two courts for kitchen and stables that are like palaces themselves,

253. Vanbrugh, a successful dramatist but an untried architect, was given the commission for Castle Howard in 1699. Assisted by Hawksmoor he was able to realize a novel and truly grandiose conception, its giant order of pilasters culminating in an eight-sided rotunda.

254. Blenheim Palace, designed by Vanbrugh only a few years later (1705), again with Hawksmoor's help, has a starker, grimmer quality, in keeping with its military hero. Its spacious layout is held together by decisive accents at crucial points – the strange, square pavilions unlike anything in ancient Rome or modern Italy, the centre marked by an equally original double pediment.

into a formal design that reads coherently and, by means of weirdly unusual decorative features (including coronets combined with fleurs-de-lis), attains a bizarre grandeur unlike anything else.

In 1693 Thomas Archer returned from several years in Italy where he had immersed himself in the Roman Baroque of Borromini and Bernini. He is the only English architect to master this style, and his churches and country houses are therefore of special interest. They all fall between 1709 and 1715. St Paul's, Deptford, has a centralized plan loosely related to Borromini's S. Agnese. St John's, Smith Square, owes as much to Hawksmoor as to Borromini, with its four corner towers and grossly overscaled details. Archer's houses were in their own way just as personal.

255. James Gibbs was the youngest of this Baroque quartet, and the one most in touch with contemporary Italian developments. His St Martin-in-the-Fields, London (1721), skilfully adapts Roman Baroque to Protestant requirements. It was to prove immensely influential in America.

The fourth architect, James Gibbs, stands apart from the others both in date (he was much younger) and in training. Between 1707 and 1709 he worked in Rome in the studio of Carlo Fontana, a survivor of the Bernini generation. This did not turn him into an Italian Baroque architect, but it did enable him to use the vocabulary of Wren with an elegance and freedom already apparent in the first church he built after his return, St Mary-le-Strand, London (1714). His masterpiece is St Martin-in-the-Fields, also in London (1721). The story of its building illustrates Gibbs's progressive retreat from Baroque towards a more classical manner. His first design was for a circular nave with aisles behind columns, balanced at either end by a chancel and an entrance bay supporting a tower fronted by a portico. The last feature remained (and was to become extraordinarily influential), but the rest was revised to the more familiar, square-ended basilican plan. Gibbs did, however, succeed in building the Radcliffe Camera at Oxford in circular form, though here quite closely based on an earlier scheme by Hawksmoor. The dome is Gibbs's most Baroque work.

Gibbs provides an easy transition to the subject of England's American colonies. His *Book of Architecture*, published in 1728, contained plans and elevations of all his works, including those unexecuted, and became a pattern-book for the Protestant builders of the New World. Mount Airey, Virginia (1755), possibly by John Ariss, is copied from it directly. Peter Harrison's King's Chapel, Boston (1749), follows St Martin-in-the-Fields fairly closely, though the interior varies by pairing the columns.

Fifty years earlier, several of the buildings at Williamsburg, the first capital of Virginia, may have been built to designs imported from England. A persistent tradition attributes the College of William and Mary (1693) to Wren himself, and that is not impossible. Not until the classical revival later in the next century, however, could North American architecture really claim a place on the world stage.

256. Gibb's Radcliffe Camera, Oxford (1739), is arguably the most genuinely Baroque building in England – significantly for secular, not religious, use. 'One cannot help thinking of S. Maria della Salute,' said John Summerson (ill. 202).

Chapter 7: The Return of Classicism

But surely classicism returned at the Renaissance and has been returning regularly ever since? How is it different this time?

One answer would be: scholarship. During the late 17th and 18th centuries knowledge of Roman architecture became increasingly systematized, spurred on eventually by the discovery of Pompeii and Herculaneum, which were particularly influential in the sphere of interior decoration, and later, the nature of Greek architecture was understood. 'Correctness' became a criterion. Theory proliferated. Freedom was curtailed. The most common criticism of Neoclassical architecture is that it is 'cold', by which people mean academic, disciplined, lacking in spontaneity and emotion. Its pleasures can nevertheless be considerable, but they have to be learned: refinement, proportion, imagination working within strict constraints, a game of skill played by the rules.

Architects were thus forced to be scholars, and scholars could without too much strain turn into architects. Hence the relatively new phenomenon of the amateur architect, who plays a major role especially in England. Lord Burlington is the best known, but there were numerous others. (Robert Adam said: 'All the gentry of the country are Architects.') Classicism was the universal language, adopted by both architects and patrons as the inevitable, rational and only way to build. Nor is it difficult to see why. The classical style was a recipe if not for achieving total success, at least for avoiding failure. Its vocabulary of the orders – Doric, Ionic, Corinthian, Composite – constituted both a system of proportion that could be applied on any scale and always produced a satisfying result and a means of articulation through ornament that was pleasing to the eye.

In the Catholic south the break between Baroque and Neoclassicism is quite obvious. In the Protestant north it is much harder to see, and indeed it has recently been questioned whether there was any break at all. This is particularly true of Britain, where what is called Baroque and what is called Palladianism (both sharing a common Roman and Renaissance vocabulary and spirit) lead imperceptibly into what is called Neoclassicism.

257. The Admiralty, one of the key buildings of St Petersburg, was rebuilt by A. D. Zakharov in 1806. In its central pavilion sculpture groups and friezes as monumental as the architecture emphasize Russia's naval strength. The stark surfaces of the lower storey and the columnar pavilion above are typical of late Neoclassicism. The spire is an allusion to Peter the Great's Baroque Admiralty, which this building replaced.

With the possible exception of Early Gothic, Neoclassicism was the first truly international style. Regional differences are minimal. Faced with a photograph of an unknown Neoclassical public building of the early 19th century, who could be sure whether it was in St Louis or St Petersburg, Birmingham or Buenos Aires? This universality was largely due to the fact that the style could be taught. Its formulae could be expressed in books: hence the rise of two new phenomena – architectural theory and architectural schools.

Theory, admittedly, goes back to Vitruvius, but 18th-century writers raised the subject to a more abstract plane. It is interesting to see how it took different forms in different countries. English books were either strictly practical, with titles like *The Master Builder's Assistant*, or consisted of models to be imitated (like Colen Campbell's *Vitruvius Britannicus*, 1716 etc., the manifesto of the Burlington school) or of an architect's own work (Gibbs, Adam, Chambers). Italy produced some very radical theorists who went back to first principles to find answers to modern needs. Carlo Lodoli was ready to abandon the whole classical vocabulary and base architecture on purely functional considerations, a true fore-runner of modernism. His ideas were given wider currency by the more fluent and persuasive Count Francesco Algarotti.

But it was in France that a true philosophy of architecture emerged, founded on the kind of rationality, clarity and certainty associated with the name of Descartes. As early as 1683 Claude Perrault had published a book on the orders making symmetry, proportion and mathematics the measure of good architecture. In 1706 the Abbé de Cordemoy presented his own logical and simple rationale for all buildings. It was essentially Vitruvian, but gener-alized, given more intellectual weight and illustrated by examples from his own time. Its emphasis was on structure: every element should express its function unadorned; the column, for instance, should be load-bearing, not used simply for effect. Cordemoy's ideas were taken up and popularized by another abbé, Marc-Antoine Laugier, whose famous 'primitive hut', roofed with branches between living trees (1752), was proposed as both the historical origin and the philosophical justification of the classical style. At a more practical level they were adopted by the great teacher Jacques-François Blondel, who contributed the articles on architecture to Diderot's *Encyclopédie* and whose principles were published in detail in his twelve-volume *Cours d'architecture*. It was through such influences that the classic French values passed from the generation of Mansart to that of Gabriel.

Blondel's work was taken further by his followers, who included Pierre Patte, Nicolas Le Camus de Mézières, Jean-Baptiste Rondelet and Jean-Nicholas-Louis Durand. Combining a strong interest in theory with a grasp of the practicalities of building (though not always in the same person), these men were united in their quest for a 'rational' architecture. Some were architects of distinction themselves. Le Camus de Mézières built the highly original Halle au Blé in Paris (1762), a circular structure with 258 double-helix oval staircases. (The subsequent covering of the courtyard by a dome produced two brilliant technical advances: the first of wood and glass by Jacques-Guillaume Legrand and Jacques Molinos in 1782, and the second of iron by François-Joseph Bélanger in 1813.) Of the many late 18th-century Parisian buildings shaped by these theories, the most interesting are Soufflot's Ste Geneviève (the Panthéon), described later, Jacques-Denis Antoine's Hôtel de la Monnaie or Mint (1767) and Jacques Gondoin's Ecole de Médecine (1769) with its anatomy theatre like the Roman Pantheon cut in half. It is this French rational tradition that somewhat paradoxically lies behind both the visionary designs of Boullée, Ledoux and the 'architects of liberty' (see below) and the long submission of French architecture to doctrinaire orthodoxy, embodied in the teaching of the Beaux-Arts.

Architectural schools go back to 1671 when the Académie Royale d'Architecture was founded in Paris. Between 1793 and 1819 this was reorganized, along with academies of painting and sculpture, into the Ecole des Beaux-Arts, where architecture continued to be taught until 1968. Similar establishments grew up in other major European cities (that of Madrid, for instance, as early as 1744), though not, significantly, in England or America. The

258. The Halle au Blé, or Granary, in Paris, was originally (1762) a circular building with an open courtyard. Twenty years later this was covered by a dome of wood and glass, prefiguring the technical advances of the next century.

259. The architecture of the Picturesque sprang from poetry and historical association rather than canons and rules. Fonthill Abbey in Wiltshire, designed for William Beckford by James Wyatt in 1796, is its epitome. This was how Beckford's generation saw Gothic – overscaled, disproportioned, sinister. Structurally Fonthill was the reverse of Gothic. Its tower collapsed (though through no fault of its architect) soon after it was finished.

result, inevitably, was a degree of standardization. The advantage of this training was that it ensured a certain level of competence, proportion and dignity; its drawback was a tendency to pompous rhetoric without imagination.

Rationality had little time for poetry (Rondelet said that architecture was not an art but a science), and although French books were quite widely translated, it was never a movement that had much of a following in England, where an alternative philosophy was developing at the same time, the Picturesque. The Picturesque movement involves so much more than architecture – gardens, landscape, the relation of man to nature – that it can only be treated very partially here, and insofar as it includes the revival of other historical styles it must wait until the next chapter. Generally speaking, Picturesque architecture appealed to the senses and the emotions rather than to the mind, relying largely on setting, association and quasi-theatrical scenic effects. John Payne Knight's medieval Downton Castle, Shropshire (1772), James Wyatt's Gothic Fonthill Abbey in Wiltshire (1796) and John Nash's rustic Blaise Hamlet, near Bristol (1811), show the wide range of references evoked by the Picturesque. To these men stylistic purity was of small account. For their justification they looked not to Cartesian logic but to Edmund Burke's *Inquiry into the Sublime and the Beautiful* (1757).

259

It would be wrong, therefore, to imply that Neoclassicism was a monolithic style, immune to change. It passed though a number of well-defined phases, as apparent to contemporaries as to us.

Phases of classicism: from Palladio to the Revolution

The story begins in England. At a time when Italy, Spain and Germany were revelling in the Baroque, England turned to Palladianism, a movement instigated and promoted by the talented amateur architect Richard Boyle, third Earl of Burlington, who had fallen under Palladio's spell when he visited Italy in 1719. Two factors probably influenced him. First, Palladio was the most classical, the most scholarly and the least Mannerist of Italian late Renaissance architects, so it was reasonable for Burlington to see him as a mediator between ancient and modern. And second, as we have seen, Palladio had already been naturalized by Inigo Jones. So in steering architecture in that direction Burlington could see himself as reviving both Antiquity and a native golden age. Two additional facts helped to make Palladio the dominant influence: his designs were conveniently available in the *Quattro Libri* and he was, specifically, a country-house architect.

The fruit of Burlington's advocacy is a group of buildings of the 1720s and 1730s which were to have a lasting influence: Mereworth Castle in Kent, by his protégé Colen Campbell, and his own villa at Chiswick, near London, designed by himself (the first 260 a near-replica of the Villa Rotonda, the second a more sophisticated variant with a sequence of highly decorated rooms around a central domed octagon); Wanstead, in Essex, also by Campbell

260. Lord Burlington's villa at Chiswick of 1725 marks a decisive movement away from the Baroque towards a revived classicism. Although suggestive of the Villa Rotonda (ill. 164). Chiswick is in fact closer to Palladio's follower Scamozzi than to the master himself.

(1713, demolished); and Holkham in Norfolk by various hands, including another protégé, William Kent. The last two were much larger than any house by Palladio but solved the problem of length by dividing the façade into discrete elements while maintaining overall unity.

Whether one chooses to call these buildings Neoclassical is largely a matter of definition. Burlington's version of Palladio was highly selective, concentrating more on elements that Palladio shared with Antiquity than on those peculiar to himself. The use of the orders, a portico and a rusticated basement was enough to merit the name 'Palladian'. Even when Burlington followed the *Quattro Libri* most literally, as in the Assembly Rooms at York (1730), he did so because Palladio was re-creating the ancient world (in that case, an 'Egyptian Hall').

Around the mid-century the move towards greater fidelity to Roman models accelerated in England and France, while in other countries, within a relatively short time, it entirely superseded the Baroque. An architect's reputation was enhanced if he had studied in Rome (prize-winners at the Beaux-Arts were sent there as part of their training) or had published original research on ancient buildings – e.g. Robert Adam on Diocletian's Palace at Split or Charles Cameron on Roman baths. Neither of these men followed their Roman models very exactly; their details can be referred to precedents but they are assembled in combinations that are personal and modern. This is not true of everyone. Thomas Jefferson advised that the Virginia State Capitol at Richmond (1785) should be a replica of the Maison Carrée at Nîmes, and Pierre-Alexandre Vignon's church of the Madeleine, in Paris (1806), for instance, is externally virtually a Roman temple out of its time.

261. Holkham Hall, Norfolk (1734), by Matthew Brettingham and William Kent (its owner, Thomas Coke, future Earl of Leicester, had met the latter in Italy during his Grand Tour). It expands the Palladian farmhouse into a palace. The central block, containing a vast pillared hall leading to the saloon – on the south front, seen here – is flanked by four square pavilions.

262. The ballroom in Lord Burlington's Assembly Rooms at York (1730) is a scholarly version of Palladio's so-called Egyptian Hall, itself based on a description by Vitruvius – a long, clearstorey-lit room surrounded by a narrow aisle behind a colonnade.

263. The Virginia State Capitol at Richmond (1785) was modelled, on Thomas Jefferson's advice, on the Maison Carrée at Nîmes (ill. 9). The side wings are later additions.

264. The church of the Madeleine in Paris (1806), by Pierre-Alexandre Vignon, is a straight-forward re-creation of a Roman temple on the largest scale.

265, 266. Two masterpieces of German Neoclassicism: Schinkel's Altes Museum, Berlin (1823), and Klenze's Walhalla, near Regensburg (1821), built to house monuments of famous Germans. Schinkel's façade, with its row of eighteen giant Ionic columns, adapts Greek forms to a wholly new purpose. Klenze's Doric temple is more archaeological, a classical tribute to Germanic genius.

A direct consequence of such initiatives was the first-hand investigation of ancient Greek architecture, which began with a few intrepid pioneers in the mid-century. The Greek Revival was to produce buildings that would have been unthinkable to any architect before 1760. The fact that the Doric order had no base came as a shock, but was soon assimilated. Doric, in fact, became the favourite, followed by Ionic. Corinthian was rarely used, and the combined orders one above the other never. Indeed, buildings could in theory not be higher than the height of the column with its entablature (plus, possibly, an attic storey). Many of its adaptations to modern uses were extremely ingenious and quite far from any Greek precedent (e.g. Heinrich Gentz's staircase of the Schloss at Weimar, 1802, or Schinkel's front of the Altes Museum, 265 Berlin, 1823). Others are more literal copies, such as Leo von Klenze's Walhalla outside Regensburg (1821), the Parthenon 266 rebuilt on a bluff above the Danube. But it was in the USA that the Greek Revival produced its most abundant crop, and there was scarcely a major city that did not have its Greek banks, capitols and churches.

The period just before and during the French Revolution saw the rise of another distinct movement, aptly characterized by the architectural historian Helen Rosenau as 'more Neo than Classical'. Pared down so that it loses almost all archaeological reference, abstract, geometrical and suited to the carrying of symbolic messages, the style produced scores of grandiose schemes, very few of which were, because of political unrest, actually realized. Its presiding genius was Etienne-Louis Boullée, all of whose great projects remained on paper; his designs for a National Library, a National Theatre and a Monument to Sir Isaac Newton, all based   267
on simple forms such as spheres and cubes, are among the most seductive of all architectural dreams. His opposite number in Germany was Friedrich Gilly, who designed a vast monument to   268
Frederick the Great (another Parthenon) and a National Theatre, both unrealized but both inspirations to later architects. Claude-Nicolas Ledoux, to be discussed shortly, was luckier, and there are

267. None of Boullée's visionary projects was ever built, but their inspired exploration of geometrical forms was to have its effect later. His cenotaph for Isaac Newton (1784) is a huge sphere encircled by pine trees, pierced by holes which from the inside evoke the starry sky.

268. Friedrich Gilly's project for a monument to Frederick the Great in Berlin (1797) likewise remained on paper. It was to stand in the Leipziger Platz, in the centre of a precinct entered by a triumphal arch.

269. Built as a barracks, Peter Speeth's forbidding structure at Würzburg (1811, 1826) was later used as a prison. With its simplified classical elements and bold disparities of scale, it is a rare example of French 'Revolutionary' architecture realized.

isolated examples by others of the same school, e.g. Peter Speeth's Guards Barracks (later Women's Prison) at Würzburg. 269

The last phase of Neoclassicism was the Empire Style, so called because of its association with Napoleon. It is most fully expressed in interiors and furniture, using motifs from imperial Rome and ancient Egypt to create an impression of monumental splendour. In its homeland, its most accomplished practitioners were Charles Percier and Pierre-François Fontaine. It was adopted with equal success in Sweden and Russia. In England it led to the style known as Regency, in Germany to Biedermeier.

The sheer quantity of notable Neoclassical architecture is daunting and it seems best not to pursue a strictly historical approach, but – after this bird's-eye view of the way it developed – to discuss types of building across frontiers and across time: public buildings and the structure of towns, private houses, cultural and commercial buildings, and churches. Finally, although anyone could learn the classical language, certain architects spoke it with a recognizably personal voice. Robert Adam was certainly one. As a coda to this chapter we shall look briefly at four very different men who belong to this category and who took Neoclassicism into the 19th century. They display both the expressive range and the highly individual character of which Neoclassicism was capable, and for that very reason fit awkwardly into both chronology and treatment by building type. They are Claude-Nicolas Ledoux (born 1736), Sir John Soane (born 1753), Karl Friedrich Schinkel (born 1781) and Alexander 'Greek' Thomson (born 1819).

Palaces, ministries, and the Neoclassical city
To begin at the top. Up to the mid-18th century the major projects
were royal. Versailles was the model for scale and grandeur. The
largest comparable palace was that of Caserta, built for the King of
Naples by Luigi Vanvitelli in the years following 1751. Classical in
its geometry and its repetitive façades, it incorporates several
bravura features, such as the staircase and theatre. One finds   270
similar ambitions realized to various degrees all over Europe,
from Spain (Aranjuez for Philip V, 1740s) to Germany and Russia,
where the numerous palaces of the nobility majestically line the
water in St Petersburg.

When, in the 18th century, central governments grew large
enough to need separate buildings to house their departments,
which had to be impressive for prestige purposes, it was to palace
architecture that their designers turned, or at least to palatial
façades; the interiors offered less scope. Numerous to the point of
monotony in virtually every capital of the Western world are the

270. Luigi Vanvitelli's palace of
Caserta (1751) for the King of
Naples rivals the Escorial in scale.
Its double staircase combines
monumental classicism with
something of the drama of
Baroque.

271. The Strand façade of William Chambers's Somerset House, London (1776), reflects only a small part of its very extensive plan. A rusticated ground storey supports demi-columns and aedicule windows, alluding to a wing by Inigo Jones in the old Somerset House.

central porticoes, the long ranges of windows, the projecting end pavilions that say 'government offices'. The commonest variant was the row of giant columns, an expressive symbol of power; so that the city of Washington, DC, for instance, suffers severely from what has been called 'columnomania'.

Self-expression is hardly to be expected in these functional and often anonymous-looking buildings, but the following list, necessarily very selective, gives an idea of their range and their potential: Somerset House, London, by Sir William Chambers (1776), a vast congeries of government offices, its façade curtailed on the landward side but fully expressed towards the river; the Custom House and Four Courts, Dublin, both by James Gandon (1776), highly original designs giving monumentality to a small city; the State House, Boston, Massachusetts, by Charles Bulfinch (1797); the Admiralty, St Petersburg, by A. D. Zakharov (1806) at the focus of Peter the Great's plan and a symbol of Russian power; the Bourse, Paris, by A. T. Brongniart (1808), an austere block of giant columns, later successfully extended; the Palais de Justice, Lyons, by L.-P. Baltard (1835), another long façade, of twenty-four giant Corinthian columns; St George's Hall, Liverpool, by H. L. Elmes (1840), an ingenious combination of law courts, assembly room and theatre; the State Parliament, Vienna, by Theophil von Hansen (1873), one of a number of grand, contrasting buildings on the new Ringstrasse; and the Capitol, Washington, begun in 1792 and continuously enlarged throughout the 19th century

271

272

257

273

274

272. Opposite, below: James Gandon gave his Four Courts building in Dublin (1776) a distinctly personal character by an imposing colonnaded drum supporting a very shallow segmental dome over the centre. Gandon was a pupil of Chambers.

273. In St George's Hall, Liverpool (1842), the young Harvey Lonsdale Elmes, faced with the problem of giving unity to several functions inside a single shell, succeeded by the ingenious manipulation of classical features. The foreground block houses the law courts and the central one the giant ceremonial hall, while at the far end is the theatre.

by a succession of architects, but undeniably impressive and worthy of its position.

All of these can be seen as adaptations of the palace façade to buildings other than palaces. And it was early realized that the palace façade could be adapted still further, for example to disguise a row of houses. One of the first of such schemes is Queen's Square, Bath (1729), where John Wood the Elder planned a speculative residential venture in the form of four palaces. Robert Adam and John Nash did likewise in London (Fitzroy Square, 1793, and the Regent's Park terraces, 1820s). In Copenhagen, the Amalienborg (1794) incorporates four real palaces for members of the royal family in an octagonal composition.

274. The United States Capitol, Washington, is the result of decades of sympathetic modification and enlargement – begun in 1792 to a design by William Thornton, continued and altered after 1814 by Benjamin Henry Latrobe, and after 1850 given its extensive wings and immense dome (like the Panthéon in Paris, ill. 297, an offspring of St Paul's in London, ill. 247) by Thomas Ustick Walter.

Monumental layouts like these were producing a new kind of city in which functional planning replaced the grand Baroque gesture: the circus and crescents of Bath; the squares of London; the sequential spaces – gridded streets, squares, crescents, circus – of Edinburgh New Town; the white colonnades of Calcutta, founded by the British in the 1690s, like a tropical outpost of imperial Rome; the new streets and *places* of Paris, notably the Place de la Concorde, bordered by two ministry buildings by Ange-Jacques Gabriel (1753) that flank a straight street leading to the Madeleine, and, later, the adjacent arcaded rue de Rivoli; the setting of Washington, planned by Pierre Charles L'Enfant to focus on the Capitol in one direction but (originally) open on the other to the Potomac River as a symbol of the new nation's infinite possibilities; the Senate Square of Helsinki in Finland (begun in 1816); and above all St Petersburg, the Neoclassical city *par excellence* – not so much the radiating avenues of Peter the Great's plan (which is Baroque) but the grand hemicycle of Palace Square (by Rossi, 1819) and the square framed by the same architect's Senate and Synod buildings beyond the Admiralty.

One of the most interesting but underrated Neoclassical cities is, appropriately, Athens, where during the 19th century Danish and Bavarian architects built a series of monumental buildings – Royal Palace, Parliament, National Library, Hellenic Academy – deliberately recalling the Periclean age and boldly incorporating the polychromy that the French architect J.-I. Hittorff had recently established as authentic.

276

Privileged domesticity

In the 18th century, for the first time, private houses became a major architectural genre – possibly the dominant genre. Order, refinement, 'politesse', educated 'taste' (all concepts inseparable from Neoclassicism) came together with wealth and technical expertise to make the lifestyle of the aristocracy and rich middle class almost an art form in itself, a combination of private comfort and public display.

275. Two symmetrical public buildings by Ange-Jacques Gabriel (1753) define the Place de la Concorde in Paris, flanking the straight street that leads to the Madeleine (ill. 264).

276. When Greece gained her independence in 1829, it was natural that this should find expression in Greek Revival buildings. Below right: the Hellenic Academy in Athens (1859), by the Danish architect Theophil von Hansen. On the column stands a giant figure of Athena.

The post-Palladian generation in Britain is dominated by the versatile and ambitious Robert Adam. Fresh from exploring Diocletian's Palace in Split, living in Rome and enjoying the friendship of Piranesi, he succeeded in persuading his patrons that Palladianism was *passé*. The result is vividly illustrated by comparing the conventional north front of Kedleston, Derbyshire, of 1757, with Adam's south front of ten years later, which incorporates a full-blown Roman triumphal arch. His façade of Stowe, Buckinghamshire (1771), a central rectangular block with portico, flanked by colonnaded ranges and ending in pavilions with large triple windows, contrasts significantly with Kent's Holkham. Both these designs embody Adam's principle of 'movement', the constant play of projection and recession, changes in height and in the scale of details, that give life to his façades and avoid the monotony that he so despised in others. Towards the end of his life, Adam (always alert to fashion) anticipates Romanticism in his Scottish 'castle-style' houses, such as Culzean (1777), poised on the edge of cliffs on the Ayrshire coast as in a painting by Claude.

277
278

261

277, 278. Robert Adam's instinct for managing classical elevations is evident in the south front of Kedleston (right) and the garden front of Stowe (below). In the first (1767) he uses the motif of the Roman triumphal arch. In the second (1771) the long façade is skilfully divided into five sections, the three main ones dominated by triple windows based on Roman precedent.

279. The Library, Kenwood, by Robert Adam (1767) uses the triple division under an arch that he later used on the exterior of Stowe. By placing it across the apsidal end of the room and by the judicious arrangement of mirrors and book-recesses, Adam plays games with space that are endlessly intriguing.

But Adam's real genius lay in interiors, whose spatial ingenuity and sophisticated, colourful ornament in paint and stucco, freely – even playfully – based on his knowledge of ancient Roman motifs (and to some extent their Renaissance derivatives), constitute a style that long outlived him. Adam and his brothers had a large country-house practice, as well as venturing into speculative building in London; Adelphi Terrace, so called because it was built on land terraced out from the Thames river bank, was their boldest undertaking and led to the generic term 'terrace' for a row of houses joined together (an English speciality). At Kenwood, near London, in the saloon of Kedleston, in his remodelled interiors of older houses (Syon and Osterley, both near London) and in his smaller town houses, Adam created rooms that had never been seen before – rich, delicate, ingeniously shaped, articulated by such devices as columnar screens across apses, moulded pilasters, mirrors, and plasterwork on walls and ceilings.

279

Home House, London, is perhaps his masterpiece, each room 28■
dense with decoration and colour, but so cleanly controlled that
the effect remains cool and poised. Almost equally inventive, if
rather quieter, are his contemporaries and successors Robert
Taylor, James Paine and James Wyatt, each concerned to make
houses into havens of aesthetic pleasure evocative of Antiquity.

The continental parallels that suggest themselves belong to a
higher social class with a more formal lifestyle, so that the houses
are more self-conscious and less domestic. In France the Petit
Trianon, a compact villa with rusticated basement and giant 28■
Corinthian columns, was intended as a place of escape from the
court of Versailles, but the exquisite precision of its design by
Gabriel (1762) and his meticulous attention to classical detail
never relax. The same can be said of a later essay in the same vein,
Bélanger's Bagatelle (1777), just outside Paris, also built for a
member of the French royal family.

Such buildings – palaces in miniature, the concentrated
essence of an architect's vision – can be quite hypnotic in their perfection. On the outskirts of Dublin, Sir William Chambers built
the Casino at Marino for Lord Charlemont (begun in 1759), where 28■
carefully calculated rooms fit together like a three-dimensional

280. Home House, London
(1775), is probably Adam's most
concentratedly decorated interior.
The elements are still essentially
Roman, but the coloured marbles,
plaster reliefs and geometrical
patterning of walls and ceiling
bring Neoclassicism within
touching distance of Rococo.

281. Gabriel's Petit Trianon in the grounds of Versailles (1762) was commissioned as a retreat for the royal family. In the interiors touches of Rococo frivolity are allowed, but none on the outside, which is marked by cubic proportions, and the absence of a pediment or lavish decoration.

282. The Marino Casino outside Dublin (1759), built by William Chambers for Lord Charlemont, is virtually architecture for architecture's sake, a condensed demonstration of the classical style in the smallest compass.

jigsaw – it is a consummate exercise displaying, on a tiny scale, all the richness, severity and plasticity of which the Roman architectural language was capable. In Spain, in the grounds of the great palace of Aranjuez, Charles IV commissioned the modestly named Casa del Labrador (Worker's Cottage), a sequence of rooms that are the ultimate expression of Neoclassical taste – cool, colourful, richly clad with marble, inlay and painting, and filled with furniture and sculpture of the same standard. Designed by Isidro González Velásquez, it was completed in 1803. In Germany, classical taste blossomed especially at Weimar under the scholarly guidance of Goethe: the Römisches Haus (Roman House), created for the Grand-Duke by Johann August Arens in 1791, is chastely Ionic to the street, starkly Doric to the park and lightly Pompeian within. In Italy, a more ambitious house on the same level of perfection is the Castello of Racconigi, with its lavish series of rooms in the Roman, Etruscan, even Chinese manner, brilliantly carried through over a long period between 1758 and the 1830s.

Northern Europe welcomed Neoclassicism with particular enthusiasm. Warsaw has its exquisite little palace of Lazienki, built between two lakes by Domenico Merlini (1775) for Stanislas August, the last king of Poland; here is true grandeur on a small scale, wall-surfaces, sculpture and furnishings creating Rome where no Roman had ever been. In Sweden Gustavus III, in conscious emulation of the Petit Trianon, built the Haga pavilion,

283. The King of Poland's little palace at Lazienki, outside Warsaw (1775). This was Stanislas August's Trianon, combining richness with elegance and charm in an idyllic garden setting.

284. The Casa del Labrador, designed for the Spanish Bourbon King Charles IV by Isidro González Velásquez at the end of the 18th century (finished in 1803), is a superbly assured statement of royal confidence at a time when thrones were falling. The Statue Gallery is ingeniously designed to display many different kinds of antique and Neoclassical sculpture.

285. Gustav III of Sweden had also fallen in love with the Petit Trianon, and in 1787 commissioned a similar country retreat for himself at Haga. Tempelman's exterior is modest, but the interior – designed by the Frenchman Louis-Adrien Masreliez – again looks to Rome and Pompeii. In the Divan Room the exoticism of ancient Rome is combined with that of the Orient.

286. The Agate Pavilion, designed
by Charles Cameron in 1780 for
the grounds of Catherine the
Great's palace of Tsarskoe Selo
outside St Petersburg, gives
Neoclassicism a Russian flavour:
the great hall is encrusted with
panels of polished agate, jasper
and malachite from the Urals.

designed by Olof Tempelman in 1787. Russia can boast the Agate 28■
Pavilion at Tsarskoe Selo (1780), created by Charles Cameron for
Catherine the Great as a pleasure house incorporating thermal
baths. As in the rooms he redesigned in the palace itself, he shows a
dazzling fertility of invention, a sort of chaste exuberance, with
motifs drawn freely from ancient Rome and Raphael.

Finally we should turn to the country where domestic classicism took deepest root and survived the longest, the United States
of America. The great houses of North America are not normally
set within the context of international Neoclassicism, but that is
where they belong. One of the key figures is Thomas Jefferson,
twice president and an all-round man of the Enlightenment.
Always obsessed by buildings, he knew Paris well just before the
Revolution (when he also paid a brief visit to England) and later
assembled the largest library of architectural books in America.
The house he built for himself, Monticello in Virginia (begun in 28■
1769), is a typically American blend of classical principles and
domestic comfort. Many of his innovations were practical (such as
revolving shelves for the delivery of food to the dining room, or a
bed in an alcove between two rooms so that he could get up either

to his dressing room or study), but he was also constantly tinkering with it architecturally, adding and subtracting parts for visual effect. These concerns were taken further at the university he founded at Charlottesville, Virginia, where the residential blocks 289 in different classical styles were intended as aids to architectural education. Jefferson took a hand in almost all the major building projects of his time. Between about 1800, when Southern prosperity began to take off, and the outbreak of the Civil War in 1861, hundreds of great mansions were built by the proud families of Virginia, the Carolinas, Georgia and Louisiana, often naive in their pretensions but frequently achieving a grand simplicity that Europe could not match. The fact that their builders were unworried about 'correctness' contributed to their quirky individuality. Most of them have porticoes with giant columns, often committing the solecism of having a balcony halfway up. Often too the pediment is omitted, leaving a high, powerful cornice (e.g. the William Cochrane House, Tuscaloosa, Alabama, c. 1855). 287 Probably the densest concentration of such columned houses is in Louisiana, for instance, in the Garden District of New Orleans.

287. The William Cochrane House, Tuscaloosa, Alabama (c. 1855, demolished), was a typical Southern stately home with columned portico and balcony.

288, 289. Thomas Jefferson began building Monticello (opposite) in 1769, modifying and extending it throughout his life. Jefferson has been called 'a belated Palladian', and in its proportions and practicality his house comes closer to its original models than most so-called Palladian buildings.

At Charlottesville, Virginia (below), he built the first university campus, begun in 1817, and originally open at the far end, the west. The library, the large rotunda in the foreground, is Stanford White's replacement of the original building, burnt in 1895.

Plasterwork and cast iron reach the highest standard with designs not mindlessly copied from the Old World but inventively adapted to the New. Oval rooms, flying staircases, lively and original ornament can be found everywhere, e.g. the Nathaniel Russell House, Charleston, South Carolina (1808). The Governor's Mansion at Jackson, Mississippi (1839), has a splendid sequence of rooms with wide Grecian doorways (too wide to be really Grecian) and Roman columns. Probably the best-known of such houses is the Lee Mansion, Arlington, Virginia, with its strong Doric portico, added by George Hadfield in 1826.

Most of these houses were designed by their owners or by builders, but occasionally the name of an architect surfaces. William Jay, a pupil of Soane, came to Georgia from London in 1817, and built a number of quite exceptional houses, many of them unhappily demolished. In a land of adventurous staircases he outdid them all. That of the Archibald Bulloch House in Savannah (1818) rose free-standing from the centre of the house inside a circular cage of six Composite columns, reminding one historian of the Choragic Monument of Lysicrates with the inner drum removed. Throughout the South, in fact, the staircase is often the showpiece of the house, as for instance in the Lyman Harding House, Natchez, Mississippi (1812), which has another free-standing spiral.

Culture and commerce

The Neoclassical period coincided with the coming-of-age of many institutions that demanded their own type of building: in the cultural sphere, museums, art galleries and theatres; in the commercial, banks, exchanges and warehouses.

Before 1750 all art galleries and museums were private though to varying degrees open to the public. The first purpose-built structures date from the 1770s: the Museum Fridericianum at Kassel by S. L. du Ry (a conventional block with central portico), the Museo Pio-Clementino in Rome, a series of monumental rooms added to the Vatican palace by M. Simonetti and G. Camporesi, and, on a smaller scale, the gallery added to Newby Hall, Yorkshire, by Robert Adam. Ten years later came the Prado, Madrid, by Juan de Villanueva, an imposing building intended for public access.

During the next forty years the idea of national museums grew up all over Europe, encouraged by Napoleon's reorganization of the Louvre, and the 1820s saw the designing of two great masterpieces of the genre, Karl Friedrich Schinkel's

8

Altes Museum in Berlin and Robert Smirke's British Museum, London, both of which use the motif of the giant free-standing Ionic colonnade. Thereafter, the classical style remained the established style for museums and picture galleries for a hundred years. Leo von Klenze, Schinkel's successor as the leader of German Neoclassicism, built a series of superb museum buildings including the Glyptothek and Alte Pinakothek in Munich (1815 and 1826) and the New Hermitage in St Petersburg (1842) to house the imperial art collection. The latter remains, in the opinion of many, the perfect museum, its outstanding merits as architecture enhancing rather than diminishing the impact of its contents. M. G. Bindesbøll's Thorvaldsen Museum, Copenhagen (1839), is also expertly adapted to its purpose, a shrine to the sculptor (he is buried in the courtyard) and his work.

George Basevi's Fitzwilliam Museum, Cambridge (1837), W. H. Playfair's National Gallery of Scotland, in Edinburgh (1850), and C. R. Cockerell's Ashmolean Museum, Oxford (1841), are all functionally efficient buildings, intentionally arousing those emotions of veneration and respect which until the 1950s were considered appropriate for the contemplation of art. The classical style was still proving its worth well into the 20th century, though by then showing some signs of fatigue.

290, 291. The early 19th century saw the rise of the public museum to a position of cultural dominance. London's British Museum, designed by Robert Smirke in 1823, spends much of its available space on a huge Ionic colonnade (below). In St Petersburg, Leo von Klenze built the New Hermitage (1842), its monumental staircase (below right) leading between marble-clad walls and Doric columns to the picture galleries on the upper floor.

The theatre too was passing through a transition from the private to the public sphere. In most European countries, but not in England or America, theatres became civic monuments, often built on prominent free-standing sites and funded by the state. Nearly all had semicircular or horseshoe-shaped auditoriums, mostly with generous circulation spaces, staircases, concert halls, back-stage areas and rehearsal rooms.

The first of the new-style theatres was Georg Wenzeslaus von Knöbelsdorf's Berlin Opera House for Frederick the Great (1741), which occupied an island site on the Unter den Linden and was entered by a classical portico. A decade later came a theatre destined to be a model for much that followed, Jacques-Germain Soufflot's Lyons Opera House (1754); and twenty years after that the culmination of the genre in the Grand Théâtre of Bordeaux 293 (1773) by Victor Louis. Occupying a key position in the city and fronted by a giant colonnade, this proclaims the cultural status of the theatre as part of urban life. (When Charles Garnier came to design the Paris Opéra a hundred years later it was to Bordeaux that he turned.) Louis used a ring of giant columns in the auditorium also, but these were generally considered too much of an intrusion on the seating capacity (the Théâtre Feydeau in Paris by Legrand and Molinos, 1788, had twenty-eight columns). But on

292. Copenhagen's Thorvaldsen Museum (1839) is devoted to the work of Denmark's greatest Neoclassical sculptor. Avoiding the orders, its architect M. G. Bindesbøll goes to archaic Greece and Mycenae for inspiration.

293. In the Grand Théâtre of Bordeaux (1773), Victor Louis made every problem seem easy. Circulation is handled by its grand staircase, taking spectators smoothly to circles and boxes. Decoration is lavish but restrained, the wonderfully precise French masonic technique satisfying the eye in every detail.

a smaller scale, in certain theatres built for royalty, the ring of columns gives a splendidly classical sense of decorum: e.g. Charles IV's theatre at Caserta (Vanvitelli, 1752), Gustavus III's at Gripsholm (Erik Palmsted, 1781) and Catherine the Great's in the Hermitage (Quarenghi, 1782). The most ambitious of these court theatres is that of Versailles, by Gabriel (1763), which houses more seats behind a semicircular colonnade at an upper level.

By the end of the 18th century, theatres and opera houses had grown to vast dimensions, holding up to 3,000 spectators and with six or seven tiers of boxes. From the architectural point of view the most notable are the San Carlo at Naples (by Antonio Niccolini, 1810 and 1816), Covent Garden, London (by Robert Smirke, 1809, later replaced by the present opera house), and Drury Lane, London (by Henry Holland, 1794; later rebuilt by Benjamin Wyatt, 1812, of which the vestibule and staircases remain). In all these examples the public rooms and staircases were at least as important as the auditorium.

Developments in commerce and industry were also leading to a demand for buildings that had no traditional precedents. The Bank of England, which goes back to the late 17th century, built itself imposing new premises in London in 1732, later much enlarged (discussion of this is postponed to the section on Sir John Soane). Other banks followed suit and by the early 19th century there were offices all over the country. Those by C. R. Cockerell for the Bank of England in Bristol and Liverpool (1830s and '40s) belong to the later age of Neoclassicism, using the Roman vocabulary to express strength, security and solid wealth. That vocabulary continued to be popular into the 20th century, and – in the rare cases where banks have resisted the urge to modernize – their interiors can still be exciting architectural experiences, from Edinburgh and Belfast to Melbourne and Chicago. In Philadelphia in the 1820s William Strickland produced a repertoire of 294 Neoclassical variants in the service of banking and business. Many great cities also needed an exchange, essentially a large open hall for the meeting of merchants. Brongniart's Bourse in Paris has already been mentioned. Thomas de Thomon's colonnaded Exchange in St Petersburg (1804), lying low on the Neva opposite 295 the Admiralty and preceded by rostral columns, lends the world of finance a nobility that it might not always deserve.

294. William Strickland's Merchants' Exchange in Philadelphia (1832) shows how the Greek Revival in the service of commerce could enhance the modern city. A curved Corinthian screen takes the corner of two streets, crowned by the Choragic Monument of Lysicrates (ill. 8).

295, 296. Two examples of the Greek Revival's versatility. The St Petersburg Stock Exchange (top, 1804) by Thomas de Thomon is a large self-contained hall with clearstorey windows derived from Roman baths surrounded by an unfluted Doric colonnade. Edinburgh Royal High School (above, 1825), by Thomas Hamilton, exploits its steep site with steps, platforms and colonnades evoking an ancient Greek acropolis.

By now it need hardly be repeated that the Neoclassical style was infinitely adaptable. Some of its most successful incarnations belong to building types for which it might seem absurd to conjure up images of ancient Rome – railway stations (Euston, London, by Philip Hardwick, 1835); markets (Padua meat market by Giuseppe Japelli, 1821); hotels (the Charleston Hotel in Charleston, South Carolina, by C. H. Reichardt, 1839); prisons (Newgate, London, by George Dance, 1770), hospitals (Albergo dei Poveri, Naples, by Ferdinando Fuga, 1751); schools (Royal High School, Edinburgh, by Thomas Hamilton, 1825) and national monuments (the Arc de Triomphe, Paris, by J. F. T. Chalgrin, 1806, and Klenze's Walhalla, already mentioned). Indeed it has never lost its appeal as a style that can unfailingly deliver both powerful associations and visual satisfaction.

296

266

Classicism and Christianity

There is no typical Neoclassical church and no consistent line of development. Each case has an element of the experimental, of problems not completely solved.

One church stands out for its ambitious scale and the novelty of its design: Soufflot's Ste Geneviève in Paris, now known as the Panthéon. Commissioned in 1754 and dedicated to the patron saint of Paris, this was to be France's answer to St Peter's in Rome and St Paul's in London. Like Wren, Soufflot planned a symmetrical Greek cross with a dome over the crossing; like Wren, he had to modify it by extending the nave; like Wren, too, he aimed to combine Gothic structure and sense of space with consistently classical forms. But whereas Wren had compromised by using concealed flying buttresses and very thick piers, Soufflot placed the whole weight of his dome on slender columns. He had gone too far. By 1806 his crossing piers had to be strengthened, and at the same time his large windows were filled in, as being unsuitable for the building's new secular purpose. The dome, outcome of a huge amount of controversy and discussion, is yet another example of Wren's influence. But for the façade Soufflot was able to avoid

297

247

298

297. Ste Geneviève, the Panthéon, Paris (1754 and later), by Soufflot. The places where the windows have been walled up can clearly be seen.

298. Left: the interior of the Panthéon. Soufflot attempted to use a basically Gothic system of forces in equilibrium, expressed in purely classical terms. In its original state, his building would have been very bright and transparent. But the windows were blocked to provide a background for monuments, and eventually his columns supporting the dome had to be replaced by solid masonry.

Wren's two-storey portico and use six giant Corinthian columns that fully express the grandeur of his conception.

Where churches of cathedral scale were required the domed church, preferably centralized, remained a favourite solution, from Ricard de Montferrand's St Isaac's in St Petersburg (1825) to Julius Raschdorf's Berlin Dom (1884). But none approached the Panthéon in architectural quality. More interesting is the form evolved by Benjamin Latrobe for the Catholic Cathedral of Baltimore, Maryland (1805). This is essentially a circle covered by a hemispherical dome based on the Roman Pantheon but enclosed within a square and with an extended nave roofed by shallow saucer domes ending in a pedimented portico.

Projects for circular churches abound in the ideal plans of Neoclassical architects, and very occasionally they were allowed to build them, e.g. St Hedwig's, Berlin, by Knöbelsdorf (designed 1747, built later under other architects), George Steuart's St

299

299. Benjamin Latrobe's Catholic Cathedral of Baltimore (right; 1805) consists of a series of squares covered by shallow domes very close to the style of his teacher Sir John Soane.

Chad's, Shrewsbury (1790), Robert Mills's Monumental Church, Richmond, Virginia (1812), and Georg Moller's Ludwigskirche in Darmstadt (1820). Moller's is the most elemental of these designs, the exterior as plain as a planetarium, the interior a simple ring of Corinthian columns. Mills has something of the same austerity; his church is octagonal, with a projecting square portico that is almost Archaic Greek in character. But the most striking example of all is the church of Possagno, in Italy, designed by the sculptor Antonio Canova, and built after his death in 1819. Here the body of the church is based on the Pantheon in Rome, but the portico is pure Greek Doric, copied from the Parthenon in Athens – a brilliant combination of scholarship and imagination. 30

Finding the right balance between these two was, in fact, the key to Neoclassical church architecture. Pure antiquarianism could go no further than the Madeleine, in Paris, designed by Pierre-Alexandre Vignon in 1806 (though later modified) as a 26

300. The sculptor Antonio Canova designed one of the most original of Neoclassical churches at his home town of Possagno (1819), combining key monuments of the Greek and Roman past.

replica of a Roman temple, surrounded on all sides by a Corinthian peristyle. In London, New St Pancras Church by W. and H. W. Inwood (1819) is equally literal, though in its parts, not its whole, and Greek this time, as befits its date. Its steeple is a combination of the Tower of the Winds and the Choragic Monument of Lysicrates in Athens and its vestries are the caryatid porch of the Erechtheion, duplicated. During the Greek Revival the Doric temple front became almost standard in Britain (St John's, Waterloo, London, by Francis Bedford, 1815) and the USA (Second Baptist Church, Charleston, South Carolina, by Edward Bricknell White, 1842). More inventive in its use of Greek elements is Joseph Bonomi's extraordinarily spare church at Great Packington, Warwickshire (1789), where a square groin vault appears to rest on four Doric columns squeezed into the corners.

6

A more straightforward option was to keep the basilican arrangement and simply replace the arcade with a classical colonnade carrying a straight entablature. The result is rarely a total success, even on the grand scale of Pierre Contant d'Ivry's Corinthian St Vaast at Arras (1775), or with the finesse of Jean-François Chalgrin's Ionic St Philippe-du-Roule in Paris (1768). The Catholic Pro-Cathedral of Dublin (1815), for which no architect can be securely named, is an unexplained offspring of St Philippe, with the Doric order replacing the Ionic. Added dignity could be achieved by giving the colonnade a second storey and pushing back the upper windows as far as the outside wall, as at Jacques-Ignace Hittorff's St Vincent-de-Paul in Paris (1824), but this inevitably darkened the church by depriving it of its clearstorey. That problem is successfully overcome in one of the purest of all Neoclassical churches, the Vor Frue (Our Lady) Church in Copenhagen by Christian Frederik Hansen (1811). Above an arcade of piers so thick that they can equally well be seen as a solid wall with openings, stands a row of unfluted quasi-Doric columns supporting a round, coffered vault. Outside, a Doric portico is set against a square tower.

To the post-Romantic, post-Gothic Revival sensibility there is a difficulty about Neoclassical churches, and it is easy to fall into the trap of speaking as if classicism and Christianity were somehow antipathetic. The Deism of the 18th century argued that Christianity was essentially rational, not a creed built on miracles and the supernatural, and this found ready expression in classicism, which was also inherently rational. The generation of St Thomas Aquinas would have sympathized, but not that of John Ruskin.

Four architectural portraits
In an age that was in many ways one of conformity, four men stand out for their assertive independence. Each had a strong personality that is immediately recognizable in his buildings. Each took Neoclassicism further than it could legitimately go, achieving a sort of abstract architecture beyond style. Each was in a sense a visionary, chafing against the restraints of what could realistically be built, yet at the same time was a practical man of affairs. And each was ready to undertake the widest possible range of projects, matching style to function like a scientist testing a hypothesis.

Claude-Nicolas Ledoux began his career designing houses for the nobility, which are already distinguished by the monumental quality of their façades and the ingenuity of their planning. His appointment in 1771 as Royal Architect and Inspector of Saltworks in Franche-Comté gave him new opportunities and released a new vein of his imagination. The saltworks that he built between the villages of Arc and Senans are laid out in a large semicircle closed by a range across the diameter. Entrance is by a big portico of six Tuscan columns, flanked by carvings representing saline water dripping from urns. The other buildings are in a strictly original style invented for the purpose by Ledoux, with heavy rustication, including columns in which round sections alternate with square. The impression of severity is not accidental, 301

301. At the saltworks of Arc-et-Senans, Ledoux was able to devise a radical style of his own, reducing the classical vocabulary to simple geometrical elements. This is the House of the Director (1775).

for this was a tightly disciplined community (there was even a prison), and Ledoux sought to determine not only its appearance but also its lifestyle. Ledoux may be the first example of the architect as social engineer. While the saltworks was being built he was playing with the idea of expanding it into a whole new town and thirty years later, in 1804, he published his final project. The semicircle has been turned into a complete circle, and a range of other buildings scattered outside it. Many are more symbolic than practical; the House of Sexual Instruction, for example, has a phallic ground-plan.

Also in the 1770s Ledoux was designing a theatre for Besançon. The auditorium was neither semicircular nor horse-shoe-shaped but bell-shaped, and instead of rising vertically with rings of boxes it stepped back on the amphitheatre principle. At the back was a colonnade of twenty-four Doric columns behind which were more seats (definitely restricted view!). The orchestra was placed below the stage, anticipating Wagner's Bayreuth. Characteristically, Ledoux published an engraving of the interior reflected in a huge eye.

302

The city of Paris received part of its revenue from customs dues on goods coming in from the country. These payments were frequently evaded and in 1784 it was decided to build a wall around Paris with fifty or so supervised gates or *barrières* which Ledoux was commissioned to design. He produced an inspired series of miniature pavilions all playing with the idea of strength and authority. Some are straightforwardly classical, with Doric

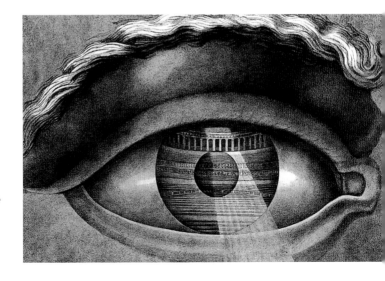

302. Peering into an enormous eye, one sees the auditorium of Ledoux's theatre at Besançon (1775), in which he abolished boxes and set back the ranges of seats as in an amphitheatre. This image comes from his visionary and influential book, *L'Architecture considérée sous le rapport de l'art, des mœurs et de la législation* (Architecture considered in relation to art, social customs, and legislation, 1804, 1847).

303. The commission to build about fifty monumental gates (*barrières*) around Paris for the collection of customs dues gave Ledoux the opportunity for an extraordinary display of architectural versatility. The Barrière de la Villette, an extreme statement of abstract classicism with a domeless drum, was the largest.

porticoes; some use the rusticated order that he invented for Arc-et-Senans; some have the Palladian motif; some have arcades of paired columns. Several were pulled down at the Revolution, many more in 1860. Today only four remain, including the grandest of all, the Barrière de la Villette, a domeless rotunda fronted by a portico of eight square piers. Ledoux died in 1806. Although most of his work was in the service of the Ancien Régime, he was architecturally a Revolutionary, using the vocabulary of Greece, Rome and the Renaissance to speak the language of his own time. 30

As much could be said of *Sir John Soane*, but he was more of a romantic, alive to the power of association. For him classical architecture was more than an authority to be followed, it was a vision to be renewed. After three years in Italy, he built up a country-house practice in which he worked out a personal style based largely on that of his highly imaginative and now underrated master, George Dance the Younger, and distinguished by spatial ingenuity (dividing rooms by shallow arches; alcoves; subtle transitions from part to part), lighting from above by skylights and domes, and a repertoire of restrained Greek ornament using incised lines and flat stylized decoration.

His great chance came in 1788 when he was appointed Surveyor to the Bank of England, at that time a random collection of buildings needing extension and renovation. Soane added new offices, replaced others and surrounded the whole by a high windowless wall. In the bank offices nearly all explicit classical references are avoided and we are left with exercises in pure geometry – shallow domes with skylights (the building was top-lit, for security), segmental arches, panels with elementary fluting, coffered semicircular niches, and complex openings into subsidiary spaces. Some rooms had more overtly classical features than others. The Bank was a succession of such richly rewarding experiences, but nearly all of Soane's work was destroyed when it was rebuilt in the 1920s.

What does survive, however, is Soane's own house in Lincoln's Inn, London, a sort of museum to his own eccentric personality. All his characteristic features appear here but on a miniature scale: concealed lighting, multiplication of surfaces, mirrors, tent-like ceilings, unexpected vistas. The house is filled with his collection of paintings, sculpture and architectural fragments, including an ancient Egyptian sarcophagus.

Nothing that Soane did, whether for private or official commissions, was predictable or ordinary. In his churches he avoided, on principle, Gibbs's combination of steeple and portico, insisting on bringing his towers down to the ground. In the Dulwich College Art Gallery, which was combined with an almshouse and the mausoleum of its founder, he adapted his spatial inventiveness to create ideal top-lit rooms for the display of paintings. He died, an old man, in 1837.

304

305

304, 305. Two characteristic interiors by Sir John Soane. Below left: the Old Dividend or Four Percent Office of the Bank of England (1818); the dome incorporates caryatids modelled on those of the Erechtheion (ill. 6). Below right: the Breakfast Room of his own house in Lincoln's Inn Fields, London (1813). Both use top-lighting, from the sides as well as the centre, and the chaste detailing that was Soane's personal signature.

Karl Friedrich Schinkel did not begin his architectural career seriously until 1815, when Prussia emerged from the Napoleonic Wars and he was already thirty-four. In the intervening years he had visited Italy, fallen in love with Gothic, and produced romantic paintings of medieval cathedrals in the sunset, panora- Frontis mas and stage sets (e.g. for *The Magic Flute*) drawing on the architecture of all periods including Greek and Egyptian. His first commissions in Berlin as the head of Prussian state building works were, however, all uncompromisingly classical: the Neue 306 Wache (a Doric-porticoed guardhouse on the Unter den Linden), the Altes Museum (already noted) and the Schauspielhaus 265 (theatre and concert hall). All combine the orders with stark, cubic massing, an emphasis on the horizontal, and window-division by plain square piers that proclaim their modernity.

The next phase of Schinkel's career was domestic. In the estates around Potsdam he built several villas, mostly for members of the royal family – Schloss Tegel, Schloss Glienicke, and his masterpiece, Charlottenhof. As much Italianate as Neoclassical, all are carefully sited in their surroundings and all provided with interiors whose classical purity does not detract from a feeling of intimacy. Charlottenhof is little more than a cottage in scale, yet its sequence of exquisitely varied and decorated rooms and the dignity of its portico and staircase-hall give it a miniature

306. Schinkel's guardhouse on the Unter den Linden, Berlin, the Neue Wache (1816), is a utilitarian building conscripted to make a symbolic statement.

monumentality. More archaeological but equally inventive is the small complex known as the Roman Baths, part of a house built for the Court Gardener at Potsdam, modelled on a Pompeian house. 307

Partly as a consequence of his official duties Schinkel became increasingly interested in the technology of architecture (he toured England in 1826 to study the achievements of the Industrial Revolution) and made free use of cast iron for such features as staircases. His Bauakademie (School of Architecture) of

307. As part of the Court Gardener's House at Potsdam (1829) Schinkel built the so-called Roman Baths, a cool evocation, on a domestic scale, of a Pompeian house.

308. In 1834 Schinkel designed a palace for the King of Greece to be built on the Acropolis in Athens. It would have been a vision of romantic classicism but, placed on the extreme eastern edge of the rock and kept to a single storey, would not have obscured views of the ancient temples.

1831 was a red-brick building with no obvious historical precedent, like the large warehouses he built behind the Altes Museum.

At the same time the romantic streak in him was not wholly suppressed. His Friedrichwerderschekirche (1824) and Schloss Babelsberg (1834), another Potsdam villa, are exercises in Gothic, not altogether convincing. But two of his last projects unite this fantasy aspect with the Neoclassical forms that came most naturally to him. His design for a palace on the Acropolis in Athens 308 (1834) was made for Otto of Wittelsbach, the newly elected king of Greece; that for a palace at Orianda in the Crimea (1838) for the Empress of Russia. Both were to be low, single-storeyed buildings, combining the informality of an asymmetrical ground-plan with a decorative formality based on the Antique. Both play with the ambiguity of interior and exterior, blurring the distinction between them as had been done to such effect at the Roman Baths or the staircase of the Altes Museum. They were unrealized dreams. Schinkel died in his prime in 1841.

Alexander Thomson is the least eminent of our four, largely because he spent all of his life in Glasgow. But his work illustrates very well how the Neoclassical style, even in the mid-19th century, was capable of repeated regeneration and renewal.

Thomson never left the British Isles and gained all his knowledge of architectural history from books. Ancient Greece, Assyria and Egypt clearly made a deep impression on him, but he was also aware of Hindu architecture and pondered the implications of the Temple of Solomon. In all he found sublimity.

For his earliest clients, the cultured Glaswegian middle class, he built a series of villas planned with considerable skill (a double villa, for instance, with entrances facing opposite directions and thus giving each owner a grander façade) and articulated in terms of Greek temple pediments, square piers and acroteria. He went on to design terraces, offices and other commercial buildings marked 309 by strong, banded rustication and restrained Greek and Egyptian decoration. The fenestration and massing have a great deal in common with Schinkel, whose published works Thomson must have studied deeply (in one of his villas, plate-glass screen windows fit within a curved classical colonnade, a combination of the Antique and the modern invented by Schinkel in his Orianda palace design).

But it is his three churches that make Thomson unforgettable. One expects a Scottish Presbyterian church to be rather grim. Quite the reverse. Thomson's were glowing with colour and rich

309, 310. Alexander Thomson brought Greek strength and Greek proportion to 19th-century Glasgow, but it was Greek reinvented for new purposes. Below: terrace housing in Moray Place (1858); its fenetration is Schinkelesque, the windows set directly, without surrounds, into bands of stone piers. Below right: the Caledonian Road Free Church (1856). The portico stands high on a podium flanked by a square tower, the two zones together representing the height of the church within. It was gutted by fire in the 1960s and is still a ruin. The apartment blocks beyond (now demolished) were also designed by Thomson.

with exotic ornament. The Caledonia Road Free Church (1856) has a Greek temple front raised up on a high basement (reflecting the arrangements inside) and flanked by a tall tower. The St Vincent Street Church (1857, the only one still intact) again has a Greek temple front and a high tower combining imagery from Asia and from Old Testament Masonic tradition. The interior, with its massive 'reredos' (centred, as was standard in Non-conformist churches, upon the pulpit, not the altar), evokes Mycenae, with galleries supported on columns with fantastic palm-like capitals. Colours are bright red and blue. The third, the Queens' Park Church (1867), had the same mixture of motifs and an even more extraordinary tower incorporating motifs from Indian architecture, but is less well documented because it was destroyed in the Second World War.

Although Thomson never fully explained the ideas behind his churches, it is certain that they were not mere fantasies. He believed strongly that Christianity was the culmination of progressive revelations made through other civilizations, and this is the iconographic programme behind his unusual choice of motifs. When he died in 1875 he already belonged to the past. Neoclassicism was over. The battle of the styles was at its height, and for that we have to go back a hundred years.

Chapter 8:   'In What Style Shall We Build?'

The title of this chapter is taken from a book published in 1828 by the German architect Heinrich Hübsch, *In welchem Style sollen wir bauen?* It was a question that was to preoccupy the architects of the early 19th century almost to the point of obsession.

It was not a question that had arisen in this stark form ever before. True, the Renaissance had been a revival, and Neoclassicism an even more self-conscious one. But it was only in the years around 1800 that knowledge of distant countries and of past ages became complete enough to allow architects seriously to contemplate building in virtually any style they chose. Both they and their patrons were assailed by new temptations which they found difficult to resist. They could select from their own past – Romanesque, Gothic – and from distant cultures as well – ancient Egyptian, Islamic (called Moorish), even Chinese. At first it was a sort of game. For his enlightened patron, the Prince of Wales (later George III), the learned classicist Sir William Chambers in the 1750s designed a whole galaxy of exotic buildings at Kew, near London, that included a Chinese pagoda, a House of Confucius, several Roman temples, a Mosque and a 'Gothic Cathedral'. For his son, later George IV, John Nash built Brighton Pavilion in a mixture of Indian and Chinese styles. Throughout the 19th century such out-of-the-way exercises could be used for some special effect: a flax mill in Leeds modelled on the temple at Edfu in Egypt (Marshall's Mill, 1838, by Joseph Bonomi Jnr); a pumping station at Potsdam disguised as a mosque (by Ludwig Persius, 1841); a mansion in Connecticut evoking a Persian palace (Iranistan, by Leopold Eidlitz, 1846); and a tea house in Moscow made to look like a Chinese temple (the Peslov Tea House by K. K. Grippius, 1895). Certain of these non-Western styles became almost standard in specific contexts – ancient Egyptian for cemeteries and Freemasons' halls (both understandable), and Islamic for synagogues (less easy to understand, except that it was non-Christian).

311. Franz Christian Gau designed Ste Clotilde in Paris as early as 1839 but it was not begun until 1846. Gau was born in Cologne and it is easy to spot the inspiration for its twin spires (see ill. 106). Iron is used in the roof.

313

312

312. The Egyptian Revival never became widespread, for fairly obvious reasons. The Temple Mill or Marshall's Mill, Leeds, was designed in 1838 by Joseph Bonomi Jnr, a noted Egyptologist, whose father and brother were architects.

313. For the Prince Regent John Nash built the ultimate folly, Brighton Pavilion (1816 onwards), the remodelling of an earlier house in a style that mixes Hindu, Islamic and Chinese, with a lavish use of concealed iron.

Why Neo-Gothic?

Only one style crossed the line between game and earnest to become a serious alternative to Classicism, and that was Gothic. The prehistory of the Gothic Revival has been much debated. It actually had three beginnings, neither of the first two leading inevitably to the third. The first was a phase in the early 18th century when Gothic (still, in many countries, a fairly recent memorÿ) was made to harmonize with earlier buildings. Such was the case in England with some of Wren's City churches (St Mary Aldermary) or Oxford college buildings (Tom Tower, Christ Church), or Hawksmoor's additions to cathedrals (the towers of Westminster Abbey). There are parallel cases elsewhere, sometimes so conservative as to be indistinguishable from the real thing, sometimes truly original. In France the west front of Orléans Cathedral is pure fantasy-Gothic. In Bohemia Santini's vaults at Sedlec and Kladruby (1703 and 1712) are as wild as anything by his model, Benedikt Ried.

222
109

The second phase, which is a largely British phenomenon, had its roots in literature as much as in architecture. The Gothic novel made the Middle Ages fashionable as a time of romance and slightly sinister beauty. It was not long before life began to imitate art. Horace Walpole, author of *The Castle of Otranto* (1765), began building Strawberry Hill, near London, as a miniature abbey even before he published his novel. William Beckford, author of *Vathek*, commissioned James Wyatt to build Fonthill Abbey (1796), the most extravagant of all Gothic fantasies. Sir Walter Scott, whose

314

259

314. In his Gothick country house outside London, Strawberry Hill, Twickenham, Horace Walpole took ideas from numerous sources, including Westminster Abbey and Old St Paul's. The library (below right) dates from 1754.

novels did more than anything to popularize the Middle Ages, built Abbotsford, a sort of compressed amalgam of Scottish history. In all these buildings there was a conscious element of make-believe. The style (today spelled 'Gothick' to indicate its frivolity) was almost as close to Rococo as to real Gothic.

This 'Rococo-Gothick' is in many ways the most enjoyable phase of the Revival. No one made authenticity a crucial consideration. By using plaster instead of stone the prettiest of fan vaults could be built at very little cost (entering Arbury Court, Warwickshire, or Shobdon church, Herefordshire, is like walking onto a stage set), and by employing the new material of cast iron architects could reduce piers to the thinnest of shafts and vaults to a network of tiny ribs, as in the charming church of Tetbury in Gloucestershire by Francis Hiorne (1781). There is little of this style outside Britain, though it can be found – for instance the little convent of the Ascension in the Kremlin in Moscow (1817, now demolished), Schloss Stolzenfels on the Rhine (begun by Schinkel, 1834) or the Caffè Pedrocchi in Padua by Giuseppe Japelli (1837). In France it continued sporadically well into the 19th century with churches such as the cast-iron St Eugène in Paris by Louis-Auguste Boileau (1854), a real *tour de force* of cross-cultural imagination.

The coming-of-age of Neo-Gothic, the moment when it passed from careless youth to responsible maturity, took place in the 1840s. This is the third phase of the Gothic Revival and neither its aesthetic course nor the ideology behind it were the same in all countries. One thing that affected them all, however, was the huge advance in historical knowledge, so that Gothic buildings were no longer remote and mysterious (in the early 18th century it was widely believed that the English cathedrals were built by the Anglo-Saxons) but precisely datable and their various phases clearly distinguished, so that standards of 'correctness' formerly confined to classical buildings could now also be applied to them. It was also, not coincidentally, the great age of church restoration. All the leading Neo-Gothic architects took part in that, learning their expertise in contact with the real thing.

In England this coincided with a religious revival which placed new emphasis on liturgical practices. Serious High Church Anglicans weighed the easy-going Georgian Church in the balance and found it wanting. To restore it meant going back to before the Reformation, stressing the sacraments and returning to ancient usages in ritual, furniture, vestments and symbolism, a movement that led inevitably to a return to ancient architecture as well, with its screens, stalls, steps, reredoses and processional paths – an area of study that became known as 'ecclesiology'. An additional factor was the growth of urban population, steeper in England than elsewhere, which in conjunction with the new missionary spirit meant the building of hundreds of new churches.

Architecture and morality

All these factors converge in the person of Augustus Welby Northmore Pugin, the man who more than any other can claim to be the father of the Gothic Revival. Pugin's quest for authentic Christianity led to his early conversion to Roman Catholicism. An interesting though not a great architect, he was a brilliant designer, incorporating medieval elements in church plate, furniture and decorative patterns, and above all a tireless propagandist through his books, beginning with *Contrasts* (1836) and *The True Principles of Christian or Pointed Architecture* (1841), soon translated 315

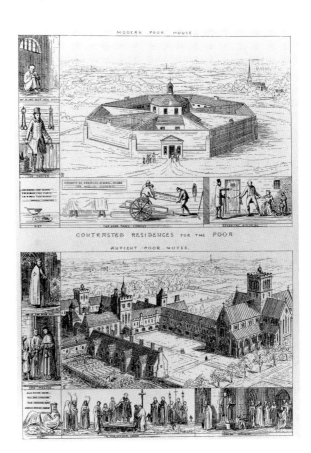

315. In *Contrasts* (1836) Pugin compared the beauty and moral soundness of the Middle Ages with the ugliness and greed of his own day. Here the 19th-century workhouse, with its brutal discipline, is contrasted with the dignity of the old almshouse.

into other languages. For him Gothic was the only truly Christian style and to adopt it – together with the values that went with it – was to remedy all the evils of the contemporary world, not just aesthetic but religious, social and moral as well. He died in 1852 at the age of 40. His idealistic view of the Middle Ages was endorsed in their different ways by the critics John Ruskin and William Morris and gave the English Gothic Revival a moral foundation and an intensity of feeling probably deeper than elsewhere.

In every country, it is fair to say, the Gothic Revival was 'church-led'. But from the very beginning it was eagerly adapted for secular buildings as well. Here historical and national associations were all-important. The great turning-point of the Revival was the competition for the new Houses of Parliament in London, 316 which had burnt down in 1834. For patriotic reasons, the new design had to be Gothic or Elizabethan, since these styles supposedly represented the ancient sources of British liberty. The winner, Charles Barry, was temperamentally a classicist, though he had built churches in the earlier Gothick mode. But he had Pugin to assist him in the details and the result is a building classical in its planning and convincingly Gothic in appearance. Its example was followed in parliaments all over the world, from Budapest to Ottawa. Other types of public building adopted the same style for

316. The Houses of Parliament, London (begun in 1840), are the happy result of collaboration between a classicist, Charles Barry, and a Goth, A. W. N. Pugin.

317. William Burges used his considerable knowledge of Gothic architecture to create a fantasy castle for Lord Bute at Cardiff (1865).

many of the same reasons, so that we get Gothic town halls at Munich (by Georg Hauberisser, 1867), Manchester (by Alfred Waterhouse, 1868), and Vienna (Friedrich Schmidt, 1868), Gothic law courts, Gothic universities, Gothic hotels, Gothic hospitals, Gothic libraries. Partisans of Gothic argued that it was a more functional style than classical because it could ignore symmetry and allow the building to follow the logic of its interior requirements, doors and windows simply coming where they were needed.

It was in the area of private commissions that the romanticism latent in all the Gothic Revival could be given free rein. Medieval castles were restored, sometimes from the ground up. Pierrefonds, in France (Viollet-le-Duc, 1858), Sintra in Portugal (Baron Eschwege, 1840s) or the Wartburg in Germany (1850s) are recreations of a past that never really existed. Cardiff Castle and Castell Coch, both in Wales, were rebuilt by William Burges (1865, 1875) to a condition that far exceeded their originals in picturesqueness. Wholly in the realm of make-believe is Ludwig II of Bavaria's fairy-tale castle of Neuschwanstein (Riedel and Jank, 1868), more Romanesque than Gothic.

Accomplished as they are, it is hard to take such buildings seriously, and to do justice to the Gothic Revival we must return to the mainstream of ecclesiastical and civic architecture. England retained the dominant position it had occupied from the start,

317

producing many talented architects who worked only in the Gothic style. Within that style England showed the greatest diversity. Certain broad generalizations can, however, be made. In the early years after the death of Pugin the favoured model was the Decorated Style (or 'Middle Pointed') of the years around 1300. Towards the middle of the century French early Gothic began to exercise a powerful influence, producing churches that were praised as 'masculine' and 'muscular'. After 1865–70 taste gradually changed towards a specifically 'English' late Gothic, returning to Decorated but now more refined and with greater delicacy of detail. Keeping pace with architecture were corresponding developments in the decorative arts, especially stone-carving, metalwork and stained glass.

George Gilbert Scott, whose career began as his contemporary Pugin's was ending, was the most learned, prolific and professionally successful of the Neo-Goths. Churches (his best, perhaps, All Souls, Halifax, of 1855), secular buildings (the Midland Grand Hotel at St Pancras, London, 1869) and restoration schemes poured out of his office. He kept fairly close to his medieval models, sometimes (e.g. the Episcopal Cathedral of Edinburgh, 1874) perhaps too close, but he could respond

318. William Butterfield's All Saints, Margaret Street, London (1849), was a model church for High Anglicans, using lavish polychromy and painting. Here we look into the aisle, which is windowless – a recommended arrangement for churches in towns, hemmed in by other buildings.

319. George Gilbert Scott's Midland Grand Hotel, St Pancras (below right, 1868), was a comparable high-water mark of secular Gothic. It fronted the station's great train-shed (visible far left; cf. ill. 360).

31

inventively to a wide range of demands, and was also influential in carrying English Neo-Gothic to Germany when he won the competition for the Nikolaikirche in Hamburg in 1844. His contemporary William Butterfield, an odd mixture of puritanical austerity and sensuous excess, made colour an integral part of his churches, most notably at All Saints, Margaret Street, London (1849). Keble 318 College, Oxford (1867), is typical of his tough – it used to be called wilful – integrity. George Edmund Street, ten years younger, makes his attack from a different direction. If his churches were shorn of all their architectural detail they would still be powerful statements of abstract geometry. Like his predecessors he built in brick for urban churches (St James the Less, London, 1859), but 320 used stone for rural ones and for the façade of his largest commission, the monumental Law Courts of London (1866). J. L. Pearson and G. F. Bodley moved from muscular strength to refined elegance and were equally successful in both. Pearson's Daylesford, Gloucestershire (1860), may be taken as representative of strength; Bodley's Hoar Cross, Staffordshire (1872), of elegance. 321

By the beginning of the 20th century the Gothic Revival in England was virtually confined to churches. E. S. Prior and Temple Moore concentrated on spatial subtlety and refinement of

320, 321. Contrasts in Victorian Gothic. Before the 1860s the favoured style derived from the churches of 12th-century France, as exemplified by G. E. Street's St James the Less, London (below, 1859). Later in the century the refinement of English Decorated was found more sympathetic, as seen in G. F. Bodley's Hoar Cross, Staffordshire (1872).

detail. Ninian Comper added non-Gothic elements to create what he called 'unity by inclusion'. The climax, and coda, of the whole movement was the Anglican Cathedral of Liverpool by Giles Gilbert Scott (1903 onwards), a church on a huge scale, genuinely Gothic in concept, yet acknowledging no prototype.

Many leading Neo-Gothic architects designed churches and cathedrals for distant parts of the British Empire: George Gilbert Scott for St John's, Newfoundland, Butterfield for Melbourne, and Pearson for Brisbane, Australia – countries which they never visited but where their works inspired local architects to emulation. Canada produced William Cumberland, who built a college for Toronto University in Ruskinian Gothic (1856), and Thomas Fuller, whose Parliament Buildings in Ottawa (1859, mostly destroyed by fire and rebuilt in a tamer style) rivalled the London Houses of Parliament. In Quebec French influence was stronger. Bruce Price's Château Frontenac Hotel (1892) outdoes everything on the Loire. In Australia a high standard was set by the English émigré W. W. Wardell, whose work was both ecclesiastical and civil (his Gothic bank in Melbourne is a striking *tour de force*). An architect of real distinction was Edmund Blacket, whose numerous Puginian churches are a feature of New South Wales (e.g. St Mark's, Darling Point, 1848). Commercial architecture at

322. The Anglican Cathedral, Liverpool, designed by Giles Gilbert Scott (a grandson of George Gilbert Scott) at the age of 22 and begun in 1903, marks the final flowering of the English Gothic Revival.

the end of the century was as opulent as anything in Europe or the United States, from the Gothic Rialto Building, Melbourne, by William Pitt (1890) to the Baroque His Majesty's Hotel and Theatre, Perth, by William Wolff (1904). British India was a world of its own. Calcutta remained faithful to classicism, culminating in the Victoria Memorial by William Emerson (1906), a vast structure in white marble with four corner towers and a central dome. The second city, Bombay, was susceptible to Gothic, often of a rather eccentric kind, and not immune to more exotic temptations. Its Victoria Railway Terminus by F. W. Stevens (1866) combines Venetian Gothic with Islamic and even a touch of Hindu.

The Gothic Revival in France and Germany was not driven by the same sense of liturgical mission as in Britain. In Germany, where political divisions often followed religious ones, Gothic became to a large extent identified with Catholicism. Its leading champion, August Reichensperger, saw it as a symbol of opposition to Prussian Protestantism, with the completion of Cologne Cathedral to the original medieval designs (1840s–'70s) as its supreme statement. Equally powerful, and not confined to Catholics, was the idea that Gothic was essentially a Germanic style, a view that originated in Goethe's romantic essay on Strasbourg Cathedral and its (supposedly) German architect. In addition, by the time Hübsch wrote his essay in 1828, German theorists were profoundly troubled by the fact that architecture had apparently reached an impasse. What was a style? they asked. Did it arise from geography, climate, technique, national character? Did it have a natural life and death of its own? Could you invent a new one? (Hübsch's own solution was a revivified Romanesque, called *Rundbogenstil*, 'round-arched style', on the grounds that Romanesque had not been allowed to work out its natural life-span but had been interrupted by Gothic.)

Controversy over theoretical issues continued throughout the century, much of it with nationalistic and regional overtones. Friedrich Schmidt, perhaps the most versatile of German-speaking Neo-Goths (he was Austrian), built several hall-churches vaulted in brick, as well as the remarkable Maria von Siege, Fünfhaus, Vienna (1867), a domed octagon with radiating chapels. Heinrich Ferstel's slightly earlier Votivkirche (1856), in the same city, is prominently placed on the Ringstrasse, Vienna's parade of grand buildings in a range of historical styles (laid out on the site of the old fortifications), but is less original. Like Ste Clotilde in Paris and St Patrick's, New York, its openwork spires reflect the west front of Cologne Cathedral. Other notable

323

311
325
106

323, 324. Above: Maria von Siege, Fünfhaus, Vienna, by Friedrich Schmidt (1867), a work of free imagination using elements from German Gothic but including a dome. Above right: Notre Dame de Fourvière, Lyons, by Pierre Bossan (1872), brings together an extraordinary array of historical styles. Once despised, such works are now being appreciated.

Neo-Gothic churches in Germany are Friedrich Zwirner's Apollinariskirke, near Remagen (1839), tall and compact, with four spires reflected in a lake, and Joseph Daniel Ohlmüller's Mariahilfkirche (1831) in Munich, a hall-church with a single openwork spire looking perhaps towards Freiburg-im-Breisgau.   104

    Belgium, where Pugin's influence was especially strong, had its own flourishing Gothic Revival, of which the two most outstanding churches are Louis van Overstraeten's Ste Marie in Brussels (1845), a domed octagon that anticipates Schmidt's Fünfhaus church in Vienna, and Notre Dame at Laeken (1854) by the versatile Joseph Poelaert, whom we shall meet again later. Standing almost alone in Holland, P. J. H. Cuypers managed to transpose Netherlandish late Gothic into a grand and florid style suitable for churches, museums (the Rijksmuseum, Amsterdam, 1877) and railway stations (Amsterdam, 1881).

    French architects were equally sure that Gothic was a French style (and here they happened to be right). But both historical and liturgical considerations were less important than technical ones. Contrasting with the spiritual Pugin and the sectarian Reichensperger stands the rational Eugène Viollet-le-Duc. A brilliant architectural historian and analyst of buildings, he was mainly responsible for the view – still widely held – that Gothic evolved in response to structural demands. For him it was neither mystical nor picturesque but logical. But by reducing Gothic to a formula, he perhaps helped to make French Neo-Gothic formulaic.

The Beaux-Arts tradition, which continued to dominate French architecture throughout the century, was not friendly to the Gothic Revival, with the result that the movement in France is far less cohesive than in England. Many of the major examples – Ste Clotilde in Paris (1839) by the German-born Franz Christian Gau, St Nicolas at Nantes (1843) by Jean-Baptiste Lassus, and St Epvre at Nancy (1863) by Mathieu-Prosper Morey – are churches where scholarship has taken precedence over inspiration. Even Viollet-le-Duc is usually too faithful to his historical models to be really interesting. Many architects clearly felt this and struck out along original paths of their own. Some sought freedom by combining several styles, e.g. Léon Vaudoyer at Marseilles Cathedral (1852). The most unpredictable of these eclectic works is Pierre Bossan's basilica of Notre Dame de Fourvière (1872) on the steep hill overlooking Lyons.

Of the Gothic Revival in America it is difficult to make a connected story. Both enthusiasm and achievement tended to be sporadic. Two New York churches led the way, Richard Upjohn's Trinity Church (1846) and James Renwick's St Patrick's (1859), both in the Pugin tradition. In the 1860s and '70s the style was

311

324

325

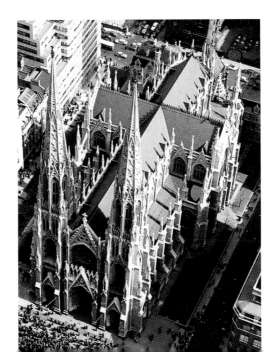

325. St Patrick's Cathedral, New York (1859), is yet another offspring of the completion of Cologne Cathedral. Its architect, James Renwick, had mastered most medieval styles (including Romanesque for the Smithsonian Institution, Washington), and here takes elements from French and English Gothic as well as German.

326. The Memorial Hall of Harvard University, Cambridge, Massachusetts (1870), is one of the infrequent successes of secular Gothic in the USA. Designed by W. R. Ware and H. Van Brunt in a 'muscular', polychrome style, it served as refectory and concert hall.

conventional for churches of almost every denomination, and for cultural institutions like universities. Ware and Van Brunt's Memorial Hall at Harvard (1870) could easily be mistaken for 326 a church. Very often the wilder spirits, like Frank Furness, by no means a committed Goth, make a more memorable impact than their sober colleagues. American Neo-Gothic, under the patronage of the Episcopal Church, is not surprisingly closer to Britain than to continental Europe, most obviously in its romantic and picturesque qualities. By the 1880s its vogue was past, but it continued to haunt some architects until well into the 20th century, mainly for churches and university buildings. Ralph Adams Cram's Cathedral of St John the Divine in New 327 York would have been a sublime, if largely derivative, building (the existing cathedral is an unsatisfactory compromise and only recently finished). The Harkness Memorial Tower at Yale 328 University (1931) by James Gamble Rogers is more whole-heartedly Gothic than anything of that date in Europe. As late as 1932 the Episcopalians of Philadelphia began a cathedral that would have been the biggest Gothic church ever built, but it was abandoned because of the Depression – the end of the Puginian dream just a century after it began.

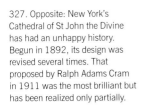

327. Opposite: New York's Cathedral of St John the Divine has had an unhappy history. Begun in 1892, its design was revised several times. That proposed by Ralph Adams Cram in 1911 was the most brilliant but has been realized only partially.

328. James Gamble Rogers's Harkness Memorial Tower for Yale University in New Haven, Connecticut (right, 1931). As in Britain, late 'refinement' based on English medieval models succeeded early 'vigour'.

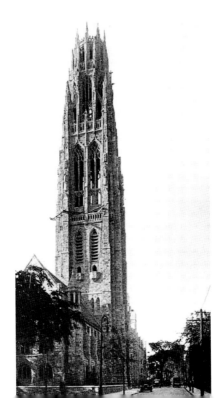

Revivals and survivals

Two other styles evocative of the Middle Ages remain to be considered, the Romanesque and the Byzantine, though neither took off like the Gothic. The Romanesque peaked early. Germany gave it a warm welcome. Friedrich von Gärtner's great Ludwigskirche, prominent on the main street of Munich, was designed in 1828 just as Hübsch was recommending *Rundbogenstil*. Pugin experimented with it. Other English architects, J. W. Wild at Streatham (1840) and T. H. Wyatt and David Brandon at Wilton (1841), used it with some fluency, though it was Italian, not British, Romanesque. Most notable of all is Ludwig Persius's Friedenskirche at Potsdam (1845), an essay in the Early Christian style of Ravenna picturesquely placed by the still waters of a lake. Alfred Waterhouse successfully adapted Romanesque to secular use in the Natural History Museum, London (1879).

But the real flowering of the Romanesque Revival came in a place where it could hardly have been predicted, the USA. In the hands of H. H. Richardson it became a modern style, suitable for churches (Trinity Church, Boston, 1872), civic buildings 330 (Allegheny County Courthouse, Pittsburgh, 1883), private houses (Glessner House, Chicago, 1885) and commercial buildings (Marshall Field Wholesale Store, Chicago, 1885). Historicist in 329 materials and detailing, modern in functional planning, these buildings are the perfect answer to those who maintain that reviving a style of the past is nothing but dressing up in period costume.

329. H. H. Richardson brought all the stony integrity of the Romanesque style to his Marshall Field Wholesale Store in Chicago (1885, demolished). It had an internal iron construction.

The Byzantine Revival produced only two memorable buildings, both of them prominent in capital cities. One is Paul Abadie's Sacré Cœur (1874), its great white domes dominating the skyline on the height of Montmartre, and by now a symbol of the city of Paris. A free and rather theatrical combination of Byzantine and Romanesque motifs, it receives more attention than its architectural merits deserve. The other is J. F. Bentley's Roman Catholic Westminster Cathedral, London (1895), a thoughtful and poetically conceived work which captures the Byzantine spirit without following any specific model. It consists of three vast domed bays with arcades along the sides supporting galleries and forming aisles, the whole of brick to be clad with marble veneer and mosaic. A number of churches built for Russian Orthodox communities in Western Europe should count as Byzantine Revival, but Russian ecclesiastical architecture is so conservative that it is hard to say where survival ends and revival begins. The huge Cathedral of Christ the Redeemer in Moscow, a building of no very obvious attractions, built between 1838 and 1880 and demolished by Stalin, has now, incredibly, been rebuilt – a revival of a revival.

Side by side with these fairly well-defined historicist revivals were a host of other initiatives, all in a sense using styles from the past but in a freer, more eclectic way. If one has to find labels for them one can specify Neoclassical, Neo-Baroque, Neo-Renaissance, Italianate and so on. But the truth is that these historical elements are like ingredients stirred into a soup; the result

331

330. Richardson was equally successful in ecclesiastical buildings. His Romanesque Trinity Church, Boston (1872), looks chiefly to Spain, but is realized with fresh vision.

331. J. F. Bentley achieved a similar feat in his Byzantine Westminster Cathedral in London (below right, 1895), its brick arches perhaps all the more impressive for being (so far) left bare.

is a new flavour of its own. When the Empress Eugénie pettishly asked the architect Charles Garnier what style he thought his opera house was in, he replied, 'C'est le style Napoléon III.'

The Paris Opéra, begun in 1861 but only completed after the Franco-Prussian War, is in fact one of the most characteristic buildings of the mid-19th century. Opulent, carefully planned, meticulously detailed, it epitomizes the confidence of the age. In its essentials it stays close to the model provided by Victor Louis's theatre at Bordeaux, but how different is the spirit! What was recti-linear and static has become rounded and dynamic, what was chaste has become voluptuous. It is a building whose only purpose is to give pleasure, and as the visitor approaches the façade, alive with dancing figures, ascends the breathtakingly grand staircase and emerges into the auditorium, that is exactly what it gives.

The Paris Opéra was a child of the Beaux-Arts, though a dis-tinctly disobedient one. More central to its continuing tradition was Louis-Joseph Duc's extension of the Palais de Justice in Paris (1857), with its logical planning, expert construction and finely organized façade of pilasters and demi-columns. Throughout the 19th century Beaux-Arts classicism proved astonishingly fertile.

332. The staircase of Charles Garnier's Paris Opéra (begun in 1861) has always been loved, though not always admired by purist critics. This is a free Baroque style drawing on classical elements and the richest of materials for a truly theatrical effect, linking four levels in a continuous movement.

333. In the Bibliothèque Ste Geneviève, Paris (1845), Henri Labrouste produced an experimental building of unusual subtlety. On the exterior the bookcases are expressed by the high walls of the upper storey. The unsuspected interior is all iron.

Two architects who demonstrate this are F. A. Duquesney and Henri Labrouste. The first built the best Parisian railway station, the Gare de l'Est (1847). The second built the Bibliothèque Ste Geneviève (1845), a startlingly personal building reflecting a peculiar intellectual concept whereby the exterior literally expresses the interior by displaying on the upper walls the names of the authors shelved inside. The interior structure is of iron, like Labrouste's later Bibliothèque Nationale. The largest public commission of 19th-century France, the completion of the Louvre by L.-T.-J. Visconti and H.-M. Lefuel, initiated by Napoleon III, is not entirely a success story. Much of the old Louvre was demolished to be replaced by buildings that are less interesting than what was there before.

Law court buildings became major vehicles for the expression of national prestige. Joseph Poelaert's Palais de Justice in Brussels (1866), in a Piranesian Baroque style, outdoes them all in grandeur, with vast halls, staircases and doorways seemingly built for giants. That of Rome (by Guglielmo Calderini, 1888), Baroque too, is nearly as overwhelming. National monuments are also richly indicative of contrasting tastes – from Chalgrin's classical Arc de Triomphe in Paris (1806 onwards) to Scott's Gothic Albert Memorial, London (1863), or Giuseppe Sacconi's Neoclassical Victor Emmanuel Monument in Rome (1885).

333

334

287

334. 'Subtle' is not the first word that comes to mind for Joseph Poelaert's Palais de Justice in Brussels (1866). But in fact its huge scale is handled with such clarity and confidence that it never becomes confusing.

335. The central hall of Charles Barry's Reform Club, London (1838), is like the courtyard of an Italian *palazzo* covered by a glass roof. Barry would have preferred to use real marble rather than scagliola, but even so, as his son rather smugly remarked, it stands 'as a model to foreigners of what a great English Club could be'.

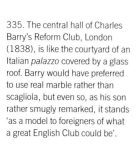

England, less lavish with official patronage and less subjected to architectural pedagogy, has a richer crop of individuals. Charles Barry's clubs in Pall Mall, London (Travellers', 1830; Reform, 1838), set a fashion for gentlemen's clubs in Italian Renaissance style, a convention that spread to America and to commercial buildings such as banks. Cuthbert Brodrick's three masterworks in the north – Leeds Town Hall (1855), Leeds Corn Exchange (1860) and the Grand Hotel, Scarborough (1863) – are strictly practical structures treated as urban monuments. In London, the institutional complex of South Kensington (Albert Hall, Imperial Institute, etc.) asserted cultural prestige; the Victoria and Albert Museum is a bizarre mixture of *Rundbogenstil* (the courtyard by Francis Fowke, 1866) and the style of the Certosa at Pavia (the façade by Aston Webb, 1904). 335

In Germany, the leading architect outside the Gothic Revival and the acknowledged heir of Schinkel was Gottfried Semper. Semper's achievements are considerable, most notably the Hoftheater at Dresden (1835), a milestone in theatre design, expressing the semicircle of the auditorium on the exterior (it was destroyed by fire in 1869 and rebuilt by Semper to a slightly different design). His Art Gallery at Dresden and the two museums in Vienna, of Art History and Natural History, which he built in collaboration with Carl von Hasenauer, are dominant, if not exactly exhilarating, accents in their urban settings. But he was even more important as a theorist and source of ideas. Semper is the Pugin of 336

336. Gottfried Semper's first Dresden Hoftheater of 1835 already incorporated the semi-circular façade expressing the auditorium.

classicism. For him it was through the Mediterranean world of Antiquity and the Renaissance that society and art were to be regenerated. The evolution of architecture reflected the evolution of civilization. That of his own time was exhausted and oppressed. Artistic freedom depended on political freedom (he ruined his career by taking part in the 1848 revolution in Saxony). Reducing architecture to its simplest elements – the hearth, the substructure, the walls and the roof – Semper offered not only an interpretation of the past but also a guide for the future. Ancient cultures – Assyrian, Egyptian, Greek, Roman – have given us a formal language of 'symbolic values that are older than history and cannot possibly be represented by something new'. Some of his most fruitful ideas concerned theatres (he built three and designed at least three more). He saw drama as a union of all the arts and a significant social ritual, thoughts which his friend Richard Wagner made his own (Semper's was the architectural mind behind the Bayreuth Festspielhaus).

American architects, many of whom studied at the Ecole des Beaux-Arts, were touchingly reluctant to bid farewell to the classical style. Even when the underlying structure belongs firmly to the age of steel and concrete it is given a respectable pedigree by its outward dress. This is the case with some of the best public buildings of McKim, Mead and White (Boston Public Library, 1888, an extended Italian *palazzo* combining elements of Alberti's Tempio Malatestiano with Labrouste's Bibliothèque Ste Geneviève, or Pennsylvania Station, New York, 1907, a close replica of the Baths of Caracalla). Faced with the problem of articulating very large surfaces, architects fell back on the formulae that came naturally to them. A high basement, a giant order and a deep attic could happily take care of nine or ten storeys that might be identical inside. There came a point, of course, when skyscrapers grew so tall that the classical dress could by no expedient be made to fit and a new fashion had to be invented. Eclecticism was perhaps happiest in the great mansions of Manhattan or Newport, Rhode Island, of which Richard Morris Hunt was the most accomplished exponent; they can still be enjoyed today, though perhaps rather as evocations of a vanished lifestyle than as great works of architecture.

The new art

In the last years of the century a new manner did quite suddenly emerge, but it proved short-lived and unsuited to works on a large scale. This was 'Art Nouveau'. It is perhaps misleading to call it 'a style'; it is many styles, and indeed it goes by many different

337, 338. The lacy metallic lightness of Horta's Tassel House, Brussels (above, 1892), contrasts with the heavy polished stone of Shekhtel's Ryabushinsky House, now the Gorky Museum, Moscow (above right, 1906), but both are equally typical of continental Art Nouveau.

names: in France, Belgium and America it is 'Art Nouveau'; in Italy 'Stile Liberty' (after the English shop); in Germany 'Jugendstil' (after a magazine); in Austria 'Secession' (after a breakaway group of artists); and in Spain 'Modernismo'. What all the architects had in common was a conscious rejection of prevailing academic styles, whether Neo-Gothic, Neoclassical or Neo-Baroque, which they condemned as heavy and pompous.

This turn-of-the-century manner may be divided into two main categories – the curvilinear and the rectilinear. The curvilinear, which prevailed in France, Belgium and Germany, is essentially decorative, like Rococo, which it closely resembles. It was based on natural forms – the serpentine, undulating line, the spiral, the tendril, and a light double or triple curve or 'whiplash' – and in some designers' hands it made lavish use of a new material that could exploit these forms: iron. Definitive examples are Victor Horta's houses in Brussels (Tassel House, 1892), where the doors, windows, staircases and furniture are like a spider's web waiting to catch anyone who enters, or the Paris Métro stations by Hector Guimard (around 1900). This variety of Art Nouveau was carried east, seeding itself in Poland and Russia, e.g. the Ryabushinsky House, Moscow, by Fyodor Shekhtel (1906).

337

338

291

In Spain 'Modernismo' gave birth to a truly amazing architectural progeny, of whom the most famous is Antoni Gaudí. Gaudí's mature buildings seem to have sprung by some strange natural process from the soil or from the depths of the sea, and to be covered in growths not unlike seaweed. His personality is fully expressed in his Barcelona apartment houses (Casa Batlló and Casa Milá, both 1905) and most ambitiously in the church of the Sagrada Familia, Barcelona (begun in 1883), left unfinished at his death and now being completed as a symbol of Catalan nationhood. This is (or will be) one of the few modern churches of cathedral scale to be a totally original work of art. Formally, it can be traced back to Gothic, but its nave vaulted in inverted catenary curves and its strange, organic towers, like the homes of giant termites, make it perhaps the most extraordinary building of its time. Gaudí did not stand alone. Josep Maria Jujol, Josep Puig i Cadafalch and Lluís Domènech i Montaner (Palace of Catalan Music, 1908) have been overshadowed by him but were almost as inventive and individual.

339

340

339, 340. Barcelona at the turn of the century became the centre of a highly individual brand of Art Nouveau, epitomized by the work of Antoni Gaudí. His Casa Batlló (right) of 1905 is typical of this undulating, organic architecture, in which all elements fuse together. But his outstanding work is the church of the Sagrada Familia (opposite), begun in 1883 and for a hundred years left a mere fragment, one single transept façade. The four towers at the back were erected in Gaudí's lifetime; the four in the foreground are new, and the whole will be completed early in the 21st century.

At the opposite end of Europe from Spain, culturally as well as geographically, Vienna looked back not to Rococo but to Biedermeier, a chaste variant of the Empire style which obeyed the discipline of straight lines, and in which exquisite passages of ornament could be played against plain surfaces. In 1897 a group of artists and architects publicly dissociated themselves from official academic conventions and called themselves 'the Secession'. Although launched by younger men, Joseph Maria Olbrich and Josef Hoffmann, the Secession's most significant figure was Otto Wagner. The undisputed leader of his profession (he was head of Vienna's Academy of Fine Arts and in charge of the city's transport system), Wagner was the dominant influence on a whole generation of architects, including not only Olbrich and Hoffmann but also Adolf Loos, Jože Plečnik and others whom we shall meet later. The emergent Secession style is seen in Wagner's Majolika House (1898) and his stations for the municipal Stadtbahn (1890s). As a theorist, he was in many ways traditional. He believed in the street, and in the façade as an expression of a building's function. Ornament was to be controlled but not banished. At first the Secession seemed to embody his ideals: flat walls, flush window-frames, free use of metal and glass. Above all, architecture had to be integral to the urban fabric, adapted to modern living as part of a larger social pattern. The culmination of this phase of his work is the Postal Savings Bank in Vienna (1904), which combines simplicity of line and surface with richness of texture, as in the sheets of marble fixed to the external walls with metal bolts; inside, bolts provide an austere ornamental feature in the glass-roofed banking 341 hall. Wagner later seceded from the Secession, but his church of the Steinhof Asylum (1905) is still very much in its spirit, with 342 its sensuous metalwork, mosaic and stained glass by leading Austrian artists. His large-scale urban schemes, in which he aimed 'to raise uniformity into monumentality', rigidly formal but carefully tailored to the needs of the inhabitants, now seem closer to Neoclassicism than they did at the time.

Josef Hoffmann went on to become an influential figure in his own right, as a teacher, designer and architect, preaching the doctrine of straight lines and abstract geometry. His most complete statement, the Palais Stoclet in Brussels (1905), built for a 343 rich connoisseur, looks forward to Modernism in its bare surfaces and freedom from traditional ornament. But it has nothing of Modernist austerity. Its interiors especially (which very few have been privileged to see) are exquisitely luxurious, lavish in their materials and lovingly precise in their details.

341. The Austrian Secession Movement in some ways anticipates the aesthetic of Modernism, aiming at clarity and the unencumbered expression of function. The banking hall of Otto Wagner's Postal Savings Bank in Vienna (1904) is fitted with purpose-designed furniture, but it might equally house machinery.

342. Wagner's church of the Steinhof Asylum (1905) outside Vienna reveals the Secession's links with classicism. Explicit reference to the orders is absent, but the cubic proportions, the dome and suggestion of a frieze look back to the Vienna of Maria Theresa.

343. Josef Hoffmann's great work is not in Vienna but Brussels, where he built the Palais Stoclet in 1905. The luxury only hinted at in its plain but dramatic exterior is made manifest within.

Italy's 'Stile Liberty' combines sharp, angular lines with massive heaviness, displayed in some weirdly eccentric buildings such as the Casa del Commercio, Mantua (1913, by Aldo Andreani), the district in Rome named after the architect Gino Coppedè (1919), the works of Giuseppe Sommaruga in Milan, or those of Ernesto Basile in Rome and Sicily.

Allusion has been made to the nationalistic implications of Gaudí's Barcelona buildings. Catalonia at this time was vigorously asserting its cultural identity, and the same is true of other small nations in other parts of Europe (in literature, art and music as much as in architecture). In Ireland the Celtic Revival used motifs from the distant past to create a rather contrived Irishness. Primitive-looking churches incorporated round towers, while inside them Art Nouveau met the Book of Kells. Scotland, too, was looking for Scottishness – one aspect that characterizes its most outstanding architect, Charles Rennie Mackintosh. But Mackintosh belonged to a wider world than Scotland. His houses

344. Straight lines, carefully restrained patterns, imaginative lighting, personalized details all bring Charles Rennie Mackintosh's Glasgow School of Art close to Otto Wagner in spirit thought not in form. Scholars and critics still argue over the source and meaning of the gallery panels in the Library of 1907.

may be harled (covered in traditional white roughcast) but their cool interiors have little that is vernacular about them, with their stencilled patterns and spare, angular furniture. His masterpiece, the Glasgow School of Art (1897 and 1907), breaks free from tradition in its ingenious manipulation of space and its novel details (e.g. the grid of galleries and hanging lamps in the library). But Mackintosh's play of fancy is always rooted in common sense, never indulged for its own sake.

344

In Hungary, whose national identity was constantly in danger of being swamped by Austria, Ödön Lechner tried to recover a specifically Hungarian style by going back to the supposed Central Asian origins of the Magyars. His Museum of Decorative Arts in Budapest (1893) is a fascinating blend of Art Nouveau and Mughal elements, which is not as absurd as it might sound. Norway and Sweden explored their Viking heritage, while in the work of Lars Sonck Finland sought to rediscover its birthright and to express its culture in the face of Russian domination; after

345

345. Hungary was one of many countries where Art Nouveau acquired overtones of nationalism. In Budapest Ödön Lechner borrowed motifs from Indian architecture in his Museum of Decorative Arts (1893) to recall the Eastern origins of the Magyars.

346. In Finland the movement known as National Romanticism also aimed to assert the nation's identity, and to this Lars Sonck's Telephone Company Building in Helsinki (1903) belongs. The material – granite – and the primitive incised ornament are in accordance with Finnish tradition, but as a later Finnish critic reasonably remarked, 'it does not suggest modern communications'.

log villas and rustic painted churches he produced such works as the Telephone Company Building in Helsinki (1903), in a gaunt granite Romanesque ornamented by folk motifs, as forceful and uncompromising as the sagas. 346

In America, where there was no patriotic subtext, Art Nouveau remained a purely ornamental style, and it is significant that before long structural engineering and decorative design came to be seen as separate disciplines. The key figure here is Louis Sullivan. His Auditorium Building, Chicago (1886), a 347 combination of office block, hotel and opera house, is cleverly articulated by means of rustication, a giant order of demi-columns and a double attic storey, but it is Sullivan's ornament that gives it unique distinction. This is carried further in his Carson, Pirie and 348 Scott Store, also in Chicago (1899), which has steel-frame construction, not loadbearing walls. Sullivan therefore belongs in the next chapter as a 'pioneer' of Modernism, but in this one as a man who believed in the crucial importance of ornament. This was where his real genius lay. Drawing their inspiration from plants and leaves, his tense, organic, expressive lines in metal or terracotta seem to turn a building into a living thing.

347. The Auditorium Building in Chicago (1886) is the fruit of co-operation between two great men, the engineer Dankmar Adler and the architect Louis Sullivan. Sullivan had not yet evolved his full style, in which Art Nouveau ornament is combined with sheer surfaces (ill. 353). The Auditorium Building's rock-like exterior comes closest to Richardson's Neo-Romanesque (ill. 329) and is still articulated in a way that disguises rather than expresses the structure.

348. Louis Sullivan's Art Nouveau affiliations are expressed entirely through his ornament, such as this cast-iron decoration around the windows of the Carson, Pirie and Scott Store in Chicago (1899). It was in Sullivan's office that Frank Lloyd Wright found his own personal style.

Houses and homes

There was one country where Art Nouveau made practically no impact and that was England. But there a quiet revolution was taking place which once again brought the ordinary private house to the centre of the architectural stage. This was due very largely to the particular lifestyle that had been evolved not by the landed gentry but by the English middle class, which demanded domestic comfort, privacy, leafy surroundings not too far from the town, informality combined with elegance, and unpretentiousness combined with 'quality'. 'Home' was the heart of the Englishman's existence, and the English house had to be the embodiment of home. The model here was the country cottage or small vernacular house, built of traditional materials (wood, brick, tile-hanging) and free from association with any 'high' styles. This 'Englishness' was so admired in Germany that in 1896 a Prussian architect and civil servant, Hermann Muthesius, was commissioned by his government to survey the whole subject and report back. The result was his classic study *Das englische Haus* (1904–5), which very perceptively analysed not only the architectural setting but also English social and cultural attitudes.

The story begins with the vicarages built by several ecclesiastical architects to go with their churches. In the 1840s and '50s, Street and Butterfield, by mixing Gothic elements with 18th-century domestic, evolved a style that was relaxed, informal and comfortable. In 1859 Philip Webb built for his friend William Morris the Red House, Bexleyheath, near London, a large,

349. Broadleys, overlooking Lake Windermere (1898), is C. F. A. Voysey's most elaborate and self-conscious house, with three bay windows corresponding to dining room, hall and drawing room, carried up into the next storey for bedrooms.

loosely planned, two-storey house in a free style which came to be widely copied by others. Webb's other houses had the same qualities, but they were too idiosyncratic to become models; he seemed to enjoy creating problems in order to solve them. His exact contemporary, Richard Norman Shaw, a better businessman, evolved a more imitable formula that drew largely on English late 17th-century precedents and has become known as the Queen Anne style. Shaw's practice was mostly in country and town houses for the upper middle class, using a variety of materials, largely derived from the vernacular of south-eastern England, to give a picturesque, traditional effect (Glen Andred, Surrey, 1866), but he also undertook larger commissions.

C. F. A. Voysey, twenty years Shaw's junior, confined himself almost entirely to fairly modest private houses, making the expression of domesticity into a fine art. A Voysey house (e.g. Broadleys, in the Lake District, 1898), for all its affectation of simplicity, is a highly artificial creation. It lies low in the landscape, its exterior surfaces covered in white render, the window surrounds of smooth unmoulded stone, the metalwork self-consciously rustic, the low spreading roof laid with carefully graded slates. Interiors are light, furnishings simple, wallpapers pretty, fireplaces welcoming – 'streamlined cottages for Quaker trolls', as they have unkindly been called. At the same time, a group of talented domestic architects (W. R. Lethaby, A. H. Mackmurdo, M. H. Baillie Scott), working for well-to-do clients, evolved a style uniting hand-craftsmanship with vernacular models that came to be known as 'Arts and Crafts'.

But now into this relatively small pond swims a much bigger fish. Edwin Lutyens designed his first major house in 1896, when he was in his twenties – Munstead Wood, for the garden designer Gertrude Jekyll. It already catches all the qualities that make his country houses so memorable. The informal mixture of brick, timber and stone; the practicality of the planning; the lack of pretentiousness together with extreme subtlety both of detailing and spatial arrangement; the effortless integration of the house into the landscape all recur in different ways in the houses he went on to build – Orchards (1898), Tigbourne Court (1899), Deanery Garden (1901) – in southern England. He called these houses 'Old English', but they are not in any way pastiches. Lutyens's way of leading into a house, of placing a staircase in relation to a hall, of conducting one via a brightly lit gallery to a sequence of bedrooms with varied views onto gardens puts him on a level with the best architects of any age. But it is all managed on such an intimate

349

350

scale that the houses are supremely congenial places to live, relaxing and exciting at the same time. Lutyens's later work takes us out of this secure little world and will have to be considered in the next chapter.

In America, the houses of the Greene brothers can be seen as part of the same movement of taste. Greene and Greene practised exclusively in Pasadena, a suburb of Los Angeles. Their houses are all of wood, wide, horizontal and open, and incorporate features from as far away as Switzerland and Japan. The Gamble House (1908), feels like a large, finely crafted piece of furniture.

We come finally in this context to the early work of Frank Lloyd Wright. Wright, who had worked in Sullivan's office, built his first house at Oak Park, outside Chicago – later to become almost a Wright precinct – in 1889. During the next fifteen years he ran a successful practice in the affluent suburbs of Chicago as

350. Edwin Lutyens's Deanery Garden, Sonning, Berkshire (1901), extends the English manor-house convention into a large country house. Built of brick, with large fireplaces and lavish use of wood in the interior, its sophisticated rusticity suggests roots going back into the past combined with every modern comfort.

351. Another variant of domesticity is that created by Greene and Greene of Pasadena, California. Their wooden houses are constructed with the finesse of a cabinet-maker, and their interiors epitomize well-being and security. The hall and living room of the Gamble House (1908) flow together in a movement subtly encouraged by the diagonally laid flooring.

352. Frank Lloyd Wright's 'Prairie Style' is another deliberate evocation of the happiness of domesticity. At the Robie House, Chicago (1909), behind the aesthetically determined horizontality of its walls, the living room, dining room and bedroom cluster around the big central chimney.

well as further afield. Of English architects it is probably Voysey who at this stage comes closest to Wright. The plans of their houses are strikingly similar, abolishing areas simply of passage and allowing spaces to flow into one another. Both take the local vernacular of their respective countries as their starting points, untouched by historicist allusions. Both stress the horizontal at the expense of the vertical, with spreading roofs and wide projecting eaves. And both give prominence to the central hearth as the domestic icon. But there the resemblance ends. Wright's idea of domesticity has nothing of Voysey's 'cosiness'. Materials are often left exposed, internally as well as externally, giving his houses a toughness in tune with his personality. Instead of quaintness and softness, the emphasis is on bare surfaces and abrupt geometry. To live in a Wright house requires a certain resolution, but they are never conventional or dull and his eye for detail never wavers. The development of his style from the Sullivanesque Winslow House, River Forest (1893), or Dana House, Springfield (1899), to the mature 'Prairie House' type at the Robie House, Chicago (1909), is marked. The elevation becomes simpler, with fewer changes of texture and colour and fewer discrete features; the sense of enclosure begins to dissolve with planes advancing and receding, reducing the distinction between exterior and interior. Shapes become more abstract, lines more orthogonal.

352

Wright continued to design private houses to the end of his life, but these and his non-domestic works must be left to the next chapter. He remained a defiant individualist, building for a cultured élite. This kind of architecture, and this kind of architect, would soon come to be seen as marginal to the world scene. To understand that situation we have to retrace our steps to the beginning of the previous century.

Chapter 9:   After Style, Modernism

Engineering – in the sense of the science and technique of construction – has always been a part of architecture, but in the 19th
century with the development of new materials it became a subject
for specialists. The two professions drew apart and for reasons of
cultural snobbery critics were reluctant to give them equal
esteem. Architecture, after all, was an art; engineering required
only technical expertise. But at a certain point it was realized
(sooner by some than by others) that while the art of
architecture was apparently heading for a cul-de-sac, the science
of engineering was only just discovering its potential. Now, in
retrospect, it seemed to many that it was the engineers who
had been the real pioneers and that the way forward was through
new technical processes, new materials and a new aesthetic of
functionalism. The search for a style was over.

Iron, glass and honesty
Iron had led a clandestine existence in architecture for centuries,
strengthening piers, giving rigidity to roofs, holding domes
together. But no one openly acknowledged it or saw that it could
have a beauty of its own until 1778, when Thomas Farnolls
Pritchard and Abraham Darby built an iron bridge at Coalbrookdale, Shropshire, which soon gave its name to the whole village
and became immensely famous all over the world. Hesitantly, iron
came out of hiding, at first in utilitarian structures like warehouses
and factories (Marshall, Benyon and Bage in Shrewsbury, 1796)
and staircases (Nash at the Brighton Pavilion, 1818) and then
more visibly in monuments (Schinkel in Berlin, 1819) and finally
in the lavish Gothick interiors of a conservatory (Carlton House,
London, by Thomas Hopper; it had coloured glass between the
ribs of a fan vault) and three churches in Liverpool (1813–16) by
Thomas Rickman and the ironmaster John Cragg. To give iron the
forms of Gothic was an extraordinary step, but not exactly in the

353. The Guaranty Building in
Buffalo, New York (1894), by
Adler and Sullivan very clearly
reflects the new aesthetic of
structure, but at the same time
retains elements of tradition –
plinth, main storey and cornice –
plus Sullivan's ornate ornament,
especially under the cornice.

right direction – even when carried out with the panache of Deane and Woodward at the University Museum, Oxford (1855) – since the whole rationale of Gothic derived from masonry. More significant for the future were those engineers who made no attempt to disguise the nature of iron but on the contrary designed the structure to express the material. Market buildings came into this category (Hungerford Market, London, by Charles Fowler, 1835, and, outshining them all, the immense and impressive Halles in Paris by Victor Baltard, 1853). So did railway stations, beginning in the late 1830s and continuing into the next century; every great European city had one. Allied to markets were 'arcades' or 'galleries', shopping malls covered with an iron-and-glass roof, which became universally popular from the 1830s, reaching an enormous size by the 1860s (Galleria Vittorio Emanuele, Milan, by Giuseppe Mengoni). Department stores followed, beginning in France and soon taken up in the rest of Europe, America and Australia. For the Coal Exchange, London (1848), J. B. Bunning built a complete iron interior with several tiers of galleries and lavish use of ornament.

354. The bridge at Coalbrookdale, Shropshire (1778), was the first iron bridge in the world, the result of collaboration between the architect T. F. Pritchard and the ironmaster Abraham Darby. It was the beginning of the specialized division of labour between architect and engineer.

355. The University Museum, Oxford (1855), by Deane and Woodward. The shell of the building is masonry, designed in Venetian Gothic with stonecarving supervised by Ruskin. The interior is entirely iron, brought as close as possible to Gothic.

356. Pioneered by Joseph Paxton at Chatsworth, the large iron and glass conservatory was a clear demonstration of how the new materials could revolutionize architecture. The Palm House at Kew (1845), by Richard Turner and Decimus Burton, remains one of its most perfect expressions.

The majority of these buildings retained a masonry exterior. For purely practical reasons this was given up in hothouses. In a very few years after the first exercise in the genre, Joseph Paxton's Great Conservatory at Chatsworth (1836) had reached a length of 277 feet (85m); the Palm House at Kew (1845), nearly as large, was produced by the ironmaster Richard Turner with contributions from the architect Decimus Burton. This tradition, and Paxton in particular, lies behind the Crystal Palace, London, built for the Great Exhibition of 1851.

356

The prominence given to the Crystal Palace in architectural history is not surprising, considering its size, the amazingly short time that it took to erect, and the fact that it was seen by so many people from all over the world. But it was not particularly innovative technically, nor was it originally entirely an iron-and-glass structure; a great deal of it was laminated wood (it was later re-erected in south London in altered form).

Perhaps its real significance was as a symbol. Coming exactly in the middle of the 19th century – the century of the Industrial

Revolution – it can be seen as marking the most radical crisis-point in the whole history of architecture. Until then, for incalculable ages, men had built in materials that nature herself supplied: stone, brick and wood. Throughout all the changes of styles and cultures, those materials had imposed their own constructional limits. Now those limits were to be overstepped. It was the great divide. Undreamed-of possibilities opened before the architects' eyes, and have continued to open, with results that defy prediction. All this was vaguely, half-unconsciously, realized at the time – hence both the passionate admiration and the passionate hostility that the Crystal Palace aroused.

To follow the origins and triumph of the Modern Movement, a process that occupied roughly a century, from 1870 to 1970, we have to abandon churches, private houses, palaces and public buildings and turn our attention to an area so far barely mentioned, the architecture of commerce, and in particular the metal-frame, high-rise office building. Around 1850 the idea of using cast and wrought iron as the frame of a building was in the air. It appeared in England and America almost simultaneously, in James Bogardus's stores in New York (1848 and later), McConnel's Jamaica Street Warehouse in Glasgow (1853), G. T. Greene's boat-store at Sheerness Naval Dockyard (1859) – in all of 358 which the metal forms the façade as well – and Peter Ellis's Oriel 359 Chambers, Liverpool (1864), where the front incorporates glass bays between masonry verticals and the back is of metal curtain-walling.

357. The Crystal Palace in London was an offspring of the iron-and-glass greenhouse, although in its original form (seen here) it made lavish use of laminated timber. Paxton's originality lay in adapting the system to a much larger building – 1,848 feet (510m) long. Designed in July 1850, it was ready for the opening of the Great Exhibition on 1 May 1851.

358. Opposite: unnoticed and unsung in architectural history, the iron-framed boat-store in Sheerness Naval Dockyard, Kent, could be mistaken for a building of the 1950s. In fact it was built in 1859 without any thought of architectural style by a naval engineer, G. T. Greene, a humble pioneer of International Modernism.

359. Peter Ellis's Oriel Chambers, Liverpool (1864), stresses its vertical lines as emphatically as Sullivan did, though they are in fact masonry. Metal, however, are the plate-glass window frames projecting from the wall.

The metal frame was as revolutionary a step as the pointed arch, and like the pointed arch it created its own aesthetic. Architects were strangely slow to recognize this, and when they did it was with many reservations. Buildings that accepted it without any qualms (like the Sheerness boat-store) were not regarded as architecture at all. For long the frame was dressed in some accepted academic style. (One reason was that for fire-safety reasons iron had to be covered.) The contrast between exposed function and architectural decorum is very neatly made by two

London railway stations standing next to each other and built within the same decade. The train-shed of St Pancras (1863), a splendid work by the engineers W. H. Barlow and R. M. Ordish, is completely hidden by George Gilbert Scott's equally splendid Gothic railway hotel (1868). Next door, the train-shed of King's Cross (1851) is openly expressed in Lewis Cubitt's pair of huge round brick arches. The esteem in which these two stations have been held is a perfect indication of the way taste has veered from the historicist to the functional and (to a degree) back again. Even a man like Louis Sullivan, who clearly saw the aesthetic potential of the new technique, gave his elevations a plinth, a middle section corresponding to a classical order, and a cornice or attic. We are therefore forced to some extent to keep structure and design in different compartments, as if they were the work of different men. Sometimes they were. The great architectural partnerships, which from now on become a major feature of the scene, could combine specialized talents of different kinds, though indeed many of the partners were competent in all of them.

360

319
361

353

Three new inventions made it possible to build higher. One was Elisha G. Otis's perfection of his elevator, an essential requirement for tall buildings. Another was Sir Henry Bessemer's new process of manufacturing steel, an alloy that provided greater strength with less weight and had tensile properties lacking in cast iron. Both these inventions date from the 1850s, but their effect was not felt until the 1870s. The third was the development of fireproofing for the iron (later steel) frame. By now architectural leadership had passed to the USA, where it would remain for several decades. The first skyscrapers went up in New York in the early 1870s (though the word did not appear until the '90s). In 1871 Chicago was devastated by a great fire, and its ensuing reconstruction drew on architects from all over the country, generating a spirit of adventure and rivalry. Richardson died aged only 48 in 1886, and so missed being part of the extraordinary fifteen years between then and 1900, which saw the creation of a series of buildings that can stand comparison with those of any similar period elsewhere in history. Faced with problems that would be daunting at any time – economic problems of competitive finance, technical problems of putting high-rise structures on the treacherous Chicago soil, and human problems of collaboration between experts – the architects produced brilliant solutions that are still as exciting as when they were built. What is surprising above all is the degree of sheer elegance and control that they achieved on a scale that had never even been imagined before.

360, 361. The railway was the most potent symbol of modernity in the 19th century, and railway stations offered the greatest technical challenges. The train-shed of St Pancras Station, London (opposite, above, 1863), by W. H. Barlow and R. M. Ordish, had the widest span in the world when it was built, but was concealed by the prestigious hotel building (ill. 319). At King's Cross, next door (opposite, 1851), by Lewis Cubitt, the double roof of the train-shed is expressed on the exterior.

In a curious parallel with the 19th-century polemics of Morris and Ruskin over 'truth to materials', the extent to which the steel skeleton was expressed on the exterior of the building was to become almost a moral issue. Those that did express it have been hailed as 'progressive' and 'honest', those that did not as 'historicist' and 'retardataire'. By now feelings have cooled and it is possible to enjoy a frankly 'dishonest' building without a feeling of shame, just as one can enjoy *Der Rosenkavalier* without worrying about how avant-garde it was.

362, 363. Two Chicago buildings of the 1890s by Burnham and Root illustrate the still-experimental nature of the steel frame. The tall, plain Monadnock Building (left) is of load-bearing brick, while the Reliance Building (above) has a steel frame clad in decorative terracotta.

Sometimes there was no steel frame to express. The story can be summarized by considering buildings in Chicago. Adler and Sullivan's Auditorium Building (1886) has load-bearing walls and 347 an essentially historicist elevation. Burnham and Root's brick-built Monadnock Building (1891), sixteen storeys high, also has 362 load-bearing walls, but virtually no ornament and is articulated only by subtle projection of the vertical bow-window bays. Visually this is a powerful design. Holabird and Roche come close to it in their Pontiac Building (1891), but in that case the masonry rests on an invisible steel frame. Should judgment depend on such knowledge? Holabird and Roche seem to have come round to thinking so, since three of their later buildings (Old Colony 1894, Marquette 1894, and Brooks 1910) express the grid more and more clearly. Burnham and Root follow an erratic course in this respect. Their early Rookery Building (1886) has a massive masonry elevation; the Reliance Building (1895) clothes its 363 skeleton in terracotta and glass; but the Fisher Building (1896), though essentially grid-like, experiments with Gothic ornament. William Le Baron Jenney had no scruples about freely expressing the frame from the beginning (e.g. in his two Leiter Buildings, 1881 and 1891, and the Fair Store), but it is interesting that this became known as the 'commercial style'. 364

It was Louis Sullivan who most consummately made the skyscraper into a work of art. His Wainwright Building in St Louis (1890) and Guaranty Building, Buffalo (1894), both built in partnership with Dankmar Adler, adopt a threefold division ultimately derived from classical precedent (plinth, order, attic) but all the stress is on verticality. The steel frame could not be openly exposed, but its presence is made manifest. Sullivan's delicate Art Nouveau ornament gives drama at close quarters but retreats from view at a distance (an exception is the cornice of the Wainwright Building). His Carson, Pirie and Scott Store, Chicago (1899), though enhanced at ground-floor level by some of his most exuberant decoration, is a yet starker expression of the frame. 365 353 348

364. The Fair Store, Chicago (1890), by William Le Baron Jenney, showing the metal frame under construction. Jenney has a claim to be the first engineer to rely wholly on a metal skeleton on a large scale. His importance, however, is purely that of a technical pioneer (he went to the Ecole Centrale des Arts et Manufactures in Paris, not the Beaux-Arts); it was left to others to exploit the new possibilities aesthetically.

365. Sullivan's first skyscraper, the Wainwright Building in St Louis (1890), is given overall unity by the classical vocabulary of plinth, column and entablature, rephrased as plain ground floor and mezzanine, rectangular piers thrusting vertically through seven floors, and an ornate attic.

After the turn of the century it was clear that New York had not lagged behind Chicago, although New York architects, whose skyscrapers are clad in stone or terracotta and in some more or less identifiable style, were more academic than Chicagoans. Because of building regulations which required the upper storeys to be set back, they also change shape. They taper towards the top, like spires, giving the old New York skyline, it has to be said, the more dramatic silhouette. In both respects Chicago followed this example. Hood and Howell's Gothic Chicago Tribune Tower (1925) follows the precedent of Cass Gilbert's Woolworth Building (1913). And they went on growing – in New York the Singer Building (1907) by Ernest Flagg had forty-seven storeys, the Woolworth fifty-two.

366

366. The Woolworth Building, New York (1913), by Cass Gilbert, technically advanced but without scruple in its appeal to picturesqueness and historicism.

The doctrine of Modernism

Meanwhile, what of Europe? Europe built no skyscrapers, and its architects looked with envy at the spectacular technological opportunities open to their American colleagues. But there was a wealth of creative talent and imagination and before long European architectural ideas were filtering back into the American context. International exhibitions continued to provide occasions for displaying new thoughts. In the Paris Exhibition of 1889 two showpieces were Dutert and Contamin's Halle des Machines, a huge structure of iron and glass resting on the most delicate of bases to allow movement, and the Eiffel Tower, for long the tallest structure on earth.

Iron and steel were also ingredients of a new material exploited early in Europe: reinforced concrete. Pioneered in England but developed by the French engineer François Hennebique, it was used in modified form to consciously artistic effect in Anatole de Baudot's church of St Jean-de-Montmartre, Paris (1897). More flexible than the steel frame, strong in both compression and tension, it allowed architects to cover vast spaces unsupported. Max Berg's Jahrhunderthalle at Breslau (now Wrocław, Poland) of 1913 is four times bigger than the dome of St Peter's. Berg used no concealment or decoration, letting the sheer sublimity of the forms speak for themselves. Such forms – rectilinear or gently curved, simplified, almost abstract in their anticipation of stream-

367. Max Berg's Jahrhunderthalle in Breslau (now Wrocław, Poland), built in 1913 to commemorate the centenary of the German states' victory over Napoleon, fully exploits the capacity of reinforced concrete to create spaces of unprecedented grandeur.

367

lining – came to symbolize the new industrial processes in the work of Walter Gropius and Adolf Meyer or the unbuilt but influential fantasy-factories of Antonio Sant'Elia (1912–14).

The years before and immediately after 1914–18 were crucial to the Modern Movement, a seedbed of ideas which came to fruition after the First World War. The name of Gropius has been mentioned and we shall have to follow his career in more detail later, and to add others – the Austrian Adolf Loos, the Frenchman Auguste Perret, the Dutchmen J. J. P. Oud and W. M. Dudok, the Germans Erich Mendelsohn and Ludwig Mies van der Rohe, the Russian Vesnin brothers and Vladimir Tatlin, and finally the maverick and unclassifiable figure of Le Corbusier. It is pointless to pretend that these men all thought the same and were working together as part of a great team. But one thing they did have in common: they all looked forward to the future rather than backward to the past, believing that the 20th century was a new era in world history, whose citizens had needs different from men and women hitherto; and that a new architecture would evolve to answer those needs which would be universal, democratic, functional, economical and beautiful, and would presumably last for ever. By the end of the Second World War it seemed to many historians and critics that this had happened, and in books written around that time the story is one of relentless progress culminating in and ending with the International Modern style. Anything that deviated from that line was dismissed as an irrelevance.

Fifty years later, and in the light of experience, this no longer rings so true. Looking back, we discover numbers of interesting, even great, architects who did not subscribe to the philosophy of Modernism, who looked to the past as much as to the future and who valued continuity more than revolution. They represent alternatives to Modernism, and their work will be described in due course. The paradox is that they may well exercise a more powerful influence on the 21st century than those who were hailed as heralds of the future.

Europe's contribution to the Modern Movement was to formulate a philosophy of architecture, all the more persuasive for being so uncompromising, and then to put it into practice. Adolf Loos claims a place in history on both counts. His ideas were not new. They can be paralleled in Ruskin, in Sullivan (Loos spent three years in America as a young man) and in Otto Wagner. But Loos was at once more extreme and more consistent. By 1908, reacting with passion against the excesses of Neo-Baroque in his native Vienna, and even against the mild indulgences of the

Secession, he proclaimed that 'Ornament is crime.' Here was the dogma of functionalism at its starkest. Nor was he afraid to follow his own precepts. The Steiner House, Vienna, with its featureless white walls, unmoulded windows and flat roof, would seem modern in 1930. For 1910 it is almost unbelievable. Yet he was no puritan. He had a dry sense of humour, a meticulous concern for quality and a taste for luxurious materials. It was ostentation he disliked, not richness. Although he designed few other complete buildings, he was responsible for several apartment and shop interiors (including the well-known Kärntner Bar, Vienna).

368

If Loos was the John the Baptist of the Modern Movement, Gropius was its Messiah. His pre-First World War industrial

368. The Austrian houses of Adolf Loos, built in the first decade of the 20th century, have become icons of Modernism. But some at least of the starkness of such works as the Steiner House, Vienna (1910), is the result of his concentrating on the interior and regarding the exterior as a mere shell.

369. Equally prophetic of the future was Gropius and Meyer's Fagus Factory at Alfeld (1911). Here the steel frame is fully expressed and, as if to demonstrate the absence of load-bearing walls, is made transparent with glass.

buildings, designed in partnership with Adolf Meyer, make construction and purpose transparently clear (e.g. the Fagus Factory, 369 Alfeld, 1911, and the Model Factory Building built for the Cologne Exhibition of 1914, with its prophetic circular staircase behind glass). In 1919 Gropius became director of the Bauhaus, a school of design, at Weimar, later moving it to Dessau. The Bauhaus deliberately avoided a programme (and its teachers were so individual that this would have been impossible anyway), but was nevertheless dedicated to certain propositions that became dogmas: the acceptance of industrial mass production, and the rejection of academic conventions derived from the past. There was also an underlying left-wing political agenda which was intolerable to the Nazis. The Modern Movement inherited all these principles, sometimes with paradoxical results.

Gropius himself designed the school at Dessau as three 370 interconnected buildings, again using concrete and uninterrupted glass walls, meticulously finished and detailed. After he resigned as director in 1928, he was able to put his social theories into practice in apartment buildings at Karlsruhe (1927) and in the Siemensstadt housing estate, Berlin (1929), a project in which several other architects were involved and which was to prove immensely influential. Indeed it is as a writer and a teacher, first at

370. Gropius's philosophy of clarity, logic and industrial production governs every detail of his Bauhaus School at Dessau (1925). From here there is a straight line to International Modernism. After 1933 ex-Bauhaus students were to be found all over the world.

the Bauhaus and then at Harvard, that Gropius will probably be best remembered. His concerns were close to those of Otto Wagner – how to design cities that would retain urban values but cater for the needs of the 20th century – and his solutions too are close to Wagner, though in a pronouncedly modern idiom: apartment blocks of five or six storeys, with large windows, zoned according to rational planning and sited to enjoy the advantages of green open space. He was an advocate of prefabrication and standardization and of architects' co-operation in working groups. With the rise of the Nazis in 1933 he settled first in England and then in the USA, returning to Germany after the War on prolonged visits. Meanwhile, in 1930 Mies van der Rohe had taken over as director of the Bauhaus; he presided over its final three years before it was closed by the Nazis and he in turn emigrated.

Modernism and national character

Throughout the 1920s and '30s each European country was pursuing its own path to the promised land. In France Auguste Perret represents the Beaux-Arts path, which almost by definition avoided a clean break with the past. It was Perret who gave reinforced concrete the *cachet* of Modernism. His flats in the rue Franklin, Paris (1903), had broken new ground by using a trabeated

371. Below: flats in the rue Franklin, Paris, by Auguste Perret (1903). The reinforced concrete frame is clad in terracotta.

372. Below right: the Bauhaus style 'on holiday' – the De La Warr Pavilion, Bexhill, Sussex (1933), by Erich Mendelsohn.

371

373. The Chrysler Building, New York (1928), by William van Alen. The spire is faced with gleaming stainless steel.

concrete skeleton clad in terracotta which, expressed on the exterior, could be mistaken for a steel frame. This is concrete used for its structural rather than its sculptural qualities. Perret continued to use concrete beams as if they were metal girders in such works as the Théâtre des Champs Elysées in Paris (1911), the church of Notre Dame at Le Raincy (1922), and the temporary theatre for the 1925 Paris exhibition of 'Arts Décoratifs et Industriels Modernes' (though that also used wood).

This exhibition brought into focus a style already current in Europe and America that has come to be called 'Art Deco'. It was a sort of pop-Modernism, Modernism made fashionable. Art Deco swiftly conquered every aspect of design, and its hallmarks – zigzags, overlapping circles, smooth curves – appeared on everything from radio sets to ocean liners. It proved eminently suited to smart hotels and to the art form that was growing to maturity simultaneously, the cinema.

Between the purely commercial products of Art Deco, the Odeons and the Roxys, and the more serious, high-minded Modernism of Gropius and the Bauhaus, there is a middle ground which shares something of both. Like the latter, the architects in question also believed in the future (or at least the present), but for them ornament was no crime. The new materials, steel, glass, reinforced concrete, were an opportunity, not a discipline. They favoured the curve rather than the straight line (the style was nicknamed 'Streamlined Moderne'); it was *chic*, it was up-to-date, it was avant-garde with a touch of élitism, the perfect background to the Jazz Age.

Demanding a place in this category are Erich Mendelsohn's cinema on the Kurfürstendamm, Berlin (1926), and his De La Warr Pavilion, Bexhill, in southern England (1933); blocks of flats by Wells Coates (Lawn Road Flats, London, 1933) and English private houses by Amyas Connell and Berthold Lubetkin; and Raymond Hood's McGraw-Hill Building, New York (1930). An Art Deco *tour de force* is the Chrysler Building, New York (1928), by William van Alen, which culminates in a Javanese-derived spire of overlapping discs and emblematic Chrysler birds gazing from the corners.

Holland had Hendrik Berlage, whose affinities were perhaps more with the New World than the Old. Via architectural magazines he knew the work of Richardson, Sullivan and especially Wright, whose European champion he became. His monumental Amsterdam Stock Exchange (1898) in the heart of the city does not reject historicism (it is built of brick with stone detailing and is full of allusions to the past), but is unmistakably a modern building, its main hall covered by an exposed steel roof. Through Berlage, the influence of Wright passed to the next generation of Dutch architects, including Willem Dudok, whose clear, rectilinear brick buildings give a unique character to the town of Hilversum, and J. J. P. Oud, whose low, streamlined housing does the same for the suburbs of Rotterdam.

Italy had Giuseppe Terragni, whose Casa del Fascio at Como (1932) can be seen as a translation of the Bauhaus into Italian (marble instead of concrete). It is also an interesting example of architectural values crossing ideological boundaries, but in the end it did not set the style that Fascism was to follow.

374. Hendrik Berlage's Amsterdam Stock Exchange (1898) stands firmly within a historical tradition (not an entirely Dutch one), but makes full use of modern structural technology.

375. The Casa del Fascio, Como, by Giuseppe Terragni (1932). It is interesting to see Mussolini's Fascist party endorsing Modernism at a time when both Nazism and Communism were turning against it.

Sweden, Norway, Denmark and Finland (which became independent in 1917) evolved a distinctively Scandinavian school of Modernism, preserving the classical virtues of restraint and proportion on a human scale. It was these qualities that made Ragnar Östberg's Stockholm Town Hall (1909) such a popular success. The material (brick), the forms (arcades of round arches, a grand balustraded staircase, a tall square tower with lantern) are reassuringly traditional, but the management of space and the lighting are adventurous and forward-looking. H. Kampmann's Police Headquarters in Copenhagen (1918) has a severe circular courtyard surrounded by coupled Doric columns. In Sweden Gunnar Asplund, with a scholar's knowledge of antiquity, evolved a personal language of classicism that eventually dispensed with overt references. One might contrast his two chapels in the Woodland Cemetery near Stockholm – one (1918) with literal Doric columns, the other (1935) reduced to elemental forms only remotely classical. Asplund's major work is the Stockholm Central Library (1924), which uses the domeless drum favoured by some 18th-century Neoclassicists (compare, for instance, Ledoux at the Barrière de la Villette).

376

377

303

It is against this background that we should see the two most influential leaders of Scandinavian Modernism, Eliel Saarinen and Alvar Aalto. Saarinen is remembered chiefly for his Helsinki Railway Station (1910), a monumental design incorporating spacious halls, a tall clock tower and an entrance flanked by sculptured figures carrying lights. Its most advanced feature was the use of reinforced concrete for the vaults. Aalto began experimenting with Modernist techniques almost as early as Gropius. His library at Viipari (1927) had a staircase behind glass screen walls reminiscent of the Bauhaus. His sanatorium at Paimio (1929) and several of his office buildings use a grid-system frankly expressed on the exterior. But Aalto soon tired of the formulaic side of Modernism. After the War his buildings, such as Säynätsalo Town Hall (1952), became increasingly varied in their shapes, using the plastic qualities of concrete and introducing a note of poetry, with brick and timber textures, lit indirectly. 'To make architecture more human', he wrote in 1960, 'means better architecture.'

378

One country where rejection of the past and faith in the future were stronger than anywhere else was Russia. Here the 1917 Revolution heralded a new age in which everything, including architecture, would be born again. The result was a huge outburst of creative energy on the part of Russian designers, most of whose projects remained on the drawing-board. Nearly all commissions,

376. Ragnar Östberg was one of many Scandinavian Modernists who had no wish to sever all links with the past: Stockholm Town Hall (1909) blends Renaissance Sweden with Byzantine Venice.

377. Like Östberg, Gunnar Asplund in the Stockholm Central Library (1924) remains within a tradition, which in this case is classicism.

378. With Alvar Aalto's library at Viipari, Finland (1927), the break has been made. This is Modernism only two years after the Bauhaus.

379. Vladimir Tatlin's Monument to the Third International (1919) was visionary architecture in the same sense as Boullée's (ill. 267). It was to be 1,300 feet (400m) high, and to contain accommodation units that revolved at different speeds.

380. Konstantin Melnikov was one of the most original talents of post-Revolutionary Russia. His Rusakov Club, Moscow, of 1927 boldly projects its three reinforced concrete auditoriums from the street façade, a totally fresh approach to an old problem.

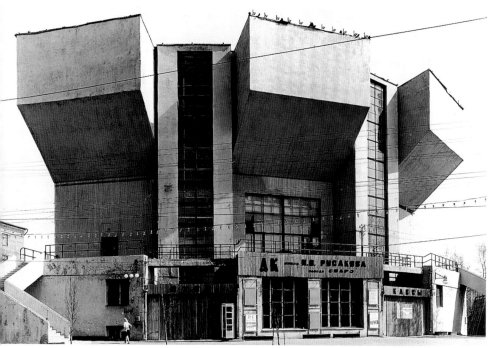

of course, came from the state, including large numbers of apartment blocks and industrial buildings that used the vocabulary of Modernism (concrete walls, horizontal walkways) in a fairly anonymous way. More interesting are those whose function was partly to proclaim an ideological message. Grigory Barkhin's Izvestiya Building, Moscow (1920), the Pravda Building, St Petersburg (1921), by the Vesnin brothers (Aleksandr, Leonid and Viktor), and their competition design for the Palace of Labour, Moscow (1922), were all either altered or not built. Ilya Golosov's Zuyev Club, Moscow (1928), has a spectacular staircase behind curving glass with a heavy concrete slab resting on it. Konstantin Melnikov's Rusakov Club, also in Moscow (1927), has triple audi- 380 toriums cantilevered out from the façade – an idea taken up later by Western theatre architects. For himself he built in 1929 a house consisting of two intersecting cylinders, an extraordinary design, never repeated. The style came to be called Constructivism because it drew attention to the way the elements of the construction are put together. Its canonical work is Vladimir Tatlin's Monument to the Third International, the skeleton of a spiral 379 cone inclined to one side; its huge specifications were quite impracticable and only a model was ever made. The most lasting offspring of Constructivism is Alexei Shchusev's Lenin Mausoleum in Red Square, Moscow (1929), a restrained and 381 impressive play of horizontals in red, black and grey granite.

381. The Lenin Mausoleum in Red Square, Moscow (1929), is a conspicuous survivor of Russian Revolutionary architecture. Alexei Shchusev's first design was classical and a vestige of this remains in the topmost storey.

Among the interwar Modernists we must include Le Corbusier, though his place is not easy to define. He was born Charles-Edouard Jeanneret in Switzerland, but spent his working life in France. Le Corbusier is without doubt one of the most important formative influences upon 20th-century architecture. Before 1939 his reputation rested partly on a small number of villas built for rich patrons, and partly on his books, especially *Vers une architecture* (1923) and *La Ville radieuse* (1935). In these he proclaimed a sort of utopianism through architecture, foreseeing an age of radical authoritarian solutions to social problems through science and technology, with populations living in planned cities where all their needs would be provided for in surroundings of sun, light and air. This dream (or nightmare) was made manifest in his Plan Voisin (1925), whereby central Paris would be replaced by twenty-four identical tower blocks for offices, and lower residential blocks. It was a vision that hypnotized postwar planners all over the world, with results that are still with us.

At the same time he saw himself as, and indeed was, an artist. His first love was painting, which he practised all his life. What fascinated him about machines — aeroplanes, cars, ocean liners, industrial plants — was their beauty. The combination of technical boldness, social idealism and aesthetic sensibility was hard to resist. Indeed his philosophy of 'Purism' can be seen as one more stage in the long French quest for a 'rational' architecture:

If we eliminate from our hearts and minds all dead concepts in regard to houses and look at the question from a critical and objective point of view, we shall arrive at the 'House Machine', the mass-production house, healthy (and morally so too) and beautiful in the same way that the working tools and instruments which accompany our existence are beautiful.

The source of Le Corbusier's faith in concrete lies in his early apprenticeship with Perret, and that of many of his ideas on town-planning in the garden-city movement in England and America (and ultimately in the Picturesque): the abolition of the street, the separation of housing from industry, the need for light, air and green countryside. What was special about Le Corbusier was the messianic style in which the message was preached, typically rising into impassioned capital letters for slogans like

A GREAT EPOCH HAS BEGUN

THERE EXISTS A NEW SPIRIT

ARCHITECTURE IS STIFLED BY CUSTOM

In his actual buildings Le Corbusier had no opportunity to work on a scale commensurate with his ideas. The closest he came was his Cité de Réfuge, Paris (1932), a functionalist design based on the grid. His villas had more personal appeal, which they retain. The Villa Savoye, just outside Paris, appears as a white box, raised 382 on stilts (*pilotis*), with a long band of horizontal windows and a flat roof, all of which would soon become clichés worldwide. The planning of this and other houses reflects his concern for the lifestyle of his clients (largely dictated by himself) and his subtle manipulation of free-flowing spaces and changing levels.

This phase of his career culminated in the Unité d'Habitation 383 at Marseilles (1947), where he was at last able to put his social ideas into practice. In complete contrast to the Miesian tower 388 block, this is a horizontal slab of reinforced concrete raised on *pilotis*, containing 337 two-storey apartments with terraces, 'villas' in the air, a formula that he had first put forward in 1922 and that was to be much copied after the War. With its careful provision of facilities such as shopping, laundries and recreation,

382. By 1929 Le Corbusier's first, 'Purist' style was fully formed. At the Villa Savoye, Poissy, the living quarters are raised up on *pilotis*. The interior spaces flow freely into one another and the lighting is by long horizontal windows without mouldings of any kind.

383. Le Corbusier's Unité d'Habitation at Marseilles (1947) embodies his ideas for communal living: two-storeyed apartments accessible by lifts, with shopping and other facilities incorporated, including a gymnasium, running track, and solarium on the roof. It proved immensely influential.

384, 385. Le Corbusier retained his faith in reinforced concrete as the material for the 20th century, but used it to express emotional qualities going beyond mere function. His pilgrimage chapel at Ronchamp (below) of 1950 is his most personal work, but his High Court Building at Chandigarh (opposite) of 1952, with its pattern of sun-baffles, has something of the same power.

the Unité aimed to be a complete environment, 'a machine for living in'. And in spite of the ostentatious roughness of its construction, it betrays the hand of the artist in its sculptural external staircase, fantastic roofscape and its colouring. Several versions of it were built with Le Corbusier's blessing.

His later works mark a change to a more personal style and in many ways a retreat from the Modern Movement. Two of them are religious buildings, the pilgrimage church at Ronchamp (1950) and the monastery of La Tourette (1957). Here he used concrete to create abstract shapes and internal spaces of great sculptural power, embodying for him and for others a sense of the numinous. Ronchamp especially is a work of amazing originality, with curved walls, billowing eaves and random window openings that owe nothing to any tradition past or present. Finally the major commission for a new capital of the Punjab at Chandigarh in India enabled Le Corbusier to return to his social concerns while retaining the expressive quality of raw concrete (*béton brut*).

Until the early 1930s the heart of the Modern Movement was still Germany, but the rise of the Nazis caused a diaspora of its architects, many of whom, including Neutra, Breuer and Mies, went to the USA, exercising a profound influence on architecture in their adopted country and establishing the conditions through which Modernism became literally International.

385

384

386, 387. The American scene was infinitely enriched through the emigration of architects from Central Europe. The Lovell House or Health House, Los Angeles (1927), by Richard Neutra, and the Whitney Museum of American Art, New York (1963), by Marcel Breuer, are two of the fruits.

Richard Neutra trained in Vienna and knew Loos and Mendelsohn. In 1923 he emigrated to America where he worked with Frank Lloyd Wright and evolved a personal style that effectively united east and west. His Lovell House, Los Angeles (1927), 386 a composition of overlapping horizontals above a steep valley, is as prophetic of the future as anything by Le Corbusier or Mies. Private houses remained his speciality, becoming more and more closely identified with International Modernism. Marcel Breuer, an early Bauhaus student originally from Hungary, came to architecture via furniture design. His first projects owed much to Le Corbusier, and when he joined Gropius at Harvard in 1937, his preference for expressive surface texture over steel and glass was already clear. Most extreme in this respect is the Whitney Museum of American Art, New York (1963), with its startling 387 series of overhanging storeys faced with granite.

The decade of the 1930s, however, was the point when definitions began to harden. Until then the concept of Modernism was still fluid and, as we have seen, could include a wide spectrum of styles and personal tastes. After the '30s, as has been well said, 'the double curse of political opposition and art-historical classification led to a regrettable ossification of modernism in the post-war world'. The result is that among critics and historians, and even among architects, the title 'International Modern' was denied to everything but the familiar abstract grid of steel or concrete and glass. Deviation from this norm was viewed with suspicion, for instance Marina City, Chicago (1967), by Bertrand Goldberg Associates, which indulged in a vulgar display of curves. There are signs that this critical vocabulary is being revised, at least insofar as it carries a value judgment with it. But for the moment it is perhaps clearer to keep to accepted popular usage.

The arrival of Ludwig Mies van der Rohe, ex-director of the Bauhaus, in the USA in 1937 was a crucial event. While still in Germany Mies had designed several strikingly prophetic projects of which few were built. His glass skyscraper of 1921 was at that time beyond available technology to construct. Three projects that did come to fruition were his contribution to the Weissenhof Siedlung, a model housing estate at Stuttgart (1927); the German Pavilion at the Barcelona Exhibition of 1928, an exercise in pure form hardly adaptable to mundane uses; and the Tugendhat House, Brno (1930), a villa with a continuous horizontal window across the whole front.

One of his first buildings in America was for the Illinois Institute of Technology, Chicago (1940); here already, fully formed, is the classic Miesian formula, the exposed metal-frame glass box, articulated only by horizontal and vertical lines. The interior space is totally flexible and has no effect on the outside. The proportions and the grid-like divisions of the surfaces are subtly calculated and meticulously detailed. Mies developed the same basic approach in his other Chicago works – Lake Shore Drive Apartments (1948), Crown Hall (1952), and Convention

388

388. In the Lake Shore Drive Apartments, Chicago (1948), Mies adapted the steel and glass skyscraper to residential use.

389, 390. The perfected International Modern style will always be associated with Mies van der Rohe, but other architects were moving in the same direction. Above: Lever House, New York, by Gordon Bunshaft of Skidmore, Owings and Merrill (1951). Above right: the Seagram Building, New York, by Mies and Philip Johnson (1954).

Hall (1953), where triangular patterns are imposed on the glass screens, and finally in the Seagram Building, New York (1954, with Philip Johnson), his most influential work, in which the glass box is sustained by an (invisible) concrete core containing the lifts. Mies produced variants for certain specialized commissions, but essentially this was the formula that conquered the world. His metal frames are usually concealed by bronze I-beams, since regulations forbade steel to be exposed. To Adolf Loos's aphorism about ornament Mies added his own, equally austere: 'Less is more.'

Whatever critical views have been or will come to be held about International Modernism, Mies's mature buildings are its climax and perfection. His refined eye; his sense of style; his feeling for proportion; his concentration on pure geometrical form; his complete mastery of scale, so that every detail slots miraculously into the framework of the whole; and his effortless, rational clarity, as if constructing a theorem of Euclid in the real world: all conveyed a finality that was both satisfying and frustrating. After

'QED' what was there left to say? In one sense, Mies was inimitable. In another he was all too easy to imitate. For his close followers, and above all for his patrons, the lure was irresistible. Undoubtedly part of the reason was financial, for in many ways Mies was the ideal developer's architect. His tower-block formula (daylighting, regular grid, identical components, lift-core, etc.) was closely geared to the commercial necessities of postwar American office-building – with the prestige of art thrown in.

Gordon Bunshaft, chief designer for the firm of Skidmore, Owings and Merrill, produced Lever House, New York (1951), 389 whose combination of tall glass tower resting on a low, wide podium – another response to New York building laws – became internationally standard for a time. In Britain Peter and Alison Smithson's misleadingly named 'New Brutalism' (a joking reference to Le Corbusier's '*béton brut*' or rough concrete) was an early attempt to follow Mies's doctrine of clarity and restraint on a smaller scale (Hunstanton School, Norfolk, 1949). In Italy Gio 391 Ponti's Pirelli Building, Milan (1956), gave the glass box a more 392 elegant silhouette of canted surfaces, while the engineer Pier Luigi

391. Peter and Alison Smithson were among those who saw that the principles of International Modernism could be used for smaller, more modest buildings. Their secondary school at Hunstanton, Norfolk, of 1949, unobtrusive as it is, proved to be a pioneering work.

392. The tapering corners of Gio Ponti's Pirelli Building, Milan (1956), are a conscious effort to avoid the rectangular slabs that were now rising in every city in the world. Pier Luigi Nervi was the consulting engineer.

Nervi, working in reinforced concrete, created unprecedentedly huge vaulted spaces. The Brazilian Oscar Niemeyer could follow the Miesian recipe when required but was also a disciple of Le Corbusier and retained a whole repertoire of diverse forms to suit different purposes (e.g. the Cathedral of Brasilia, 1970, a circular, half-sunken glazed structure whose dome opens like the corona of a flower). In Japan the International Style arrived via Kenzo Tange. His Kugawa Prefectural Office Building, Tahamatsu (1955), is squarely in the Miesian orbit, but he later struck out on paths of his own, seeking for a new Japanese national style.

Back in Germany Hans Scharoun, in a career stretching from the 1920s to the 1970s, produced a body of work which is completely different from that of Mies. It had far less influence, but is equally representative of the Modern Movement at its most brilliant. Scharoun, a few years younger than Mies, shared his intellectual background, and was also deprived of commissions under the Nazis. He spent the 1930s and '40s in small-scale private practice in Berlin where he designed a series of highly individual houses, and where he rose to a dominant position after 1945. In some ways Scharoun was Mies's antithesis. Instead of seeking a formula that could be applied universally, he conceived every building freshly for its purpose. Fully sympathetic as he was towards the

393. Oscar Niemeyer is the Brazilian Le Corbusier, equally wedded to reinforced concrete and nearly as unpredictable. His buildings for the new capital of Brasilia are in a variety of styles including International Modern; his Cathedral (1970) is a flamboyant and totally original gesture comparable to Ronchamp.

ideals of Modernism, he shunned rigid mechanistic solutions and aimed at a much more 'organic' architecture – 'the spiritual basis of building, the structure in space and time'. These semi-mystical qualities are recognizably present from his earliest works (residential hall for the Deutsche Werkbund Exhibition, Breslau, now Wroclaw, 1929), to his great Philharmonie in Berlin (1956), with a series of interrelated interior spaces of great subtlety (and therefore hard to photograph), generated from the concept of 'music in the centre'.

Alternatives to Modernism

By the 1960s the International Style had prevailed all over the world, and the common complaint was that every city looked the same. Architects might hanker in vain for opportunities to express their own personalities. To some this was a healthy development, the submission of aesthetic standards to universal criteria of rationality and efficiency. Only in the 1970s did doubts begin to set in, doubts not only about the way buildings looked (Kenzo Tange was not the only one to rail against 'boring modern architecture') but even about Modernist ideology.

Partly through the verbal and graphic skills of its advocates like Le Corbusier, partly through the accident of its being persecuted by the Nazis, International Modernism was widely accepted as the egalitarian style, the style of the people, the only style suited to mass culture. The fact that its greatest triumphs occurred in capitalist countries and were financed by capitalist enterprise was largely ignored. It was only the belated realization that as a style for mass housing it was a near-total disaster that led to its other credentials being scrutinized and a search for alternatives seriously to begin.

These alternatives to Modernism, as has been hinted already, had existed all through the 20th century, and it is to them that we now turn. None of the architects, it must be emphasized, was opposed to change, and most, perhaps all, would have seen themselves, and were seen by others, as belonging to the architectural avant-garde. What, to our Post-Modern eyes, distinguishes them is that they were not, on the whole, committed to radical solutions but sought to graft innovation onto tradition and to continue what had been meaningful in the past.

Born within five years of each other (between 1863 and 1868), Henry van de Velde (Belgian), Joseph Maria Olbrich (Austrian) and Peter Behrens (German) all had their roots in that immensely fertile soil of pre-1914 continental Europe, from which so much of

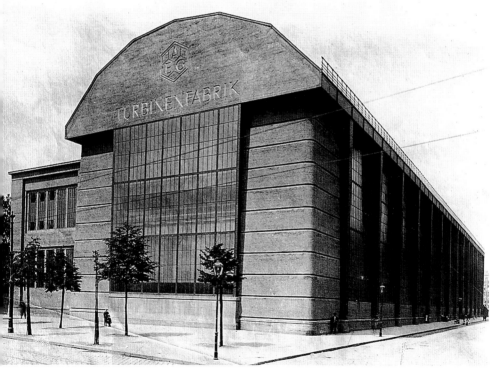

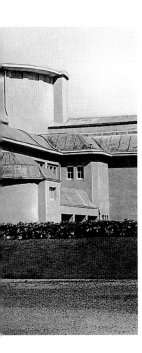

394. Henry van de Velde's Werkbund Theatre at Cologne (1914) was designed as a model theatre for an exhibition demonstrating new ideas in the field. Architecturally, the emphasis was on unity, the concrete construction welding together the foyer, auditorium and fly tower.

395. Peter Behrens was appointed architect to AEG (General Electric Company), a vast German industrial concern, in 1907. For them he designed not only buildings but kettles, coffee-pots, clocks, radiators and a range of other products. His Turbine Hall in Berlin was built in 1909.

20th-century culture seems to spring (including painting, literature and music). Each man contributed significantly to the evolution of architecture, yet the exact nature of his influence is hard to define. To the next generation they were seen as the sources of challenging ideas rather than as models to be imitated.

For Van de Velde, architecture was almost a form of abstract sculpture. His affinities are primarily with Art Nouveau, but he has a massive, masonic quality foreign to that style. His Werkbund Theatre, Cologne (1914, destroyed), organic in its forms but virtually bare of ornament, reflected his interest in the drama through its innovations in both stage and auditorium. The School of Applied Arts at Weimar (1906), which he both built and directed, became the first Bauhaus and promoted some of the same ideas and methods. Olbrich's background was Vienna. After working with Otto Wagner he became a member of the Secession and actually designed its exhibition premises (1897), a distantly classical building surmounted by a golden openwork sphere of foliage. In 1899 he joined the Grand Duke of Hesse's artistic colony at Darmstadt, where his most notable work was the Wedding Tower, a strange structure crowned by rising curvilinear shapes rather like an organ. Peter Behrens was also part of the Darmstadt group, building a few highly individual, somewhat romantic houses before moving to Berlin to work for a large electrical company. Behrens's industrial buildings for AEG are his best-known works and are often seen as proto-Modern. This is true of the Turbine Hall (1909), which is essentially steel and glass, though styled in such a way as to suggest a classical temple front. His high-tension plant, also in Berlin (1910), has two stripped-down porticoes, but the interior court of his building for the Hoechst Dyeworks, Frankfurt (1920), is openly Expressionist in its sharp brick detailing and sense of aggressive energy.

What is Expressionism? One is tempted to say, the opposite of everything that Modernism stood for: emotion rather than reason, revolt rather than conformity, assertive personality rather than 'functional' anonymity. With Expressionist buildings, it seems, the imaginative impulse came first, fresh from the artist's subconscious, and was then adapted for use in the real world. In a rejection of steel and glass, the chosen materials are brick (used in highly inventive ways that recall German late Gothic) and concrete, which of all materials comes closest to natural rock. The result is always, to a degree, eccentric, and was intended to be.

Expressionism began in Germany before the First World War. Hans Poelzig's bulbous and disturbing combination of water tower and exhibition hall at Posen (Poznań, Poland) was designed as early as 1911. His Grosses Schauspielhaus in Berlin, with its tree-like piers and stalactite-hung roof (also demolished), dated from 1918. Some early Modernists sowed their Expressionist wild oats before settling down. Mies van der Rohe's Monument to Karl Liebknecht and Rosa Luxemburg in Berlin (1926), a layered composition of textured brick, and Erich Mendelsohn's Einstein Tower at Potsdam (1917) can only be called Expressionist. Other classics of the style are Fritz Höger's Chilehaus, Hamburg (1922), where the far-projecting cornice is brought out at the corner like the point of an arrow, and the anthroposophist Rudolf Steiner's Goetheanum near Basel (1924), whose strange concrete forms seem to grow from the soil like a giant fungus.

Two church architects of the 1920s and '30s, Dominikus Böhm and Otto Bartning, discovered affinities between Expressionism and the angular Gothic of north Germany, reflected for instance in Böhm's church at Frielingsdorf (1926). It was not by chance that Expressionism became a favourite of German

396. Hans Poelzig's remodelling of an old circus building into the Grosses Schauspielhaus, Berlin (1918), turned it into an early theatre-in-the-round. The stalactite-like shapes were put there for acoustic reasons.

397. In 1926 the 40-year-old Mies van der Rohe had still not found his definitive style. His monument to the socialist martyrs Karl Liebknecht and Rosa Luxemburg and reflects an affinity with Frank Lloyd Wright that he was soon to outgrow.

398. Erich Mendelsohn's Einstein Tower at Potsdam (1917) was built to serve a scientific programme testing the theory of relativity. Designed for poured concrete, it is actually built of brick covered in cement.

makers of atmospheric silent films like *The Cabinet of Dr Caligari*. Nor is it without significance that some of the boldest Expressionist designs were conceived on paper and remained there. Hermann Finsterlin, for instance, produced a number of quick, extempore, passionate sketches for buildings which he did not seriously consider could be built, but which stimulated later architects. Bruno Taut was a similar visionary, fascinated by glass and by visions of buildings crowning mountains or cities.

Expressionism was essentially a German movement. It had some vogue in Holland, in Denmark and in Czechoslovakia, but not much elsewhere. In Holland it produced J. M. van der Meij's Scheepvaarthuis in Amsterdam (1912), almost as wild and wonderful as anything by Gaudí, and in an only slightly more 399 sober vein the community housing of Michael de Klerk and Piet 400 Kramer. They were in charge of a series of medium-sized housing estates in Amsterdam during and after the First World War (Holland remained neutral in the conflict). In complete contrast to the rational approach of Oud in Rotterdam, only a few miles away, they designed a series of façades whose brick surfaces undulate,

expand and multiply like the segments of a telescope, contract as if pinched into a point, and generally behave unpredictably. Once considered an 'aberration' which held up the progress of modern architecture, these estates now seem enviably humane as well as visually exciting.

In Denmark the only notable Expressionist was Peter Jensen Klint, who built the Grundvig Church in Copenhagen (1913). This looks back to medieval Danish parish churches, exaggerating and dramatizing their forms in its huge organ-like façade. The Gothic connection is also strong in Czechoslovakia, where a movement known as Czech Cubism flourished in the same postwar period and took its inspiration largely from the cellular vaults of the Bohemian late Middle Ages. Its chief exponents were Josef Chochol and Josef Gočar, with, for instance, the House of the Black Virgin in Prague (1911).

As the 1930s succeeded the '20s and in many countries of Europe dictatorships succeeded democracy, the face of architecture changed. The connection between these events is still under debate, but one consequence was a revived classicism that was

401

explicitly opposed to Modernism and was once bitterly reviled by historians of that persuasion.

It was in Russia that the change, always associated with Stalin's rise to power, though it is difficult to pin the blame entirely on him, seems most abrupt. Certainly nothing could be more different from the heady days of revolutionary experiment than the prize-winning entry (the work of three architects) for the (unbuilt) Palace of the Soviets in 1932, a monumental structure of five superimposed circular colonnades, culminating in a gigantic statue of Lenin. In that same year, all architects were obliged to join a single union, a move bound to promote conformity. Architecture now had to express the power of the people in a language that the people could understand. It is often forgotten, however, that the Russian taste for megalomaniac classicism is older than the Revolution. An apartment block of 1911 in St Petersburg by one of its pioneers, B. A. Shchuko, could easily be mistaken for a Stalinist building of twenty-five years later, for instance I. V. Zholtovsky's Moscow apartments of 1934 with their giant Corinthian columns rising through six storeys. A masterplan for Moscow, only realized in fragments, envisaged wholesale demolition and the creation of wide boulevards lined with such monumental buildings. The most lasting legacies of the Stalinist era, however, are the seven spectacular high-rise blocks that encircle Moscow (including the Ministry of Foreign Affairs and the University) evoking the towers of the Kremlin, and the Moscow Metro (underground, or subway) system. This latter, still the pride of the city, is an architectural experience of a high order. Each station has its own style, usually loosely classical, but all bearing a common stamp of heroic symbolism and excellently crafted high-quality materials, often including sculpture.

Mussolini's Italy also looked to Roman architecture, but in a form shorn of details, reducing the orders to bare cylinders and pediments to triangles. The resulting style is abstract and timeless, and with its pale travertine gleaming in the hot sun, still impressive. One enjoys many Fascist railway stations and particularly the EUR near Rome, an area built for a planned exhibition (Esposizione Universale Roma) due to happen in 1942. It includes a range of monumental buildings in a stark, marmoreal style that seems immune to political change. Italy did not outlaw Modernism, and successful mainstream designs are not hard to find, e.g. Florence Railway Station by Giovanni Michelucci (1933).

Nazi Germany adopted a pared-down classicism that was similar to that of Italy, and applied it more single-mindedly.

402. Classicism under Stalin: Komsomolskaya Metro Station, Moscow (1952), palatial luxury for the common man.

403. Proto-Stalinism: an apartment building in St Petersburg of 1911 by B. A. Shchuko, with a free version of the giant order that looks forward to Stalinist classicism and to Post-Modernism (cf. ill. 429).

40

40

40

404. Ideological opposites, Communism and Nazism both adopted classicism as their official style, an indication that the symbolism of architecture can never be anything but arbitrary. Paul Ludwig Troost's Haus der Kunst, Munich (1933), can be seen as a stripped-down version of Schinkel's Altes Museum in Berlin (ill. 265).

Paul Ludwig Troost's Haus der Kunst in Munich (1933), with its 404 long façade of stone columns and flat entablature, has undeniable dignity. This was the style inherited by Albert Speer, Hitler's architect, who compromised it by heavy detail and exaggerated scale.

We have seen how easy it is for certain architectural styles to become tainted by association with unpopular ideologies. This was the case with classicism, and between 1945 and 1980 one may look in vain in the West for Doric, Ionic or Corinthian. What such politicized views overlook, however, is that in the 1930s classicism was very widely accepted as an alternative to Modernism, in the democratic as well as the totalitarian states; it kept its popularity in the United States, especially in Washington, until much later (e.g. the National Gallery, by John Russell Pope, 1941).

That architecture does not necessarily carry fixed political connotations is proved by the fact that even at the height of the Cold War Stalinist architects looked for models to America (sometimes over a considerable time-gap). There is little to choose between the Moscow Ministry of Foreign Affairs (Gelfreich and 405 Minkus) of 1956 and the Wrigley Building in Chicago, or the Municipal Building in New York (McKim, Mead and White) of 406 fifty years earlier.

405, 406. From opposite ends of the political spectrum, Stalinist Russia was influenced by capitalist America. The ornately decorated skyscrapers which encircle Moscow (above: the Ministry of Foreign Affairs, 1956) evoke the towers of the Kremlin, but in their form they are clearly inspired by American skyscrapers of the early 20th century such as (right) McKim, Mead and White's Municipal Building, New York, (1906), or the Woolworth Building (ill. 366).

407. The Marin County Administrative Building and Hall of Justice, San Rafael, California (1957), shows Frank Lloyd Wright at the end of his life still inventing new solutions.

Three nonconformists

During these years Frank Lloyd Wright continued vigorously at work. He lived to be over ninety (he died in 1959), joining no school, subscribing to no doctrine outside his own inspiration. He designed (among dozens of commissions) private houses; an office building (the Larkin Building, Buffalo, 1904); a church (Unity Church, Oak Park, Illinois, 1905); a hotel (Imperial Hotel, Tokyo, 1915); an industrial complex (S. C. Johnson Wax, Racine, Wisconsin, 1936–56); a museum (Guggenheim Museum, New York, 1956); and a civic centre (San Rafael, California, 1957). Each 407 one was a new challenge for which Wright devised a new solution. His concerns were, first, to integrate the building into its setting, whether rural or urban, and second to provide interior spaces that were functional, yet sensuously and intellectually satisfying. For the Unity Church this meant a cool, orthogonal room in harmonious colours, lit by abstract patterns of stained glass; for Johnson Wax, a large hall supported on mushroom pillars; for the Guggenheim Museum, a continuous spiral ramp. His quest for the 409 union of art and nature found its expression in the three versions of his own house, Taliesin, and in his most famous house, Fallingwater, Pennsylvania (1935), a composition of concrete horizontals 408 balanced over a waterfall. As a theorist and as a practising architect Wright attracted a band of disciples, who continue to acknowledge his mastery and for whom his authority is almost mystical. Their headquarters is in his last house, Taliesin West, Arizona.

408. Opposite: Fallingwater, Pennsylvania (1935), 'the apotheosis of the horizontal', is Wright's most famous private house, and his most successful reconciliation of the two roots of his personal style – Modernism and Romanticism.

409. At the Guggenheim Museum, New York (1956), Wright rethought the concept of an art gallery as a spiral.

410, 411. In his later work, Lutyens turned from his 'Old English' style to a form of classicism that put him even more out of touch with the avant-garde. Above: the Viceroy's (now President's) House, New Delhi (1920), which incorporates elements from Hindu and Buddhist architecture. Right: the Memorial to the Missing on the Somme, or Thiepval Arch (1927), in eastern France.

In England, Edwin Lutyens had experimented with classicism before the First World War; in his later years he came to find it increasingly congenial in solving formal architectural problems, especially on a large scale. Above all, it provided a system of proportions that enabled him to organize and articulate volumes and spaces in ways entirely beyond his earlier vernacular style. It underpins three of his greatest works – the Memorial to the Missing on the Somme, known as the Thiepval Arch (1927), a superbly rational build-up of arches which is at the same time strangely emotional in effect; the government buildings of New Delhi, notably the Viceroy's House (now the President's), finished in 1929, where he combined Roman and Indian features; and the Catholic Cathedral of Liverpool, designed about 1933. The Second World War brought Lutyens's cathedral to a halt and it was eventually completed to a different design by Frederick Gibberd. Of his project only the crypt exists (finished in 1958) and a large model, which gives a vivid idea of its splendour. (One is irresistibly reminded of the model of that other unbuilt masterpiece, Wren's St Paul's.) The cathedral, centred upon a great dome, was an amalgam of elements from ancient Rome, Byzantium and the Renaissance, handled with such confidence and originality that it would surely have outlasted changes in fashion.

412. Model of Lutyens's unbuilt Catholic Cathedral, Liverpool, begun in the early 1930s but halted by the Second World War.

And so finally to a figure who has yet to find his place in architectural history: Jože Plečnik. Hopelessly out of touch with his own age or its truest representative? A die-hard traditionalist or a prophet of the future? The 21st century will have to answer these questions. In the meantime this account of his career – perhaps disproportionately long – is offered to compensate for the fact that he has gone entirely unmentioned in all the standard histories of architecture.

What distinguishes Plečnik's work is his fertility of invention and the range and depth of his ideas. His invention flowed so copiously that one could easily mistake it for the exercise of pure fantasy were it not for the seriousness of his thinking. These ideas, acquired largely through the writings of Gottfried Semper, transform architecture into a summing up of civilization, an expression of human progress, through the adaptation of motifs from the past. Thus, nothing in Plečnik's work is original, yet everything is. His starting point is the classical tradition of Greece and Rome, and before Greece, Minoan Crete. He was also a devout Catholic, so that everything was in a sense a confession of faith.

Plečnik spent his long life in the territories of the old Austro-Hungarian Empire, divided in his lifetime into Austria, Hungary, Czechoslovakia and Yugoslavia. In Vienna he built the Zacherl apartment house (1903) in a personal version of the Secession style. In Prague he built a series of additions to the Castle and its gardens (1929–31), harmonizing with the existing structures but

413. The church of the Sacred Heart, Prague (1928), by Jože Plečnik.

414, 415. Two works from the
last phase of Plečnik's life,
when he returned to his native
Ljubljana, in Slovenia: the
staircase of the University Library
(left, 1936) and the sluice on the
edge of town (1940). Both use
classical elements with a degree
of originality that takes them
beyond Neoclassicism
into a language all his own.

constantly surprising by unexpected details (a canopy of sheet-metal resting on miniature bulls protects the steps from the courtyard to the ramparts). His church of the Sacred Heart (1928) is a single unified space, dominated on the exterior by its bell tower, a sheer wall of brick incorporating a transparent clock the size of a three-storey house. His major works in or near his native city of Ljubljana are the Chamber of Trade, Industry and Commerce (1925), a building in which classical architecture seems to have been reinvented in the 20th century without losing its imperial past; the church of St Francis (1930), its interior defined by a rectangle of huge Doric columns; the University Library (1936), which has a staircase rising between bare walls to galleries whose balustrades are Doric and Ionic column-tops and capitals; the church of St Michael (1937), built economically, using industrial components painted to give it a rustic local flavour; and several bridges and a sluice, each individualized by the classical orders magnified and diminished as if seen through the two ends of a telescope. Finally just outside the town he built Žale (1938), a collection of cemetery chapels for funerals of different denominations, which are like a series of musical variations on an original theme, always different but always recognizably the same. Plečnik's imagination was extraordinarily fertile in both forms and details. It is as if he were trying to provide a future generation of architects with every idea they would ever need. Perhaps that is what he did.

413

414

415

Epilogue

Chapter 10: After Modernism, Style

Had this book been written in 1498 instead of 1998, how would the last chapter have summarized the contemporary situation and looked into the future? 'Clearly the international modern style (pointed arches, rib vaults, flying buttresses) is destined to continue indefinitely, and in view of the unchallenged leadership of the Catholic Church, churches will remain the dominant building type. It is not very likely that the strange Italian experiment of imitating ancient Roman temples will get very far, and already eccentric young men seem to be undermining it by indulging in bizarre fantasies of their own. New technology, such as the fan-vaults of King's College Chapel, still in the development stage, points to the shape of things to come.'

In other words, speculation is asking for trouble. This brief Epilogue (which tries to give the last forty years no more space than any other forty years) will therefore not venture upon generalizations. A pattern that is obvious when one looks back from a distance is not at all obvious when it is only a few inches from one's face. All we can do is to persevere with the method used hitherto and trace connections between past and present. One of the lessons that history teaches is that everything has a history. However unprecedented a design is thought to be, even (or especially) by its designer, there is always a precedent.

The legacy of Modernism
International Modern, in spite of the writings of several would-be obituarists, is not dead, but in its old Miesian guise it interests fewer and fewer major architects. Its principal legatee is High-Tech, the aesthetic of which is equally dependent on the engineering aspect of architecture and the open display of structure, but which is more versatile in its forms and more varied in its results. Mies himself was tending to escape from an over-rigid formula at the end of his life (New National Gallery, West Berlin, 1962). The Danish architect Arne Jacobsen similarly emerged from orthodox Modernism to build the still disciplined but imaginative Danish National Bank at Copenhagen (1961) and the City Hall at Mainz (1970).

416. Michael Graves's Public Services Building, Portland, Oregon (1980), was a revolutionary work, not simply because of its formal challenges (others had anticipated his subversive attitude to Modernism) but because of its prominence and prestige.

417, 418. After the 1960s the technical capabilities of International Modernism, and in particular its complete mastery of the steel frame and transparent wall, began to lead beyond the geometrical clarity of Mies van der Rohe towards new realms of the imagination. An early work of Norman Foster was the Willis Faber Dumas Building in Ipswich, Suffolk (above, 1974), which wraps its irregular site in a sheath of undulating tinted glass. In total contrast is his Hong Kong and Shanghai Banking Corporation Headquarters in Hong Kong (right, 1979), a deft and daring composition of verticals.

The old charge of anonymity levelled against the school of Mies is no longer valid. A building by Norman Foster is recognizably different from one by Richard Rogers. Whatever its size, a Foster building is calculatedly controlled, from the early days of his Willis Faber Dumas Building in Ipswich (1974), with its rounded forms sheathed in dark glass held by almost invisible Neoprene joints, to the radiating struts of Stansted Airport (1991). A Rogers building aims at strength rather than elegance, proclaiming its affinity with industrial plant by exposing the service features (cables, ducts, pipes); instances are the Centre Pompidou in Paris (designed in partnership with Renzo Piano, 1970) and the Lloyds Building in London (1978).

417

419

420

Reinforced concrete continued to play a leading role in Modernism, largely owing to Le Corbusier's influence. The sculptural qualities of moulded concrete went on being exploited after the Second World War (the gun emplacements built by the Germans along the French coast enjoyed a brief burst of architectural popularity), and a new technique was invented by which a façade was constructed from pre-cast units, which could take any shape – circles, squares or triangles – to produce an overall pattern. This was used, for instance, in two American embassies in Europe, that of Dublin (1950, by John M. Johansen) and of London

421

419, 420. Richard Rogers has exploited the newly recognized beauty of industrial installations (there are now books of art photographs featuring blast-furnaces and pit-head machinery) to base the whole aesthetic of his buildings on their service elements. Below: Centre Georges Pompidou, Paris (1970), by Rogers with Renzo Piano. Below right: Lloyds Building, London (1978).

421. An alternative to the steel frame is the pre-cast concrete unit, which achieves a more organic, deliberately sculptural effect. The Embassy of the United States, Dublin, by John M. Johansen (1950), is an early example of the genre, which also favoured circular or otherwise curved plans.

(1965, by Eero Saarinen), as well as another London landmark, Centre Point (1963, by Richard Seifert). In America it was taken up by Marcel Breuer, Edward Durrell Stone and Minoru Yamasaki.

More often, concrete, left with the marks of wooden shuttering showing, was relished for its uncompromising starkness and strength. This may have been appropriate for monasteries (La Tourette); it was less so for theatres, concert halls and art galleries (London's National Theatre, Hayward Gallery and Queen Elizabeth Hall), and depressingly inappropriate for large housing estates in poor areas, many of which became hated by their inhabitants and are now threatened with demolition, even when designed by architects like Denys Lasdun, Erno Goldfinger and Basil Spence. In America concrete's most prominent exponents were Paul Rudolph, whose Yale School of Art and Architecture (1958) is a formal composition of some subtlety, and Louis Kahn, whose conscious aim was to restore an element of monumentality to Modernism (he was even accused of 'poetry' and 'medieval romanticism'). His Alfred Newton Richards Medical Research Building, Philadelphia (1957 and 1961), and Jonas Salk Institute, La Jolla, California (1959), show a mastery of geometrical logic and a play of volumes reminiscent of the Beaux-Arts, qualities also exemplified in his two museums, the Kimbell Art Museum, Fort Worth, Texas (1966), and the Yale Center for British Art, New Haven (1969). Shortly before his death in 1974 he drew up plans for large-scale developments in India and Bangladesh.

422. The School of Art and Architecture of Yale University (1958), New Haven, by Paul Rudolph, displays a different aesthetic of concrete. Trained under Gropius at Harvard, Rudolph initiated a concept of 'new freedom' in form, and his Yale building uses concrete for its ability to produce exciting aggressive shapes and a free outline .

423. In the Jonas Salk Institute, La Jolla, California (1959), Louis Kahn achieved a restrained, symmetrical monumentality in concrete finished with great care.

Ingredients of Post-Modernism

All the architects mentioned so far would claim that their work was the product of logic and reason, not of 'style'. At the opposite extreme are those for whom style is everything and logic nothing, a movement for which no better term has been invented than 'Post-Modern'. What the Post-Modernists have in common is easier to define negatively than positively. They find International Modern boring. They deny that 'less is more', they have no great fondness for rationality. Their work is colourful, controversial, exciting, witty… In their search for novelty they have looked at the styles of the past, especially classicism, but use them in ways that are deliberately incongruous. In a sense theirs is a learned style, since the viewer is expected to recognize solecism as a Neoclassical patron was expected to recognize correctness. Proportions are disturbed. Heavy Doric columns are suspended against glass walls. Rows of pilasters, whose essence is regularity, lose their rhythm and huddle together. Pediments expand to embrace whole buildings. Giant columns are revealed as blocks of flats. Ionic volutes turn into crude circles like dartboards.

424. Even before he built the AT&T Building in New York, with its 'Chippendale' pediment (1978), Philip Johnson had run into criticism for his 'whimsical changeability', 'frivolity' and 'craving for the spectacular'. Two years later he went on to build the 'Crystal Cathedral' in Los Angeles, an exercise in Pop-Architecture designed for mass evangelism.

How did all this begin? In the late 1960s and '70s one finds a number of designers outside the main architectural establishment playing games almost in the spirit of the style known as 'California Crazy', where one might see a snack bar in the shape of a giant hamburger. The American James Wines invented something called 'De-architecture'. His works have names like 'Peeling Project', 'Indeterminate Façade' and the 'Tilt Showroom' (in the last, in Tonson, Maryland, 1976, the whole front appears detached and leans dangerously against the side walls). In Europe Günther Domenig's bank in Vienna (1975) seems to have collapsed as if struck by an earthquake. Hans Hollein's jewelry shop in the same city (1976) looks as if it has been damaged by gunfire, while his travel agency (1976) outfaced vulgarity with golden palm trees, a bronze Indian dome and a classical ruin. The same cheerful defiance of all canons of taste appeared in shopping malls and reached its epitome in Disneyland.

Serious, prestige architecture by men with solid reputations was slower to follow. In 1978 Philip Johnson (who had been Mies's assistant on the cool Seagram Building in 1954) designed a skyscraper with a top like a Georgian bookcase, the AT&T Building, New York. Then in 1980 Michael Graves offended the architectural establishment by designing the Public Services Building for Portland, Oregon, a tall, nearly cubic block articulated by a massive wedge-shape at the top like a giant keystone. It was originally to be crowned by three miniature temples concealing machinery, but he was persuaded to omit these. The building was revolutionary in at least three ways. First, it entirely renounced the Modernist aesthetic of unity. Secondly, it returned to heavy masonry, something thought to have been relegated to the past forever; its small square windows seemed an insult to the Modernist ideals of light and transparency. And thirdly, it reintroduced colour into architecture, a quality that had come to seem as shocking as polychromy did to the early Neoclassicists.

After the shock waves had subsided, architects on both sides of the Atlantic began to realize that their Miesian prison doors had been thrown open and they were free. It would be misleading to refer to Plečnik in this context, but it is a fact that his uninhibited use of classicism did anticipate to an astonishing degree the ambitions of the Post-Modernists. He cannot, however, be called the father of Post-Modernism – partly because he has only recently been widely publicized and, more importantly, because of his intense seriousness. For him, this was not a game. For many Post-Modernists the element of game is not something they would

390

424

416

361

425. In 1956 the competition for Sydney Opera House was won by the 30-year-old Jørn Utzon of Denmark with a design that was completely unlike any other opera house in the world. Its shell roofs, unrelated to the auditoriums below, struck the engineer Pier Luigi Nervi as 'the most straightforward anti-functionalism from the point of view of statics as well as construction'.

wish to deny. At the Venice Biennale of 1980, a number of architects (Hollein, Kleihues, Leon Krier, and Venturi, Rauch and Scott-Brown) put together a semi-serious 'Strada Novissima' consisting of classical adaptations of their own, plus Adolf Loos's Chicago Tribune Tower of 1920, a project in the form of a giant Doric column (once dismissed as a joke, now hailed as a prophecy).

There is another derivative of classicism where definitely no joke is intended, and that is the straightforward classical revival that has gained a limited popularity in the United States and Britain. Its patrons, who include the Prince of Wales, are criticized for admiring mere pastiche. This would not in itself be a ground for complaint were the pastiche carried out competently, but too often the proportions are mishandled and the plans inept. Among the best is Norman Neuerberg's (first) Getty Museum at Malibu, California (1970), a scholarly reconstruction of a Roman villa.

Alongside this parodic historicism has grown another, far more philosophical strain of Post-Modernism which (borrowing from literary theory) calls itself Deconstructionist. Its key idea seems to go back to a book by Robert Venturi, himself a practising architect who never renounced historicist allusions, *Complexity and Contradiction in Architecture* (1966). This and its successor, *Learning from Las Vegas* (1972), not only accepted the apparently ugly aspects of American pop culture (neon signs, the 'mall', the 'strip', the eight-lane highway) as serious architecture, finding in them qualities of irony and ambiguity previously unrecognised, but offered a way forward that was neither rationalist nor historicist. Based on the actual language of architecture itself, this is in its extreme form entirely intellectual, and its premises make it virtually impossible to put into practice. Its chief advocate is the American Peter Eisenman, for whom architecture is an abstract, self-referential activity, remote from the needs of real life.

Expressionism provides a further strand in the texture of Post-Modernism. It is an open question, for instance, whether one should call two famous buildings of the 1950s – Jørn Utzon's 425 Sydney Opera House and Eero Saarinen's TWA Terminal at 426 Kennedy Airport, New York – late Expressionist or early Post-Modern. Certainly in the case of the former the closest analogues are the sketches of Hermann Finsterlin, but it could only have been turned into reality with the most advanced engineering techniques (by the firm of Ove Arup and Partners). In Mexico City, the Church of the Miraculous Virgin by Felix Candela (1954) similarly looks back to Bartning and Böhm.

There were of course more serious reasons than desire for change for rebelling against Modernism. One was its 'failure to communicate'. An apartment building, its critics maintained, looked exactly the same as an office block, a chapel the same as a boiler house. For many 'functionalist' architects, actual function

426. Eero Saarinen chose to give his TWA Terminal at John F. Kennedy Airport, New York (1956), the outline of a bird to 'express the excitement of flight'. It was a foretaste of a return to symbolism by modern architects.

427. In London's Docklands development all the extremes of modern architectural styles can be studied within a few square miles. John Outram's Storm Water Pumping Station (1988), 'a temple to summer storms', represents a rejection of Miesian logic in favour of a personal symbolic language.

was an irrelevance. The Post-Modernists do indeed communicate, but often in such arcane codes that the public does not get the message. Their means of communication – their language – consists of signs, symbols, metaphors drawn from private mythologies and the architecture of the past. John Outram's Storm Water Pumping Station in London's Docklands (completed 1988), one of the canonical works of English Post-Modernism, is intended to be understood as follows: 'The design of this building is derived from the idea that it should imitate a river and a landscape, from which the storm-water flowed. Thus the walls are stratified like the sides of a mountain. The central section of the front wall is made of blue bricks to imitate the river that flows between the tree-trunks, represented by the big round, red, central columns. The round hole of the ventilating fan which splits the gable into two triangular "peaks" contains the source of the river as if within a cave between two mountain peaks.' One consequence of this wealth of allusion has been the multiplication of expository and theoretical writing, which now occupies a much more prominent place on architects' bookshelves than before.

Variety and scale
Two things which will surely strike historians of the future about the last forty years are the increase in variety and the increase in scale – an increase not only of the building as a whole but also of its parts.

First, variety: no longer can it be said that cities all over the world look the same. The range of forms, styles, ideas and materials is quite bewildering. On the other hand, there has been no return to identifiable nationalism. Architecture is still international, with great cosmopolitan firms operating in every part of the world and every innovation becoming instantly known and assimilated.

Some ideas genuinely are new. One is the exploitation of steel in tension. As an engineering principle it has a long history (e.g. in suspension bridges), but to have the roof of a major building suspended like a tent from upright poles by steel cables is a novel, and to some a slightly unsettling, innovation. It has appealed to several modern architects, especially for sports stadiums and grandstands. Others are membrane structures, either cable-hung or inflatable (membranes are made of teflon-coated fibreglass and other such materials), concrete shells, and the structural use of toughened glass.

More often variety is achieved either by devising new ways of using existing techniques and materials, or by the deliberate manipulation of historical styles to provoke new reactions. In the Financial Times Building, London (1988), Nicholas Grimshaw, within the parameters of High Tech, saw the possibility of making the familiar steel-and-glass box one vast, unified, transparent space, displaying the printing presses inside like installation art. Terry Farrell, also in High-Tech mode, confounds expectation by a sudden disruption of logic in the centre of the TVam Building, London (1980). In Paris, Jean Nouvel has taken High Tech into new regions of the imagination in his Institut du Monde Arabe (1987), a steel-and-glass building that explores ideas of access and

428. For Jean Nouvel High Tech is a means to an end and that end is ultimately poetic. His Institut du Monde Arabe in Paris (1987) combines the clarity of International Modernism (nearly all steel and glass) with a highly individual spatial imagination alluding to such features as the Islamic pierced screen.

impenetrability. In his later Galeries Lafayette in Berlin (1990) he constructs an iridescent glass interior which seems to rise and descend into infinite heights and depths.

In Europe, the years from the late 1960s onwards have produced a series of extreme, even eccentric, initiatives which have been given generic titles by their practitioners or critics, each provided with its own programme, theory or credo – Populism, Neo-Rigorism, Critical Regionalism, etc. – few of which seem likely to stick. If these tell us nothing else, however, they do convey a sense of the disparity of styles into which architecture has plunged. It has been an age of constant experiment. Ralph Erskine built the Byker Wall, Newcastle (1968), a housing estate in the form of undulating lines of eight- or nine-storey blocks, blank and intimidating on the outer side, intimate and welcoming on the inner. Richard Meier, who has in some ways inherited Mies's mantle, combining stylistic flair with commercial success, has applied his refined modular system to a variety of commissions, including the Museum for Decorative Arts, Frankfurt (1979). Meier, who has been called a 'Neo-Purist', stands opposed to Post-Modernism in all its forms, and still marches under the banner of clarity and logic. Rafael Moneo's Museo Nacional de Arte Romana, Mérida, Spain (1980), brilliantly matched style and content by its

unequivocally modern invocation of the Roman past. Hans Hollein's Neue Haus Haas, Vienna (1985), a big shopping complex opposite the Cathedral, also builds, literally, on Roman foundations, but confounds expectations by its self-conscious avoidance of finality. Paul Chemetov and Borja Huidobro built the Ministry of Economy and Finance, Paris (1982), in the form of a 'horizontal skyscraper' spanning an eight-lane highway... The fruits of these experiments lie in the future rather than the present.

Stylistic novelty is easier than technological to track, though sometimes harder to analyse. The boldest of those who have appropriated (or should we say plundered?) the classical heritage is Ricardo Bofill. A Spaniard working also in France, he has designed public-housing developments at St Quentin-en-Yvelines (1974), Marne-la-Vallée (1978), and elsewhere consisting of vast classical colonnades, exaggeratedly, impossibly, Roman, which, he says, 'reconstruct the collective unconscious'. In America Charles Moore has been (at least once) equally enamoured of the ancient world (Piazza d'Italia, New Orleans, 1974). More unusually, Paolo Portoghesi, an architectural historian as well as an architect, revived Baroque forms in his Casa Baldi in Rome (1959).

Lastly, scale. There are still architect-designed private houses, and they can sometimes encapsulate an architect's genius in a way that is not possible in a more public domain. The house that Gropius designed for himself outside Boston (1938), for instance, is full of intimate and ingenious touches and subtle spatial ideas reflecting the personality of its owner. At other times, one cannot help feeling, the more eccentric the patron the happier the architect, because only on this small scale can theoretical issues be directly explored. Michael Graves's Benaceraf House, Princeton, New Jersey (1969), deconstructs the concept 'house' into its semantic elements, so that 'the syntax calls attention to itself'. Clotet and Tusquets's Georgina Belvedere at Gerona, Spain (1971), puts the bedroom on the ground floor and the garage on the roof, all surrounded by double-height piers supporting a trellis. 'The syncopation of verticals is masterful,' we are told, 'the layering of space a surprise, the contrast of meanings a delight.' It cannot be easy to live in. Peter Eisenman's houses are the most extreme of all, including, for instance, such features as staircases that lead nowhere: 'He brushes aside the client's expectations in order to criticize them.'

More often the problem is one of bigness. Architects, or teams of architects, are now being required to design buildings as large as towns, or towns under the guise of buildings. The Italian Paolo

429

429. The classical orders return, hugely magnified as if in a dream, in Ricardo Bofill's Espaces d'Abraxas, a block of social housing at Marne-la-Vallée, France (1978).

430. At the centre of London's
Docklands stands Canary Wharf
(initial design 1985, modified
after 1988), exemplifying a worldwide phenomenon, the large-
scale development on a cleared
site, with buildings in all styles
thrown together in a mêlée that
can be seen optimistically as a
vision of the future. Supervising
architects are Skidmore, Owings
and Merrill; the tower – the tallest
in Britain to date, and visible from
central London – is by Cesar Pelli.

Soleri has specialized in ideas for 'arcologies' ('architecture' + 'ecology') for up to six million inhabitants. The only one actually realized is his Arcosanti in Arizona (begun 1972) for a mere 1,500, a sort of space-age fantasy come true. Comparable to it in some ways (not ideologically) is Walt Disney World, Florida, where a whole range of buildings, including two huge Post-Modern hotels by Michael Graves, do indeed create a 'world' of their own. In Britain the nearest equivalent is the subsidized development of Docklands, in east London, an architectural free-for-all covering many square miles, centring on Canary Wharf (1985 onwards), 430 a collection of buildings exemplifying every fashionable and contemporary style, masterminded by the firm of Skidmore, Owings and Merrill and dominated by a tall skyscraper by Cesar Pelli with a squat pyramidal roof and gleaming stainless steel surface.

Also larger than conventional single buildings are commissions like new towns, university campuses and airports, schemes that create their own micro-environment, demanding skills in town-planning and landscaping. Rockefeller Center, New York (1930–40), was an early example of this. In a sense James Stirling's very influential Staatsgalerie at Stuttgart (1977) belongs to this category, since it reveals itself gradually as a sequence of spaces – 431 ramps, platforms, domes open to the sky. At a more formal level Ed Jones and Michael Kirkland's Mississauga Civic Center (1982) consists of several interrelated buildings, their forms playing with historical allusions (pediments, rotundas, etc.).

431. James Stirling's Staatsgalerie at Stuttgart (1977) was an architectural landmark because it rediscovered ways of manipulating space that could be applied on any scale, using a variety of textures, changes of level and unexpected vistas.

432. The Grande Arche de la Défense, Paris, by Johann Otto von Spreckelsen (competition winner in 1982) and Paul Andreu, completed in 1989. It was intended by President Mitterand to make a bold modern statement on the axis of the Arc de Triomphe, but has not succeeded in winning popular favour as his predecessor's Pompidou Centre has.

In France a custom has grown up whereby each president sets his mark on Paris by a *'grand projet'*. The Centre Pompidou was one. Others are the Grande Arche de la Défense by Johann Otto von Spreckelsen and Paul Andreu (completed 1989), not an arch at all but a huge post-and-lintel structure containing offices; the steel-and-glass pyramid forming the new entrance to the Louvre by I. M. Pei (1993); the Parc de la Villette, begun by Bernard Tschumi in the late '70s on the site of an abandoned abattoir, consisting of a museum and sundry small buildings and sculptures, a sort of avant-garde Disneyland; and the new Bibliothèque Nationale de France by Dominique Perrault (opened 1996), a quadrangle with four L-shaped towers at the corners and a sunken forest in the middle.

432

Present dilemmas
There is always a temptation in surveys of this kind to choose the exceptional and eccentric examples at the expense of the typical and the run-of-the-mill. But the innovations described above do quite rapidly seep down to the high street and the market-place, if only in diluted form.

Possibly the most crucial development of recent years is one that has nothing to do with engineering or construction, but purely with the process of design. This is the computer. It is now comparatively easy to generate graphics of which the mathematics (constant changes of scale, proportion, dimensions, curvatures, etc.) are so complicated that they would have been virtually impossible to draw by the old method. It is to the computer rather than to any technical advances that we owe the extraordinary shapes and apparent defiance of structural logic of such architects as Zaha Hadid, Daniel Libeskind and Frank Gehry.

One very noticeable development in modern Western cities, though not in the rest of the world, has been the virtual disappearance of the high-rise building (flagship of the International Modern style) except for prestige office blocks. As a solution to mass housing it proved a costly failure, for both practical and social reasons. This is just one instance of architecture being subjected to pressures that did not apply in the past, and of architects being forced to shoulder heavier and heavier responsibilities. Planning laws and safety regulations are more demanding than ever before. Dozens of technical aspects (access, circulation, car parking, waste disposal) are delegated to teams of experts. Modern buildings use huge amounts of energy (for maintenance, heating, air-conditioning, etc.) and a whole new discipline of 'green architecture' has arisen to minimize such consumption.

'Cabined, cribbed, confined' as he is by all these considerations, it is a matter for surprise that the architect is still so evidently in control, and that buildings are not as faceless and depersonalized as computers. Whatever else architecture has become, it remains an art, a unique expression of visual and spatial experience and a unique source of both instinctual and intellectual pleasure.

433

433. Nearly all buildings can be given an architectural pedigree, but at present it seems impossible to provide one for Frank Gehry's Guggenheim Museum at Bilbao, opened in 1998. Clad in shining titanium, its forms are said to have been suggested by 20th-century painting, especially Picasso, and 'envisioned' by semi-automatic drawing.

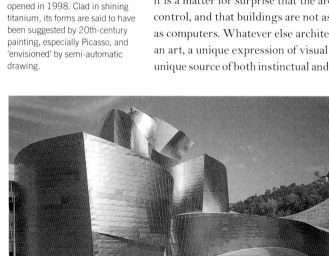

Glossary

abacus Stone slab between the **capital** and **entablature**. See fig. 2.

aisle In a **basilican** building, a passage between the **arcade** and the outside wall.

ambulatory A semicircular **aisle**, the passage round the **east end** of a church between the **arcade** and the outside wall.

apse/apsidal Part of a building that is semicircular in plan.

arcade A series of **arches**. See fig. 1.

arch Masonry construction, curved in outline, spanning an opening. See fig. 1.

> **diaphragm arch** Masonry arch spanning an interior space of which the roof is wood.
> **horseshoe arch** Arch narrowing at the bottom like a horseshoe.
> **quadrant arch** A half-arch, a quarter of a circle.
> **stilted arch** An arch raised on elongated straight sides.

architrave The lowest element of a classical **entablature**.

ashlar Smooth, squared stone masonry.

Baroque A style prevalent in Europe and Latin America in the 17th and 18th centuries. See p. 168.

base The lowest part of a classical **order** supporting a column. See fig. 2.

basilica (1) Architecturally, a building with an **arcade**, **aisles** and **clearstorey**, i.e. consisting of a central vessel flanked by **aisles** and defined by **arcades**, above which rise walls containing windows. (2) Ecclesiastically, a Roman Catholic church of a certain status.

bay A single compartment of a building, defined by the placing of windows or, especially in a church, the space between one **pier** or column and the next.

blind arch/arcade An **arch** or series of arches against a solid wall. See fig. 1.

capital Element derived from classical architecture that forms the top part of a column, standing between the column or **pier** and what it supports. See fig. 2.

caryatid Support in the form of a female figure.

cella The main enclosed room of a Greek or Roman temple.

centering Temporary wooden support for an arch or rib during the process of building.

centralized/centrally planned Said of a building whose plan is symmetrical in all four directions.

chancel The easternmost part of a church, reserved for the clergy, where the altar is situated; by extension, the eastern arm.

choir That part of a church near the **chancel**, where the choir sit; by extension, the eastern arm.

Churrigueresque Style popular in Spain in the 18th century, named after the Churriguera family. See p. 201.

clearstorey The upper part of a **basilica**, the wall above the **arcade** containing windows. See fig. 1.

cloister A courtyard surrounded by an open **arcade**.

coffer/coffering Sunk panels in a ceiling or **vault**.

Composite A classical **order** combining **Corinthian** and **Ionic**. See fig. 2.

console A **corbel** in the form of a scroll.

corbel A stone bracket.

Corinthian A classical **order** characterized by its acanthus-leaf **capital**. See fig. 2.

cornice The top projecting section of a classical **entablature**; by extension, a continuous projection along the top of a building. See fig. 2.

crocket A medieval ornament consisting of a spur-like projection.

crossing The space where the four arms of a cruciform church meet.

Decorated A phase of English **Gothic**, c. 1280–1350. See p. 94.

diaphragm arch See **arch**.

Doric One of the **orders** of Greek architecture, marked by a plain moulded **capital** and the absence of a **base**. In Roman Doric a base is added. See fig. 2.

Early English A phase of English **Gothic**, c. 1170–1280. See p. 90.

east end Term conventionally used for the altar end of a church, even when the church is orientated differently.

egg-and-dart Classical ornament in which these two motifs alternate.

elevation A representation of the vertical dimension of a building.

entablature In classical architecture, the horizontal layer (composed of **architrave**, **frieze** and **cornice**) above the columns. A Doric entablature includes **metopes** and **triglyphs**. See fig. 2.

entasis The slight swelling in the middle and narrowing towards the top of a classical column, most noticeable in **Doric**.

exedra A very large niche.

fan vault See **vault**.

Flamboyant Last phase of French **Gothic**, prevalent in the 15th and 16th centuries. See p. 96.

flute/fluting Parallel vertical grooves in a column or **pilaster**. See fig. 2.

flying buttress A form of buttress consisting of a half-arch meeting the thrust of a **vault**. See fig. 1.

frieze The central element of a classical **entablature**.

gallery An enclosed upper space opening to the exterior or into a larger interior. In a medieval church, the storey above the **arcade**. See fig. 1.

giant order An **order** of columns extending through two or more storeys.

Gothic The architectural style of medieval Europe c. 1150–1550. See p. 74.

Greek cross A cross with four equal arms.

groin vault See **vault**.

guttae Rows of stone studs on the underside of a classical **entablature**. See fig. 2.

hall-church A church of which the **aisles** are as tall, or nearly as tall, as the central vessel.

hammerbeam A type of timber roof in which the beams rest on brackets projecting from the wall.

horseshoe arch See **arch**.

Ionic One of the **orders** of classical architecture, characterized by its **volute capitals**. See fig. 2.

lantern A glazed vertical feature on a roof or the apex of a dome to admit light.

Latin cross A cross of which one arm is longer than the other three.

lierne A subsidiary vaulting rib connecting two other ribs.

lintel A horizontal slab over a door or window.

loggia A roofed space with an open **arcade** on one or more sides.

longitudinal Of a plan, longer in one direction than another; the opposite of **centralized**.

lunette A window or recess in the shape of a half-circle.

metope Part of a **Doric frieze**; a section, usually carved in relief, that alternates with **triglyphs**. See fig. 2.

mezzanine A subsidiary storey inserted between two major ones.

moulding A decorative profile, either projecting or incised.

narthex A vestibule or porch attached to the front of a church.

nave The part of a church west of the **crossing** or **chancel**, where the congregation assembles.

ogee A double curve, like an elongated letter S.

orders The categories into which classical architecture has been divided, defined chiefly by the column and its **capital**. See p. 13 and fig. 2.

Figure 1

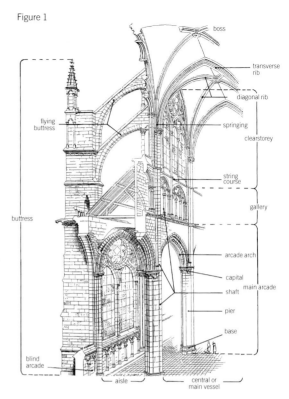

Figure 2

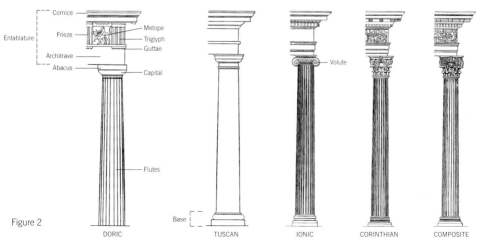

DORIC   TUSCAN   IONIC   CORINTHIAN   COMPOSITE

pediment A triangular feature crowning a building (or on a smaller scale a door- or window-opening), originally corresponding to the gable end of a roof.

pendant vault See **vault**.

pendentive A triangular fragment of a sphere, serving to support the circular ring of a dome on a square or polygonal lower structure.

peristyle A row of columns surrounding a building on all sides.

Perpendicular A phase of English **Gothic**, c. 1330–1550. See p. 97.

pier A free-standing masonry support usually for an **arch**. See fig. 1.

pilaster A flattened version of a column set against a wall.

Plateresque A style popular in Renaissance Spain, characterized by lavish ornament. See p. 164.

quadrant arch/vault See **arch**, **vault**.

quadripartite vault See **vault**.

Rayonnant Phase of French **Gothic**, 13th and 14th centuries. See p. 87.

reredos (Spanish *retablo*) A carved or painted back, behind and above an altar.

rib vault See **vault**.

ridge rib Rib running along the apex of a **vault**, normally longitudinal but can also be transverse.

Rococo Late **Baroque** style, prevalent in the 18th century. See p. 185.

Romanesque Style of European architecture prevalent in the early Middle Ages, c. 1000–1200, using the forms of Roman architecture. See p. 43.

rustication Leaving blocks of masonry in a rough state, as if straight from the quarry.

section The representation of a building as if sliced through.

sexpartite vault See **vault**.

springing Point at which an arch or vault leaves the wall or vertical support. See fig. 1.

stilted arch See **arch**.

string-course A continuous horizontal **moulding**. See fig. 1.

stylobate Platform on which a classical temple rests.

tabernacle Classical frame around a window or niche consisting of a pair of columns and a **pediment**.

tie-rod/beam An iron rod or wooden beam placed between two walls or supports to prevent them from leaning outwards.

tierceron Vaulting rib additional to the diagonal ribs, which goes from the **springing** to a **ridge rib**.

transept An 'arm' of a cruciform church, at right angles to **nave** and **chancel**.

transverse arch/rib An **arch** or vaulting rib across a space at right angles to the walls.

triforium Open wall-passage above the **arcade** of a Gothic church, sometimes used synonymously with **gallery**. See p. 81.

triglyph Part of the **Doric entablature** consisting of a panel with three vertical grooves. See fig. 2.

tunnel vault See **vault**.

Tuscan One of the classical **orders**, added to the Greek originals. It resembles Roman **Doric**, but has a simpler capital and is unfluted. See fig. 2.

tympanum Semicircular space above a doorway between the **lintel** and the **arch**.

vault An arched masonry ceiling. See fig. 3.

fan vault A tunnel vault shaped into inverted cones and half-cones and carved with a pattern of ribs.

groin vault A vault formed by the meeting of two tunnel vaults at right angles, the surfaces forming a sharp edge (groin).

pendant vault The most elaborate form of fan vault, where the cones or ornamental shapes seem to hang from the ceiling.

quadrant vault Half a tunnel vault.

rib vault Vault in which the edges (groins) are reinforced by a **moulding**, the rib. The commonest kinds of rib vault are: **quadripartite**, with four ribs meeting at the centre of a bay; **sexpartite**, with six ribs meeting at the centre of a bay; **tierceron**, a quadripartite vault with extra ribs starting from the **springing** (see **tierceron**); lierne, a tierceron vault with short extra ribs connecting other ribs (see **lierne**).

tunnel vault A continuous vault, either semicircular or pointed in section.

volute A spiral **moulding**, the characterizing feature of the **Ionic capital**. See fig. 2.

west end/front The term conventionally used for the entrance front of a church, even when it faces another direction.

westwork A tower-like feature characteristic of Carolingian, Ottonian and German **Romanesque** churches, built at the **west end** and containing rooms opening onto the **nave**.

Figure 3

Tunnel vault

Groin vault

Quadripartite vault

Tierceron vault

Sexpartite vault

Further Reading

General

Fletcher, B., *A History of Architecture*, 20th edn, London, 1996

Kostoff, S., *A History of Architecture*, Oxford/New York, 1985

Pevsner, N., *An Outline of European Architecture*, Harmondsworth/Baltimore, 1943 (numerous later edns)

Watkin, D., *A History of Western Architecture*, London, 1986

Countries

The following contain useful material relating to all periods:

Britain: Kidson, P., P. Murray and P. Thompson, *A History of English Architecture*, Harmondsworth, 1965

Watkin, D., *English Architecture*, London, 1979

France: Lavedan, P., *French Architecture*, Harmondsworth, 1956

Russia: Brumfield, W. L., *A History of Russian Architecture*, Cambridge, 1993

Hamilton, G. H., *The Art and Architecture of Russia*, Harmondsworth/Baltimore, 1954

Spain: Bevan, B., *History of Spanish Architecture*, London, 1938

USA: Whiffen, M., and E. Koeper, *American Architecture, 1607–1976*, Boston/London, 1981

Architects

Biographies and studies of individual architects are too numerous to be included in this list, but can be found in the bibliographies following the entries in A. K. Placzek (ed.), *Macmillan Encyclopaedia of Architects*, London/New York, 1982

Greece and Rome

Berve, H., C. Gruben and M. Hirmer, *Greek Temples, Theatres and Shrines*, London, 1963

Brown, T. E., *Roman Architecture*, New York, 1961

Coulton, J. J., *Ancient Greek Architects at Work*, London, 1977

Dinsmoor, W. B., *The Architecture of Ancient Greece*, 3rd edn, New York, 1975

Lawrence, A. W., *Greek Architecture*, 5th edn, London/New Haven, 1996

MacDonald, W. I., *The Architecture of the Roman Empire*, New Haven, 1986

Plommer, W. H., *Ancient Greek Architecture*, London, 1956

Sear, F., *Roman Architecture*, London, 1989

Ward-Perkins, J. B., *Roman Imperial Architecture*, Harmondsworth, 1981

Early Christian and Byzantine

Krautheimer, R., *Early Christian and Byzantine Architecture*, Harmondsworth/Baltimore, 1965

Mainstone, R., *Hagia Sophia: Architecture, Structure and Liturgy*, London, 1980

Mango, C., *Byzantine Architecture*, London, 1978

Carolingian and Romanesque

Clapham, A. W., *Romanesque Architecture in Western Europe*, Oxford, 1936

Conant, K. J., *Carolingian and Romanesque Architecture*, Harmondsworth/Baltimore, 1959

Gothic

Acland, J. H., *The Gothic Vault*, Toronto, 1972

Bony, J., *French Gothic Architecture of the 12th and 13th Centuries*, Berkeley/London, 1983

Fitchen, J., *The Construction of Gothic Cathedrals*, Oxford, 1901

Frankel, P., *Gothic Architecture*, Harmondsworth/Baltimore, 1972

Gimpel, J., *The Cathedral Builders*, London, 1983

Grodecki, L., *Gothic Architecture*, London, 1986

Harvey, J., *The Cathedrals of Spain*, London, 1957

— *The Medieval Architect*, London, 1972

Webb, G. F., *Architecture in Britain in the Middle Ages*, Harmondsworth/Baltimore, 1965

White, J., *Art and Architecture in Italy, 1250–1400*, Harmondsworth/Baltimore, 1966

Wilson, C., *The Gothic Cathedral*, London/New York, 1990

Renaissance

Bialostocki, J., *The Art of the Renaissance in Eastern Europe*, London/New York, 1971

Blunt, A., *Art and Architecture in France, 1500–1700*, Harmondsworth/Baltimore, 1953

Burckhardt, J., *The Architecture of the Italian Renaissance*, trans., London, 1985

Heydenreich, L., *Architecture in Italy, 1400–1500*, New Haven/London, 1996

Hitchcock, H.-R., *German Renaissance Architecture*, Princeton, 1981

Lotz, W., *Architecture in Italy, 1500–1600*, New Haven/London, 1995

Murray, P., *The Architecture of the Italian Renaissance*, London/New York, 1989

Summerson, J., *Architecture in Britain, 1530–1830*, New Haven/London, 1993

Baroque

Blunt, A. (ed), *Baroque and Rococo*, London/New York, 1978

Downes, K., *English Baroque Architecture*, London, 1966

Hempel, E., *Baroque Art and Architecture in Central Europe*, Harmondsworth/Baltimore, 1965

Kubler, G., and M. Soria, *Art and Architecture in Spain and Portugal, 1500–1800*, Harmondsworth/Baltimore, 1959

Lees-Milne, J., *Baroque in Spain and Portugal*, London, 1960

Norberg-Schulz, C., *Baroque Architecture*, London/New York, 1972

— *Later Baroque and Rococo Architecture*, London/New York, 1974

Wittkower, R., *Art and Architecture in Italy, 1600–1750*, 3rd rev. edn, Harmondsworth/Baltimore, 1980

Neoclassical

Braham, A., *The Architecture of the French Enlightenment*, London, 1980

Crook J. M., *The Greek Revival*, London, 1972

Kaufmann, E., *Architecture in the Age of Reason*, New York, 1955

Kennedy, R. G., *Greek Revival in America*, New York, 1989

Kalnein, W. von, *Architecture in France to the Eighteenth Century*, New Haven/London, 1995

Stillman, D., *English Neo-Classical Architecture*, London, 1988

Watkin, D., and T. Mellinghoff, *German Architecture and the Classical Ideal, 1740–1840*, London, 1987

Nineteenth Century

Dixon, R., and S. Muthesius, *Victorian Architecture*, London/New York, 1978

Hitchcock, H.-R., *Architecture: 19th and 20th Centuries*, Harmondsworth/Baltimore, 1958

Middleton, R., and D. Watkin, *Neoclassical and Nineteenth Century Architecture*, London/New York, 1980

Mignot, C., *Architecture of the 19th Century in Europe*, New York, 1984

Russell, F., *Art Nouveau Architecture*, London, 1979

Twentieth Century

Banham, R., *Theory and Design in the First Machine Age*, London, 1972

Benevolo, L., *History of Modern Architecture*, London, 1971

Collins, P., *Changing Ideals in Modern Architecture*, London, 1985

Frampton, K., *Modern Architecture, A Critical History*, 3rd edn, London/New York, 1992

Jencks, C., *Modern Movements in Architecture*, Harmondsworth, 1988

— *Post-Modern Architecture*, London/New York, 1987

Kidder Smith, G. E., *The New Architecture of Europe*, Harmondsworth, 1962

Lampugnani, V. M., *Encyclopaedia of 20th Century Architecture*, London/New York, 1986

Richards, J. M., *The Functional Tradition in Early Industrial Buildings*, London, 1958

Sharp, D., *Twentieth-Century Architecture*, London/New York, 1991

Tafuri, M., and F. Dal Co, *Modern Architecture*, London/New York, 1980

Acknowledgments

This book has benefited from the comments of Andrew Saint, Robert Thorne, Michael Hall and Peter Howell, who kindly read the text at an early stage. From them I have stolen ideas and even whole sentences, with only minor twinges of guilt. My greatest debt, by a very long way, is to my dedicated dedicatee.

Illustration Credits

Index

Figures in *italic* type refer to illustration numbers

Aachen, Germany: Palatine Chapel 38, *26*
Aalto, Alvar (1898–1976) 324, *378*
Abadie, Paul (1812–84) 285
Abbeville, France: St Wulfran 96
Abbotsford, Scotland 272
Adam, Robert (1728–92) 224, 230, 238, 240, 241, 249, *277–80*
Adler, Dankmar (1844–1900) 314, *347*, *353, 365*
Admont abbey, Austria: library 191, *215*
Aegina, Greece: temple 13
Agrigento, Sicily: temples 14, 15, *5*
Alberti, Leon Battista (1404–72) 130–31, *144–45*
Albi, France: Cathedral 97, *97*
Alcalá, Spain: Bernardas church 200
Alfeld, Germany: Fagus Factory 320
Algarotti, Count Francesco 226
Almazán, Spain: S. Miguel 72, *70*
Amiens, France: Cathedral 80, 84, 87, *78, 83*
Amsterdam, Netherlands: Eigen Haard Estate 341, *400*; Railway Station 280; Rijksmuseum 280; Scheepvaarthuis 341, *399*; Spanish and Portuguese Synagogue 215; Stock Exchange 322, *374*
Ancy-le-Franc, France: château 162
Andreani, Aldo (1887–after 1945) 296
Andreu, Paul (b. 1938) 370
Anet, France: château 162
Angers, France: Cathedral 55, *48*; Hospital 119
Angoulême, France: Cathedral 55, *47*
Ani, Turkey: Cathedral 32
Annaberg, Germany: St Anne 102, *108*
Anthemius of Tralles (6th c.) 27
Antoine, Jacques-Denis (1733–1801) 227
Antuñes, João (*fl.* 1683–1734) 204
Antwerp, Belgium: Cathedral 104; St Charles Borromeo 213, *243*; Town Hall 156, *174*
Aranjuez, Spain: Palace 235; Casa del Labrador 244, *284*
Araujo, José Alvarez de (d. 1762) 204
Arbury Court, England 272
Arc-et-Senans, France 260–61, *301*
Archer, Thomas (1668–1743) 222, *252*
Arcosanti, Ariz., USA 369
Arens, Johann August (1757–1806) 244
Arlington, Va., USA: Lee Mansion 249
Arnold of Westphalia (15th c.) 103, 117
Arras, France: St Vaast 259
Arup, Ove (1895–1988) 363
Asam, Cosmas Damian (1686–1739) and Egid Quirin (1692–1750) 193, *220, 221*
Asfeld, France: St Didier 210, *241*
Aspendos, Turkey 20
Asplund, Gunnar (1885–1940) 324, *377*
Assisi, Italy: S. Francesco 105

Athens: Choragic Monument of Lysicrates 16, *249, 8*; Erechtheion 15, *6*; Hellenic Academy 239, *276*; Parthenon 13, *2*; Schinkel's designs for palace 266, *308*; Temple of Olympian Zeus 15; 'Theseion' (Temple of Hephaestos) 13, *3*; Tower of the Winds 16–17
Augsburg, Germany: St Anna 155; Rathaus 156
Autun, France: Cathedral 54, *44*
Averbode Abbey, Belgium 213
Avignon, France: Chapel of the Oratoire 211; Hôtel des Monnaies 210; Palace of the Popes 117
Ávila, Spain: S. Vicente 72; walls 113

Baalbek, Lebanon: Temple of Bacchus 17, *10*
Bähr, Georg (1666–1738) 168, *212*
Baillie Scott *see* Scott, M. H. Baillie
Baltard, Louis-Pierre (1764–1846) 237
Baltard, Victor (1805–74) 306
Baltimore, Md., USA: Roman Catholic Cathedral 257, *299*
Bamberg, Germany: Cathedral 48
Banz, Germany: abbey church 195, *225*
Barcelona, Spain: Casa Batlló 292, *339*; Casa Milá 292; Cathedral 111; Exhibition Pavilion 333; Palace of Catalan Music 292; Sagrada Familia 8, 292, *340*; S. Maria del Mar 111, *120*; Tinell 117, *130*
Barcelos, Portugal: Bom Jesus 204
Barfreston, England: church 63
Bari, Italy: S. Nicola 69
Barkhin, Grigory (1880–1969) 327
Barlow, W. H. (1812–1902) 311, *360*
Barry, Charles (1795–1860) 274, 289, *316, 335*
Bartning, Otto (1883–1959) 340, 363
Basel, Switzerland: Cathedral 48
Basevi, George (1794–1845) 250
Basile, Ernesto (1857–1932) 296
Bassae, Greece: temple 14, *4*
Bath, England: Abbey 89; Queen's Square 238
Baudot, Anatole de (1834–1915) 317
Bayreuth, Germany: court theatre 191, *214*; Festspielhaus 290
Beaumaris, Wales: castle 115, *128*
Beaune, France: Hospital 119
Beauvais, France: Cathedral 80, 82, 96, *80*
Beckford, William 271
Bedford, Francis (1784–1858) 259
Behrens, Peter (1868–1940) 317, 339, 395
Bélanger, François-Joseph (1744–1818) 227, 242
Bellver, Mallorca: castle 115
Bentley, J. F. (1839–1902) 285, *331*
Berg, Max (1870–1947) 317, *367*
Berlage, Hendrik (1856–1934) 322, *374*
Berlin: Altes Museum 232, 264, *265*; cinema on Kurfürstendamm 322; Dom 257; Friedrichwerderschekirche 266; Galeries Lafayette 366; Grosses Schauspielhaus 340, *396*; Monument to Karl Liebknecht and Rosa Luxemburg 340, *397*; Neue Wache 264, *306*;

Berlin, cont.
New National Gallery 354; Opera House 251; Philharmonie 337; St Hedwig 257; Schauspielhaus 264; Schloss 8; Siemensstadt Estate 320; Turbine Hall 339, *395*
Bernini, Gianlorenzo (1598–1680) 173, 175, *166, 195, 196, 197*
Bernward, Bishop 43
Berrecci, Bartolommeo (d. 1537) 154, *172*
Berwick-on-Tweed, England 151
Besançon, France: Theatre 261, *302*
Bethlehem, Israel: Church of the Nativity 24
Bexhill, England: De La Warr Pavilion 322, *372*
Bexleyheath, England: Red House 300
Bilbao, Spain: Guggenheim Museum 371, *433*
Bindesbøll, M. G. (1800–56) 250, *292*
Bishapur, Iran 27
Blacket, Edmund (1817–83) 278
Blaise Hamlet, England 228
Blanqui, Andrés (1677–1740) 204
Blenheim Palace, England 221–22, *254*
Blois, France: château 207
Blondel, Jacques-François (1705–74) 226
Böblinger, Matthäus (d. 1505) 72
Bodley, George Frederick (1827–1907) 277, *321*
Boffiy, Guillermo (15th c.) 111
Boffrand, Germain (1667–1754) 211
Bofill, Ricardo (b. 1939) 367
Bogardus, James (1800–74) 309
Böhm, Dominikus (1880–1955) 340, 363
Boileau, Louis-Auguste (1812–96) 272
Bologna, Italy: S. Petronio 105
Bombay, India: Victoria Railway Terminus 279
Bonomi, Joseph (1739–1808) 259
Bonomi, Joseph, Jnr (1796–1878) 268, *312*
Boppard, Germany 48
Bordeaux, France: Grand Théâtre 251, 286, *293*
Borromini, Francesco (1599–1667) 175–77, *198–200*
Bossan, Pierre (1814–88) 281, *324*
Bossi, Antonio 188
Boston, Mass., USA: King's Chapel 168, 223, *189*; Public Library 290; State House 237; Trinity Church 284, *330*
Boullée, Etienne-Louis (1728–99) 233, 267
Bourges, France: Cathedral 82, *71*; House of Jacques Coeur 121
Braga, Portugal: Bom Jesus 204, *232*
Bramante, Donato (1444–1514) 132–36, *146–49*
Brandon, David (1813–97) 284
Brasília, Brazil: Cathedral 336, *393*
Breslau *see* Wrocław
Breuer, Marcel (1902–81) 332, 358, *387*
Břevnov, Czech Republic: abbey church 195
Brighton, England: Pavilion 268, 304, *313*
Brisbane, Australia: Cathedral 278
Bristol, England: Bank of England 253; Cathedral 94, *95*
Brixworth, England: church 37

Brno, Czech Republic: Tugendhat House 333
Broadleys, Lake District, England 301, 349
Brodrick, Cuthbert (1822–1905) 289
Brongniart, A. T. (1739–1813) 237
Bruant, Libéral (c. 1635–97) 208
Bruchsal, Germany: Schloss 185, 210
Bruges, Belgium: Cloth Hall 121
Brühl, Germany: Schloss 185
Brunelleschi, Filippo (1377–1446) 126–30, 141–43
Brunswick, Germany: St Blasius 102, 107; Town Hall 121
Brussels: Grand' Place 215, 245; Notre Dame-du-Bon-Secours 213, 242; Palais de Justice 287, 334; Palais Stoclet 294, 343; Ste Marie 280; Tassel House 291, 337
Budapest, Hungary: Museum of Decorative Arts 297, 345
Buffalo, N.Y., USA: Guaranty Building 314, 353; Larkin Building 349
Bulfinch, Charles (1763–1844) 237
Bunning, J. B. (1802–63) 306
Bunshaft, Gordon (b. 1909) 335, 390
Buontalenti, Bernardo (1531–1608) 137, 150
Burges, William (1827–81) 275, 317
Burghley House, England 159
Burgos, Spain: Cathedral 109, 164, 117, 119
Burke, Edmund 228
Burlington, Richard Boyle, third Earl of 224, 229, 230
Burnham, Daniel H. (1846–1912) 313, 362, 363
Burton, Decimus (1800–81) 307, 356
Butterfield, William (1814–1900) 277, 278, 300, 318

Caen, France: La Trinité 57; St Etienne 57, 50, 51; St Pierre 97, 161
Caernarvon, Wales: Castle 115
Cahors, France: Cathedral 55
Calcutta, India: Victoria Memorial 279
Calderini, Guglielmo (1837–1916) 287
Cambridge, England: Fitzwilliam Museum 250; King's College Chapel 99, 101; Trinity College 219, 135, 250
Cambridge, Mass., USA: Harvard Memorial Hall 283, 326
Cameron, Charles (c. 1740–1812) 230, 246, 286
Camicia, Chimenti (1431–before 1505) 152
Campbell, Colen (1676–1729) 226, 229
Camporesi, Giuseppe (1763–1822) 249
Candela, Felix (b. 1910) 363
Canosa di Puglia, Italy 68
Canova, Antonio (1753–1819) 258, 300
Canterbury, England: Cathedral 63, 77, 79, 88, 89, 98, 87, 100
Caprarola, Italy: Villa Farnese 150
Carcassonne, France: walls 113, 126
Cardiff, Wales: Castle 275
Carlone, Carlo Antonio (d. 1708) 181
Casas y Navoa, Fernando de (d. 1794) 200, 230

Caserta, Italy: Palace 235, 270; Theatre 252
Castel del Monte, Italy 117, 129
Castell Coch, Wales 275
Castilho, João de (fl.1515–52) 167
Castle Hedingham, England 64, 60
Castle Howard, England 220, 221, 253
Cefalù, Sicily: Cathedral 70
Centula, France 40, 27
Chalgrin, J. F. T. (1739–1814) 254, 259, 287
Chambers, Sir William (1723–96) 237, 242, 268, 271, 282
Chambord, France: château 161, 180
Chandigarh, Punjab: Government Buildings 331, 384
Charleston, S. C., USA: Charleston Hotel 254; Nathaniel Russell House 249; Second Baptist Church 259
Charlottesville, Va., USA: University of Virginia 247, 289
Chartres, France: Cathedral 77, 80, 76
Chatsworth, England: Conservatory 307
Chelles, Jean de 84
Chemetov, Paul (b. 1928) 367
Chernigov, Russia: Cathedral of the Transfiguration 33
Chevakinski, S. I. (1713–83) 198
Chicago, Ill., USA: Auditorium Building 298, 313, 347; Brooks Building 313; Carson, Pirie and Scott Store 298, 348; Convention Hall 333; Crown Hall 333; Fisher Building 313; Glessner House 284; Illinois Institute of Technology 333; Lake Shore Drive Apartements 333, 388; Leiter Buildings 314; Marina City 332; Marquette Building 313; Marshall Field Wholesale Store 284, 329; Monadnock Building 313, 362; Oak Park 302, 349; Old Colony Building 313; Pontiac Building 313; Reliance Building 313, 363; Robie House 303, 352; Rookery Building 313; Tribune Tower 315, 362
Chochol, Josef (1880–1956) 343
Churriguera family 201, 202
Ciudad Rodrigo, Spain 72
Clotet, Lluis (b. 1941) 367
Cluny, France: abbey church 51, 40
Coalbrookdale, England: iron bridge 304, 354
Coates, Wells (1895–1958) 322
Cobergher, Wenceslas (16th–17th c.) 213
Coca, Spain: castle 117
Cockerell, C. R. (1788–1863) 250, 253
Codussi, Mauro (c. 1440–1504) 143
Coimbra, Portugal: university library 183
Cola da Caprarola 154
Cologne, Germany: Cathedral 8, 84, 101, 279, 105, 106; Great St Martin 47; Holy Apostles 47, 34; Rathaus 155; St Gereon 47; Werkbund Theatre 339, 394
Como, Italy: Casa del Fascio 323, 375; S. Abbondio 65
Connell, Amyas (1900–80) 322
Conques, France: Ste Foy 49, 38, 39

Constantinople: Hagia Sophia 27, 29, 16; Holy Apostles 30; St Irene 29; St John of Studion 26; SS. Sergius and Bacchus 29, 30, 17
Contamin, Victor (1840–93) 317
Contant d'Ivry, Pierre (1698–1777) 259
Contini, Giovanni Battista (1641–1723) 201
Conway Castle, Wales 115
Copenhagen: Amalienborg 238; Grundvig Church 343, 401; Danish National Bank 354; Police Headquarters 324; Thorvaldsen Museum 250, 292; Vor Frue Church 259
Coppedè, Gino (1866–1927) 296
Cordemoy, Abbé de 226
Córdoba, Argentina: Cathedral 204
Cortona, Pietro da (1596–1669) 173, 194
Corvey, Germany: abbey church 41, 29
Courtvriendt, Jan 213, 242
Coutances, France: Cathedral 80, 82, 79
Cracow, Poland: Cathedral, Sigismund Chapel 154, 172; Wawel Castle 154
Cragg, John (1767–1854) 304
Cram, Ralph Adams (1863–1942) 283, 327
Cubitt, Lewis (1799–1883) 311, 361
Culzean Castle, Scotland 240
Cumberland, William (1821–88) 278
Cuvilliés, François (1695–1768) 188, 191, 211
Cuypers, P. J. H. (1827–1921) 280
Cuzco, Peru: Cathedral 167

Dance, George (1741–1825) 254
Danzig see Gdańsk
Darby, Abraham (1750–89) 304, 354
Darmstadt, Germany: Ludwigskirche 258; Wedding Tower 339
Deane, Thomas (1792–1871) 306, 355
Deerhurst, England: church 37
Delamonce, Ferdinand (1678–1753) 211
Delorme, Philibert (c. 1510–70) 161, 162
Dessau, Germany: Bauhaus 320, 374
Didyma, Turkey: Temple of Apollo 15
Dientzenhofer, Georg (1643–89) 192
Dientzenhofer, Johann (1663–1726) 195, 225
Dietterlin, Wendel (c. 1550–99) 156
Dijon, France: St Bénigne 41
Domènech i Montaner, Lluís (1850–1923) 292
Domenico da Cortona (1470?–1549?) 181
Domenig, Günther (b. 1934) 361
Dornach, Switzerland: Goetheanum 340
Downton Castle, England 228
Dresden, Germany: Art Gallery 289, 213; Frauenkirche 168, 212; Hoftheater 289, 336; Zwinger 188, 213
Dublin, Ireland: Catholic Pro-Cathedral 259; Custom House 237; Four Courts 237, 272; Marino Casino 242, 282; US Embassy 357, 421
Duc, Louis-Joseph (1802–79) 286
Dudok, Willem Marinus (1884–1974) 318, 323
Duquesney, F. A. (1790–1849) 287

Durand, Jean-Nicolas-Louis (1760–1834) 227

Durham, England: Cathedral 61, 63, 93, *54, 55, 58*

Du Ry, S. L. (1726–99) 249

Dutert, C. L. F. (1845–1906) 317

Edinburgh, Scotland: Episcopal Cathedral 276; National Gallery of Scotland 250; New Town 238; Royal High School 254, *296*

Eidlitz, Leopold (1823–1908) 268

Einsiedeln, Switzerland: abbey 192

Eisenman, Peter (b. 1932) 363, 367

Ellis, Peter (1804–84) 309, *359*

Elmes, Harvey Lonsdale (1814–47) 237, 273

Ely, England: Cathedral 63, 89, 94, *94*

Emerson, William (1833–1917) 279

Emo, Villa, Italy 147, *163*

Ephesus, Turkey: Temple of Artemis 13; St John 29

Epidaurus, Greece: theatre 16, *7*

Erskine, Ralph (b. 1914) 366

Eschwege, Baron Wilhelm Ludwig (1777–1855) 275

Escorial, Spain 166, *187*

Esztergom, Hungary: Cathedral, Bakócz Chapel 152, *169*

Exeter, England: Cathedral *93*

Eyndes, Jean van der (*fl.* 17th c.) 213

Fallingwater, Pa., USA 349, *408*

Farrell, Terry (b. 1938) 365

Faydherbe, Lucas (1617–97) 213

Ferstel, Heinrich (1828–83) 279

Figueroa, Leonardo de (*c.* 1650–1730) 201

Finsterlin, Hermann (1887–1973) 341, 363

Fioravanti, Aristotele (1415?–1486?) 153

Fischer von Erlach, Johann Bernhard (1656–1723) 181–83, *207, 208*

Flagg, Ernest (1857–1947) 315

Florence, Italy: Cathedral 105, 126, 128, *113, 142*; Foundling Hospital 129, *143*; Palazzo Medici 131; Palazzo Rucellai 130, *145*; Palazzo Vecchio 121; Pazzi Chapel 129; Railway Station 344; S. Lorenzo 129, (Laurentian Library) 139, *152*, (Medici Chapel) 136, 139, *151*; S. Maria degli Angeli 129; S. Maria Novella 130; S. Miniato al Monte 67, *63*; S. Spirito 129, *141*; S. Stefano 137; Uffizi 137, *150*

Floris, Cornelis (1514–75) 155, 156, *174*

Fontaine, Pierre-François (1762–1853) 234

Fontainebleau, France: château 162

Fontana, Carlo (1638–1714) 201, 222

Fontana, Paolo Antonio (1696–1765) 198, *226*

Fontenay, France: abbey church 53, *42*

Fonthill Abbey, England 228, 271, *259*

Fort Worth, Tex., USA: Kimbell Art Museum 358

Foster, Sir Norman (b. 1935) 357, *417, 418*

Fountains Abbey, England 119

Fowke, Francis (1823–65) 289

Fowler, Charles (1791–1867) 306

Frankfurt, Germany: Hoechst Dyeworks 339; Museum for Decorative Arts 366

Freiburg-im-Breisgau, Germany: church 101, *104*

Frielingsdorf, Germany: church 340

Fuga, Ferdinando (1699–1781) 254

Fuller, Thomas (1822–98) 278

Furness, Frank (1839–1912) 283

Gabriel, Ange-Jacques (1698–1782) 211, 238, 242, 252, 275, *281*

Galli-Bibiena, Giuseppe (1695–1747) and Carlo (1728–87) 191, *214*

Gandon, James (1742–1823) 237, *272*

Garnier, Charles (1825–98) 286, *332*

Gärtner, Friedrich von (1792–1847) 284

Gau, Franz Christian (1790–1853) 281, *311*

Gaudí, Antoni (1852–1926) 8, 292, *339, 340*

Gdańsk (Danzig), Poland 123, *140*; St Mary 103, *111*

Gehry, Frank (b. 1929) 371, *433*

Gelfreich, Vladimir (1885–1967) 346

Gentz, Heinrich (1766–1811) 232

Geoffrey de Noiers (late 12th c.) 91

Germigny-des-Prés, France: chapel 38

Gernrode, Germany: abbey church 41

Gerona, Spain: Cathedral 111, *122*; Georgina Belvedere 367

Gervase of Canterbury 79, 88

Ghent, Belgium: St Peter 213

Gibberd, Frederick (b. 1908) 351

Gibbs, James (1682–1754) 222–23, *255, 256*

Gilbert, Cass (1859–1934) 315, 366

Gilly, Friedrich (1772–1800) 233, 268

Giulio Romano (*c.* 1499–1546) 139, *153*

Glasgow, Scotland: Caledonia Road Free Church 267, *310*; double villa 266; Jamaica Street Warehouse 309; Moray Place 266, *309*; Queen's Park Church 267; St Vincent Street Church 267; School of Art 297, *344*

Gloucester, England: Cathedral 62, 89, 97, 57, 98

Gočar, Josef (1880–1945) 343

Goldberg, Bertrand (b. 1913) 332

Goldfinger, Erno (1902–87) 358

Gondoin, Jacques (1737–1818) 227

Göttweig, Austria: monastery 191, *217*

Gračanica, Serbia 33, *22*

Granada, Spain: Cathedral 165, *185*; Charterhouse 202, 231; Palace of Charles V 165, *184*

Graves, Michael (b. 1934) 361, 367, 369, *416*

Great Packington, England: church 259

Greene, G. T. (*fl.* 1850–64) 309, *358*

Greene and Greene (Charles S., 1868–1957, and Henry M., 1870–1954) 302, *351*

Greenwich, England: Hospital 219; Queen's House 161, *179*

Grimshaw, Nicholas (b. 1939) 365

Grippius, K. K. 268

Gripsholm, Sweden: castle 252

Gropius, Walter (1883–1969) 318–21, 367, *369, 370*

Guadalajara, Spain: Cathedral 167

Guarini, Guarino (1624–83) 179, 201, 210, *203–04*

Guimard, Hector (1867–1942) 291

Haarlem, Netherlands: Nieuwe Kirk 215

Hadfield, George (1763–1826) 249

Hadid, Zaha (b. 1950) 371

Haga, Sweden 244, *285*

The Hague, Netherlands: Mauritshuis 215, *244*

Halifax, England: All Souls 276

Halle, Germany: Marktkirche 102

Hamburg, Germany: Chilehaus 340; Nicolaikirche 277

Hamilton, Thomas (1784–1858) 254, *296*

Hampton Court Palace, England 157, 219, 249

Hansen, Christian Frederik (1746–1845) 259

Hansen, Theophil von (1813–91) 237, 239, 276

Hardouin-Mansart, Jules (1646–1708) 208, *238, 239*

Hardwick Hall, England 159

Hardwick, Philip (1792–1870) 254

Harlech, Wales: Castle 113, 115

Harrison, Peter (1716–75) 223, *189*

Hasenauer, Carl von (1833–94) 289

Hauberisser, Georg (1841–1922) 275

Hawksmoor, Nicholas (1661–1736) 168, 220, 271, *251*

Hayberger, Gotthard (1695–1764) 191, *215*

Heidelberg, Germany: Castle 155, 156, *173*

Helsinki, Finland: Railway Station 324; Senate Square 239; Telephone Company Building 298, *346*

Hennebique, François (1842–1921) 317

Henry of Reyns (13th c.) 93

Héré, Emmanuel (1705–63) 211

Herrera, Juan de (1530–97) 166, 167, *187*

Het Loo, Netherlands 215

Hildebrandt, Lukas von (1668–1745) 181, 184, 191, *209, 217*

Hildesheim, Germany: St Michael 42–43

Hilversum, Netherlands 323

Hiorne, Francis (1744–89) 272

Hittorff, Jacques-Ignace (1792–1867) 239, 259

Hoar Cross, England: church 277, *321*

Hoffmann, Josef (1870–1956) 294, *343*

Höger, Fritz (1877–1949) 340

Holabird, William (1854–1923) 313

Holkham Hall, England 230, *261*

Holl, Elias (1573–1646) 156

Holland, Henry (1745–1806) 252

Hollein, Hans (b. 1934) 361, 362, 367

Hong Kong: Hong Kong and Shanghai Bank *418*

Hood, Raymond (1881–1934) 315, 322

Hopper, Thomas (1776–1856) 304

Horta, Victor (1861–1947) 291, 337

Howells, John Mead (1868–1959) 315

Hübsch, Heinrich (1795–1863) 268, 279

Huidobro, Borja (b. 1928) 367
Huis ten Bosch, Netherlands 215
Hunstanton, England: School 335, *391*
Hunt, Richard Morris (1827–95) 290
Hurtado, Francisco (1669–1725) 201
Huyssens, Pieter (1577–1637) 213, *243*

Ingolstadt, Germany: St Mary 102
Inwood, W. (1771–1843) and H. W.
  (1794–1843) 259
Ipswich, England: Willis Faber Dumas
  Building 357, *417*
Iranistan, USA 268
Isidore of Miletus (6th c.) 27
Istanbul *see* Constantinople

Jaca, Spain: Cathedral 72
Jackson, Miss., USA: Governor's
  Mansion 249
Jacobsen, Arne (1902–71) 354
Jaén, Spain: Cathedral 165
Jank, Christian (1833–80) 275
Japelli, Giuseppe (1783–1852) 254, 272
Jay, William (*c.* 1793–1837) 249
Jefferson, Thomas (1743–1826) 230,
  246–47, *263*, 288, 289
Jenney, William Le Baron (1832–1907)
  314, *364*
Jerusalem, Israel: Church of the Holy
  Sepulchre 24, 42, 73
Johansen, John M. (b. 1916) 357, *421*
Johnson, Philip (b. 1906) 334, 361, *390*
Jones, Ed 369
Jones, Inigo (1573–1652) 156, 159–61,
  229, *178–79*
Juan de Colonia (15th c.) 109
Jujol, Josep Maria (1879–1949) 292
Jumièges, France: abbey church 57
Juvarra, Filippo (1678–1736) 180, *205*

Kahn, Louis (1901–74) 358, *423*
Kampmann, Hack (1856–1920) 324
Karlsruhe, Germany: apartment buildings
  320
Kassel, Germany: Museum
  Fridericianum 249
Kedleston, England 240, 277
Kent, William (1685–1748) 230, *261*
Kew, England 268; Palm House 307, *356*
Kiev, Russia: Hagia Sophia 33
Kirby Hall, England 159, *177*
Kirkland, Michael 369
Kladruby, Czech Republic: abbey church
  195, 271, *222*
Kleihues, Josef Paul (b. 1933) 362
Klenze, Leo von (1784–1864) 232, 250,
  266, *291*
Klerk, Michael de (1884–1923) 341–43,
  400
Klimontów, Poland: church 198
Klint, Peter Jensen (1853–1930) 343, *401*
Knight, John Payne 228
Knöbelsdorf, Georg Wenzeslaus von
  (1699–1753) 251, 257
Krak des Chevaliers, Syria 115
Kramer, Piet (1881–1961) 341–43, *400*
Krier, Leon (b. 1946) 362
Kuen, Hans Georg (1642–91) 192

Labrouste, Henri (1801–75) 287, *333*
Laeken, Belgium: Notre Dame 280
La Jolla, Calif., USA: Jonas Salk Institute
  358, *423*
Lamego, Portugal 204
Landshut, Germany: Stadtresidenz 155
Laon, France: Cathedral 80, 84, *81*
Lasdun, Sir Denys (b. 1914) 358
Lassus, Jean-Baptiste (1807–57) 281
La Tourette, France: monastery 331
Latrobe, Benjamin (1764–1820) 257,
  299
Laugier, Abbé Marc-Antoine 226
Laurana, Luciano (*c.* 1425–79) 131, 132
Le Camus de Mézières, Nicolas 227, *258*
Lechner, Ödön (1845–1914) 297, *345*
Le Corbusier (Charles-Edouard Jeanneret,
  1887–1965) 318, 328–31, *382–85*
Ledoux, Claude-Nicolas (1736–1806) 8,
  233, 260–62, *301–03*
Leeds, England: Corn Exchange 289;
  Marshall's Mill 268, *312*; Town Hall
  289
Lefuel, H.-M. (1810–80) 287
Legrand, Jacques-Guillaume
  (1753–1809) 227, 251, *258*
Lemercier, Jacques (*c.* 1582–1654) 205,
  235
Le Muet, Pierre (1591–1669) 207, *235*
L'Enfant, Pierre Charles (1754–1825)
  239
Le Nôtre, André (1613–1700) 207
León, Spain: Cathedral 107, *118*;
  S. Isidore 72
Leptis Magna, Libya 20, 22
Lérida, Spain: Cathedral 72, 119
Lescot, Pierre (*c.* 1515–78) 163, *182*
Lethaby, W. R. (1857–1931) 301
Leuven (Louvain), Belgium: Town Hall
  121; St Michael 213
Le Vau, Louis (1612–70) 207, 208, *236*,
  237
Libeskind, Daniel (b. 1946) 371
Lima, Peru: Cathedral 167
Limburg-an-der-Lahn, Germany: abbey
  church 47
Lincoln, England: Cathedral 91, 93, *89*,
  90
Lincoln, Mass., USA: Gropius House 367
Lisbon, Portugal: Belém monastery *124*
Liverpool, England: Anglican Cathedral
  278, *322*; Bank of England 253; Catholic
  Cathedral 351, *412*; Oriel Chambers
  309, *359*; Rickman churches 304; St
  George's Hall 237, 273
Ljubljana, Slovenia: Chamber of Trade,
  Industry and Commerce 353; St
  Francis 353; St Michael 353; Sluice
  Gates 353, *415*; University Library
  353, *414*; Žale Cemetery 353
Lodoli, Carlo 226
London, England: Adelphi Terrace 241;
  Albert Hall 289; Albert Memorial 287;
  Bank of England 262–63, *304*;
  Banqueting House 159, *178*; British
  Museum 250, 290; Canary Wharf 369,
  430; Carlton House 304; Centre
  Point 358; Coal Exchange 306;

London, cont.
  Covent Garden Theatre 252; Crystal
  Palace 308–09, *357*; Drury Lane
  Theatre 252; Dulwich College Art
  Gallery 263; Euston Station 254;
  Financial Times Building 365; Fitzroy
  Square 238; Home House 242, *280*;
  Houses of Parliament 274, *316*;
  Hungerford Market 306; Kenwood 241,
  279; King's Cross Station 311, *361*;
  Law Courts 277; Lawn Road Flats 322;
  Lloyds Building 357, *420*; National
  Theatre 358; Natural History Museum
  284; Newgate Prison 254; Osterley
  House 241; Reform Club 289, *335*;
  Regent's Park terraces 238; St Pancras
  Station 311, 360, (Midland Grand
  Hotel) 276, *319*; Sir John Soane's
  house, Lincoln's Inn Fields 263, *305*;
  Somerset House (old) 159, (new) 237,
  271; Syon House 241; Tower of
  London 64; Travellers' Club 289;
  TVam building 365; US Embassy 357;
  Victoria and Albert Museum 289;
  Westminster Hall 64, 117, *131*
  CHURCHES: All Saints, Margaret Street
  277, *318*; Christ Church, Spitalfields
  220, *251*; Christ Church, Streatham,
  284; Queen's Chapel, St James's 161;
  St Benet Fink 216; St George's,
  Bloomsbury 220; St James the Less
  277, *320*; St John's, Smith Square 222;
  St John's, Waterloo 259; St Martin-in-
  the-Fields 223, *255*; St Mary, Abchurch
  216; St Mary Aldermary 271; St Mary-
  le-Strand 223; St Pancras 259; St Paul's
  Cathedral (old) 161, (new) 216, *246–47*;
  St Paul's, Covent Garden 161; St Paul's,
  Deptford 222, 252; St Stephen's Chapel,
  Westminster 86; St Stephen, Walbrook
  216, *248*; St Swithin, Cannon Street
  216; St Vedast, Foster Lane 216;
  Westminster Abbey 84, 93, 99, 271, *92*,
  102; Westminster Cathedral 285, *331*
Longhena, Baldassare (*c.* 1599–1682) 178,
  202
Longhi, Martino (1602–60) 171, *192*
Longleat House, England 157, *176*
Loos, Adolf (1870–1933) 294, 318, 319,
  362, 368
Lorsch, Germany: monastery 38
Los Angeles, Calif., USA: Gamble House,
  Pasadena 302, *351*; Getty Museum
  362; Lovell House 332, *386*
Loscher, Sebastian (d. 1548) 155
Louis, Victor (1731–1800) 251, 286, *293*
Louvain *see* Leuven
Lubartów, Poland: St Anne 198, *226*
Lubetkin, Berthold (1901–90) 322
Lucca, Italy 67, 151, *168*
Ludovice, J. F. (1670–1752) 204
Lunéville, France: abbey 211
Lurago, Carlo (1615–84) 181
Lutyens, Sir Edwin (1869–1944) 301–02,
  351, *350*, *410–12*
Lyons, France: Notre Dame de Fourvière
  281, *324*; Opera House 251; Palais de
  Justice 237; St Bruno 211

Machuca, Pedro (1485?–1550) 165, *184*
Mackintosh, Charles Rennie (1868–1928) 296–97, *344*
Mackmurdo, A. H. (1851–1942) 301
Maderno, Carlo (*c.* 1556–1629) 172, *193*
Madrid, Spain: Hospicio de S. Fernando 202; Prado 249
Mafra, Portugal: monastery 204
Mainz, Germany: Cathedral 46, *32*; City Hall 354
Maisons, France: château 207
Málaga, Spain: Cathedral 165
Malbork (Marienburg), Poland 115, 117, *127*
Manchester, England: Town Hall 275
Mansart, François (1598–1666) 207, *234*, *235*
Mantua, Italy: Casa del Commercio 296; Palazzo del Tè 139, *153*; S. Andrea 130; S. Sebastiano 130
Maria Laach, Germany 47, *35*
Marienburg *see* Malbork
Marne-la-Vallée, France: housing 367
Marot, Daniel (1661–1752) 215
Marseilles, France: Cathedral 281; Unité d'Habitation 329, *383*; Vieille Charité 211
Masreliez, Louis-Adrien (1748–1810) *285*
Matthew of Arras (14th c.) 99
Maulbronn, Germany: monastery 119, *132*
McKim, Charles Follen (1847–1909) 290, 346, *406*
Mead, William Rutherford (1846–1928) 290, 346, *406*
Mechelen (Malines), Belgium: Cathedral 104; Our Lady of Hanswijk 213
Meier, Richard (b. 1934) 366
Meissen, Germany: Albrechtsburg 117
Melbourne, Australia: Cathedral 278; Rialto Building 279
Melk, Austria: monastery 191, *216*
Melnikov, Konstantin (1890–1974) 327, *380*
Mendelsohn, Erich (1887–1953) 318, 322, 340, *372*, *398*
Mengoni, Giuseppe (1829–77) 306
Mereworth Castle, England 229
Merguete, José Gonzáles 204
Mérida, Spain: Cathedral 167; Museo Nacional de Arte Romana 366
Merlini, Domenico (1730–97) 244, *283*
Mexico City: Cathedral 167; Church of the Miraculous Virgin 363; Sagrario Metropolitano 204
Meyer, Adolf (1881–1929) 318, 369
Michelangelo Buonarroti (1475–1564) 136–39, 141, 149, *151–52*, *165–67*
Michelozzo Michelozzi (1396–1472) 131
Michelucci, Giovanni (1891–1990) 344
Mies van der Rohe, Ludwig (1886–1969) 318, 321, 333–35, 340, 354, 361, *388*, *389*, *397*
Milan, Italy: Cathedral 106–07, *115–16*; Galleria Vittorio 306; Pirelli Building 335, *392*; S. Ambrogio 65, *61*; S. Lorenzo 24; S. Maria delle Grazie 132; S. Maria presso S. Satiro 132

Mills, Robert (1781–1855) 258
Minkus, Mikhail 346
Mississauga, Ont., Canada: Civic Center 369
Mistra, Greece: Hodeghetria 32, *21*
Molfetta, Italy: Cathedral 69
Molinos, Jacques (1743–1831) 227, 251, *258*
Moller, Georg (1784–1852) 258
Moneo, Rafael (b. 1937) 366
Monreale, Sicily: Cathedral 69, 70, *66*
Montepulciano, Italy: Madonna di S. Biagio 140
Montferrand, Ricard de (1786–1858) 257
Monticello, Va., USA 246, *288*
Moore, Charles (1925–94) 367
Moore, Temple (1856–1920) 277
Moosbrugger, Caspar (1656–1723) 192
Morey, Mathieu-Prosper (1805–86) 281
Morris, William 300
Moscow: Cathedral of Christ the Redeemer 285; Cathedral of the Dormition 153; Cathedral of St Michael 153, *170*; Convent of the Ascension 272; Izvestiya Building 327; Lenin Mausoleum 327, *381*; Melnikov House 327; Ministry of Foreign Affairs 346, *405*; Palace of the Soviets project 344; Peslov Tea House 268; Rusakov Club 327, *380*; Ryabushinsky House 291, *338*; Underground (Metro) 344, *402*
Moszynski, Count Augustus (1731–86) 198
Mount Airey, Va., USA 223
Munich: Alte Pinakothek 250; Amalienburg 186, *211*; Glyptothek 250; Haus der Kunst 346, *404*; Ludwigskirche 284; Mariahilfkirche 280; Residenztheater 191; St John Nepomuk 193, *221*; St Michael 156
Muthesius, Hermann (1861–1927) 300

Nancy, France: town plan 211; St Epvre 281
Nantes, France: St Nicolas 281
Naples, Italy: Albergo dei Poveri 254; S. Carlo Opera House 252
Nash, John (1752–1837) 228, 238, 268, 304, *313*
Nasoni, Niccolò (1691–1773) 204
Natchez, Miss., USA: Lyman Harding House 249
Neresheim, Germany: church 192
Nerezi, Serbia: church 33
Nervi, Pier Luigi (1891–1979) 336, *392*, *425*
Neuerberg, Norman (1927–97) 362
Neuf-Brisach, France 151
Neumann, Balthasar (1687–1753) 184, 188, 192, *188*, *210*
Neuschwanstein Castle, Germany 275
Neutra, Richard (1892–1970) 332, *386*
Nevers, France: St Etienne 54
Newby Hall, England 249
Newcastle, England: Byker Wall 366

New Delhi, India: Viceroy's House 351, *410*
New Haven, Conn., USA: Harkness Memorial Tower 283, *328*; School of Art and Architecture 358, *422*; Yale Center for British Art 358
New Orleans, La., USA: Garden District 247; Piazza d'Italia 367
New York, USA: AT&T Building 361, *424*; Bogardus stores 309; Chrysler Building 322, *373*; Guggenheim Museum 349, *409*; Lever House 335, *389*; McGraw-Hill Building 322; Municipal Building 346, *406*; Pennsylvania Station 290; Rockefeller Center 369; St John the Divine 283, *327*; St Patrick's Cathedral 279, 281, *325*; Seagram Building 334, *390*; Singer Building 315; Trinity Church 281; TWA Terminal 363, *426*; Whitney Museum of American Art 332, *387*; Woolworth Building 315, *366*
Niccolini, Antonio (1772–1850) 252
Nice, France: St Pons 211
Niemeyer, Oscar (b. 1907) 336, *393*
Nîmes, France: Maison Carrée 17, 230, 9; Pont du Gard 22
Nonsuch Palace, England 157
Norwich, England: Cathedral 89
Nouvel, Jean (b. 1945) 365, *428*
Novgorod, Russia 33
Nuremberg, Germany 101, 123

Oak Park, Ill., USA 302, 349
Ocotlán, Mexico: Sanctuary 200, *229*
Ohlmüller, Joseph Daniel (1791–1839) 280
Olbrich, Joseph Maria (1867–1908) 294, 337, 339
Orange, France 20
Orcival, France: church 49
Orford, England: Castle 77
Orgaz, Spain 202
Orléans, France: Cathedral 271
Östberg, Ragnar (1866–1945) 324, *376*
Ostia, Italy 22
Ottawa, Canada: Parliament Buildings 278
Ottery St Mary, England: church 102
Oud, J. J. P. (1890–1963) 318, 323, 341
Ouro Preto, Brazil: Rosano Chapel 204
Outram, John (b. 1934) 364, *427*
Oviedo, Spain: S. Julián de los Prados 37; S. Maria de Naranco 37, *24*
Oxford, England: Ashmolean Museum 250; Christ Church 219, 271; Keble College 277; Radcliffe Camera 223, *256*; University Museum 306, *355*

Padua, Italy: Caffè Pedrocchi 272; meat market 254
Paestum, Italy: temples 13, 14, *1*
Paimio, Finland: sanatorium 324
Paine, James (1717–89) 242
Palermo, Sicily: Martorana 70; Palatine Chapel 69, *67*; S. Cataldo 70; S. Giovanni degli Eremiti 70; La Zisa 70

Palladio, Andrea (1508–80) 143–47, 159, 171, 229, 230, 160–64, 190
Palma de Mallorca, Spain: Cathedral 111, 121
Palmanova, Italy 151
Palmsted, Erik (1741–1803) 252
Palmyra, Syria 22
Pamplona, Spain: Cathedral 71
Paray-le-Monial, France: abbey church 53, 43
Paris, France: Arc de Triomphe 254, 287; barrières 8, 261, 303; Bibliothèque Nationale (old) 287, (new) 370; Bibliothèque Ste Geneviève 287, 333; Bourse 237; Centre Pompidou 357, 419; Ecole des Beaux-Arts 227; Ecole de Médecine 227; Eiffel Tower 317; Gare de l'Est 287; Grande Arche de la Défense 370, 432; Halles, Les 306; Halle au Blé 227, 258; Halle des Machines 317; Hôtel de Cluny 20, 121; Hôtel de la Monnaie 227; Hôtel de Soubise 211; Institut du Monde Arabe 365, 428; Louvre 163, 175, 208–09, 287, 370, 163, 197, 240; Madrid, Château de 161; Ministry of Economy and Finance 367; Opéra 286, 332; Palais de Justice 286; Parc de la Villette 370; Place de la Concorde 238, 275; Place des Vosges 163; rue Franklin flats 321, 371; Salpêtrière 208; Sorbonne 207; Théâtre des Champs-Elysées 322; Théâtre Feydeau 251; Tuileries 162 CHURCHES: Invalides 208, 239; Madeleine 230, 258, 264; Notre Dame 80, 87, 75, 84; Panthéon (Ste Geneviève) 227, 255, 257, 297–98; Sacré Cœur 285; Sainte Chapelle 86, 96, 85; Ste Clotilde 279, 281, 311; St Eugène 272; St Eustache 161, 181; St Gervais 205; St Jean-de-Montmartre 317; Ste Marie-de-la-Visitation 207, 234; St Paul-St Louis 205; St Philippe-du-Roule 259; St Vincent-de-Paul 259; Val de Grâce 207, 235
Parler, Peter (c. 1330–99) 99, 102
Passau, Germany: Cathedral 181
Patte, Pierre 227
Pavia, Italy: Cathedral 132; Certosa 147, 161
Paxton, Joseph (1803–65) 307–08, 357
Pearson, John Loughborough (1817–97) 277, 278
Pei, I. M. (b. 1917) 370
Pelli, Cesar (b. 1926) 369
Percier, Charles (1764–1838) 234
Périgueux, France: St Front 55
Perrault, Claude (1613–88) 208, 226, 240
Perrault, Dominique (b. 1955) 370
Perret, Auguste (1874–1954) 318, 321–22, 371
Persius, Ludwig (1803–45) 268, 284
Perth, Australia: His Majesty's Hotel and Theatre 279
Peruzzi, Baldassare (1481–1536) 140, 149, 155
Peterborough, England: Cathedral 58, 53

Philadelphia, Pa., USA: Alfred Newton Richards Medical Research Building 358; Episcopal Cathedral 283; Merchants' Exchange 253, 294
Piano, Renzo (b. 1937) 357, 419
Pienza, Italy 131
Pierrefonds, France: château 275
Pirna, Germany: church 102
Pisa, Italy: Cathedral 67, 64
Pitt, William (1855–1918) 279
Pittsburgh, Pa., USA: Allegheny County Courthouse 284
Playfair, W. H. (1790–1857) 250
Plaza, Sebastián de la (fl. 1617–30) 200
Plečnik, Jože (1872–1957) 9, 294, 352–53, 361, 413–15
Poblet, Spain: monastery 119, 133
Poelaert, Joseph (1817–79) 280, 287, 334
Poelzig, Hans (1869–1936) 339–40, 396
Poitiers, France: Notre Dame-la-Grande 55; Palace of the Counts 117
Pommersfelden, Germany: Schloss 184, 209
Pompeii, Italy 19, 22
Ponti, Gio (1891–1979) 335, 392
Pontigny, France: church 53, 41
Pope, John Russell (1874–1937) 346
Pöppelmann, Daniel Mathaeus (1662–1736) 188, 213
Porta, Giacomo della (1533–1602) 156, 171, 191
Portland, Ore., USA: Public Services Building 361, 416
Porto, Portugal: Clérigos church 204
Portoghesi, Paolo (b. 1931) 367
Possagno, Italy: church 258, 300
Post, Pieter (1608–69) 215
Potsdam, Germany: Charlottenhof 264; Einstein Tower 340, 398; Friedenskirche 284; Pumping Station 268; Roman Baths 265, 307; Sans Souci 188; Schloss Babelsberg 266; Schloss Glienicke 264; Schloss Tegel 264
Poznań (Posen), Poland 340
Prague, Czech Republic: Castle 102, 352, 109, 171; Cathedral 99, 103; Church of the Sacred Heart 353, 413; Clam-Galas Palace 184; House of the Black Virgin 343; Hvezda Castle 154; Villa Belvedere 154
Prandtauer, Jakob (1658–1726) 191, 216
Prato, Italy: S. Maria delle Carceri 131
Price, Bruce (1845–1903) 278
Priego de Córdoba, Spain 203, 233
Primaticcio, Francesco (1594–70) 161, 162
Princeton, N.J., USA: Benaceraf House 367
Prior, E. S. (1852–1932) 277
Pritchard, Thomas Farnolls (1723–77) 304, 354
Prunner, Johann Michael (1669–1739) 192, 424
Puebla, Mexico: Cathedral 167
Puget, Pierre (1620–94) 211
Pugin, Augustus Welby Northmore (1812–52) 273, 315, 316
Puig i Cadafalch, Josep (1867–1957) 292

Qalat Siman, Syria 24
Quarenghi, Giacomo (1744–1817) 252
Quebec, Canada: Château Frontenac Hotel 278
Quedlinburg, Germany 41
Queluz, Portugal 204

Racconigi, Italy 244
Racine, Wis., USA: S. C. Johnson Wax Building 349
Le Raincy: Notre Dame 322
Rajhrad, Czech Republic: abbey church 195
Raphael (1483–1520) 139, 149
Raschdorf, Julius (1823–1914) 257
Rastrelli, Bartolommeo (1700–71) 34, 198, 227, 228
Ravenna, Italy: S. Apollinare Nuovo 36, S. Vitale 30, 19
Regensburg, Germany: St Jakob 48; Walhalla 232, 266
Reichardt, Charles H. 254
Reichenau, Germany 41
Reichensperger, August 279
Reims, France: Cathedral 80, 84, 86, 77, 82
Remagen, Germany: Apollinariskirche 280
Renwick, James (1818–95) 281, 325
Ribera, Pedro de (c. 1683–1742) 202
Richardson, Henry Hobson (1838–86) 284, 311, 329, 330
Richmond, Va., USA: Monumental Church 258; State Capitol 230, 263
Rickman, Thomas (1776–1841) 304
Ried, Benedikt (1454–1534) 102, 153, 109, 171
Riedel, Edouard (1813–85) 275
Rimini, Italy: S. Francesco (Tempio Malatestiano) 130, 290, 144
Ripoll, Spain: monastery church 71, 68
River Forest, Ill., USA: Winslow House 303
Rivolta d'Adda, Italy: S. Sigismondo 67
Roche, Martin (1853–1927) 313
Rodriguez, Lorenzo (c. 1704–74) 204
Rogers, James Gamble (1867–1947) 283, 328
Rogers, Sir Richard (b. 1933) 357, 419–20
Rohr, Germany: church 193
Roman, Jacob (1650–1715) 215
Rome, Italy: Arch of Constantine 22; Basilica of Maxentius 18, 12; Basilica of Trajan 19, 24; Baths of Caracalla 19, 290; Baths of Diocletian 10, 19; Campidoglio 149, 167; Casa Baldi 367; Colosseum 21, 13; Coppedè district 296; EUR buildings 344; House of Raphael 183, 134, 148; Market of Trajan 22; Palazzo della Cancelleria 132; Palazzo Farnese 140; Palazzo di Giustizia 287; Palazzo Massimo alle Colonne 140, 155; Pantheon 18, 11; Piazza del Popolo 177; Piazza S. Ignazio 177; Piazza S. Pietro 175, 196; Spanish Steps 177, 201; 'Temple of Minerva Medica' 26; Vatican (Belvedere Courtyard) 133, 135,

Rome, cont.
(Museo Pio-Clementino) 249; Victor Emmanuel Monument 287; Villa Giulia 150; Villa Madama 139 CHURCHES: Gesù 150, *191*; S. Andrea al Quirinale 173, *195*; S. Anna dei Palafrenieri 150; S. Carlo alle Quattro Fontane 175, *198–99*; S. Clemente 68, *65*; S. Eligio degli Orefici 139; S. Filippo Neri 176; S. Ivo della Sapienza 176, *200*; St John Lateran 24; S. Maria in Cosmedin 68; S. Maria Maggiore 24, *15*; S. Maria della Pace 133, 173, *146*, *194*; S. Maria in Via Lata 173; SS. Martina e Luca 173; St Paul without the Walls 26; St Peter's (old) 24, *14*, (new) 135, 149, 172, 173, *149*, 165, *166*; S. Sabina 26; S. Susanna 172, *193*; SS. Vincenzo ed Anastasio 171, *192*; Tempietto, S. Pietro in Montorio 133–34, *147*
Ronchamp, France: Chapel 331, *385*
Rondelet, Jean-Baptiste 227, 228
Root, John Wellborn (1850–91) 313, *362*, *363*
Rossellino, Bernardo (1409–64) 131
Rossi, Karl I. (1775–1849) 239
Rosso Fiorentino 161
Rotterdam, Netherlands: housing 318, 323, 341–42
Rouen, France: St Maclou 77, 96; St Ouen 96
Rudolph, Paul (b. 1918) 358, *422*
Rueda, Spain: church 202

Saarinen, Eero (1910–61) 358, 363, *426*
Saarinen, Eliel (1873–1950) 324
Sabratha, Libya 20
Sacconi, Giuseppe (1854–1905) 287
Saffron Walden, England: church 99
St Denis, France: abbey 79, 87, *74*, (Bourbon Mausoleum) 207, (Valois Mausoleum) 162
St Florian, Austria: abbey 181
St Gall, Switzerland: library 191; monastic plan 41, *28*
St Gilles-du-Gard, France 54, *46*
St John's, Newfoundland: Cathedral 278
St Louis, Mo., USA: Wainwright Building 314, *365*
S. Maria de Lebeña, Spain 70
S. Pere de Roda, Spain 70
St Petersburg, Russia 239; Admiralty 237, *257*; apartment blocks 327, *403*; Exchange 253, *295*; Hermitage theatre 252; New Hermitage Museum 250, *291*; Palace Square 239; Pravda Building 327; St Isaac's Cathedral 257; St Nicholas 198; Smolny Convent 34, 198, 228; Tsarskoe Selo 198, 246, *286*; Winter Palace 198, 227
St Quentin-en-Yvelines, France: housing 367
St Savin-sur-Gartempe, France: church 55
Salamanca, Spain: Cathedral 72, 73, 164; Plaza Major 202; S. Sebastián 202; University 165, *183*

Salisbury, England: Cathedral 92, *91*
Salonika, Greece: St Demetrius 26
Salzburg, Austria: Cathedral 181; Schloss Mirabell 184
Sanfelice, Ferdinando (1675–1750) 178
Sangallo, Antonio da, the Elder (1453–1534) 140
Sangallo, Antonio da, the Younger (1484–1546) 140, 149
Sangallo, Giuliano da (1443–1516) 131
Sanmicheli, Michele (1484–1559) 141, *157*
San Rafael, Calif., USA: Marin County Administrative Building 349, *407*
Sansovino, Jacopo (1486–1570) 143, *158*, *159*
Santo Domingo, West Indies 167
Sant'Elia, Antonio (1888–1916) 318
Santiago de Compostela, Spain 49, 200, 36, *230*
Santiago de Peñalba, Spain 70
Santini-Aichel, Johann (1677–1723) 9, 195, 271, *222–24*
Sarvistan, Iran 27
Savannah, Ga., USA: Archibald Bulloch House 249
Säynätsalo, Finland: Town Hall 324
Scamozzi, Vincenzo (1548–1616) 159
Scarborough, England: Grand Hotel 289
Scharoun, Hans (1893–1972) 336–37
Scherpenheuvel, Belgium 213
Schinkel, Karl Friedrich (1781–1841) 232, 264–66, 272, *frontis.*, *265*, *306–08*
Schmidt, Friedrich (1825–91) 275, 279, *323*
Schwäbisch Gmund, Germany: church 101
Scott, George Gilbert (1811–78) 276, 278, 287, *319*
Scott, Giles Gilbert (1880–1960) 278, *322*
Scott, M. H. Baillie (1865–1945) 301
Scott, Sir Walter 271–72
Sedlec, Czech Republic: abbey church 195, 271
Segesta, Sicily: temple 14
Segovia, Spain: Cathedral 164
Seifert, Richard (b. 1910) 358
Semper, Gottfried (1803–79) 289, 290, 352, *213*, *336*
Sent, Laurentius Muretto de 198
Seo de Urgel, Spain 71
Serlio, Sebastiano (1475–1555) 137, 157, 159, 161, 162
Seville, Spain: Cathedral 111, *123*
Shaw, Richard Norman (1831–1912) 301
Shchuko, B. A. (1878–1939) 344, *403*
Shchusev, Alexei (1873–1949) 327, *381*
Sheerness, England: boat-store 9, 309, *358*
Shekhtel, Fyodor (1859–1926) 291, *338*
s'Hertogenbosch, Netherlands: St John 105, *112*
Shobdon, England: church 272
Shrewsbury, England: Marshall, Benyon and Bage mill 304; St Chad 258
Shute, John 157
Siena, Italy: Cathedral 105; Palazzo Pubblico 121, *136*

Siloé, Diego de (c. 1495–1563) 165, 167, *185*
Simón de Colonia (15th c.) 109, 119
Simonetti, M. (1724–81) 249
Sintra, Portugal 275
Skidmore, Owings and Merrill 335, 369, *389*
Smirke, Robert (1781–1867) 250, 252, *290*
Smithson, Alison (1928–93) and Peter (b. 1923) 335, *391*
Smythson, Robert (c. 1535–1614) 157, *175*
Soane, Sir John (1753–1837) 262–63, *304–05*
Solari, Pietro 153
Solari, Santino (1576–1646) 181
Soleri, Paolo (b. 1919) 367–69
Sommaruga, Giuseppe (1867–1917) 296
Sonck, Lars (1870–1956) 297, *346*
Sonning, England: Deanery Garden 301, *350*
Soufflot, Jacques-Germain (1713–80) 227, 251, 255–57, 297, *298*
Specchi, Alessandro (1668–1729) 177, *201*
Speer, Albert (1905–81) 346
Speeth, Peter (1772–1831) 234, *269*
Spence, Sir Basil (1907–76) 358
Speyer, Germany: Cathedral 44–46, 25, *31*
Split, Croatia: Palace of Diocletian 22, 230
Spreckelsen, Johann Otto von (1929–87) 370
Springfield, Ill., USA: Dana House 303
Stadl Paura, Austria: church 192, *218*
Stalpaert, Daniel (1615–76) 215
Stansted, England: airport 357
Steiner, Rudolf (1861–1925) 340
Steinhausen, Germany: church 192
Stella, Paolo della (c. 1450–93) 154
Steuart, George (c. 1730–1806) 257
Stevens, F. W. (1848–1900) 279
Stirling, Sir James (1926–94) 369
Stockholm: Central Library 324, *377*; Town Hall 324, *376*; Woodland Cemetery 324
Stolzenfels, Germany: Schloss 272
Stone, Edward Durrell (1902–78) 358
Stowe, England 240, *278*
Strawberry Hill, England 271, *314*
Street, George Edmund (1824–81) 277, 300, *320*
Strickland, William (1788–1854) 253, *294*
Stuttgart, Germany: Staatsgalerie 369, *431*; Weissenhof Siedlung 333
Suger, Abbot 79
Sullivan, Louis (1856–1924) 298, 311, 313, 314, *347*, *348*, *353*, 365
Sydney, Australia: Opera House 363, *425*

Tahamatsu, Japan: Kugawa Prefectural Office Building 336
Taliesin East and West, USA 349
Tange, Kenzo (b. 1913) 336, 337
Tarnopól, Poland: church 198
Tarragona, Spain: Cathedral 72
Tatlin, Vladimir (1885–1953) 318, 327, *379*

Taut, Bruno (1880–1938) 341
Taylor, Sir Robert (1714–88) 242
Tempelman, Olof (1745–1816) 246, 285
Terragni, Giuseppe (1904–43) 323, 375
Tetbury, England: church 272
Tewkesbury, England: Abbey 62, 56
Thiepval Arch, France 351, 411
Thomon, Thomas de (1754–1813) 253, 295
Thomson, Alexander (1817–75) 266–67, 309–10
Timgad, Algeria 22
Tivoli, Italy: Hadrian's Villa 22
Todi, Italy: S. Maria della Consolazione 140, 154
Toledo, Juan Bautista de (d. 1567) 166
Toledo, Spain: Cathedral 107–09, 201
Tomar, Portugal: Conceição Chapel 167; Cristo Monastery 112, 167, 125, 186; Templar church 73
Tomé, Narciso (fl. 1715–42) 201
Tonson, Md., USA: Tilt Showroom 361
Toro, Spain: S. Maria 73, 69
Torralva, Diogo de (1500–66) 167, 186
Toulouse, France: St Sernin 49, 37
Tournai, Belgium: Cathedral 47
Tournus, France: St Philibert 42, 30
Tours, France: St Martin 37
Trani, Italy: S. Francesco 69
Trier, Germany: Porta Nigra 22
Troost, Paul Ludwig (1878–1934) 346, 404
Troyes, France: St Urbain 87, 86
Tschumi, Bernard (b. 1944) 370
Turin, Italy: Cathedral, Chapel of the Holy Shroud 179, 203; Palazzo Carignano 179; Palazzo Madama 180; S. Lorenzo 179, 204; Stupinigi 180; Superga 180, 205
Turner, Richard (1798–1881) 307, 356
Tuscaloosa, Ala., USA: William Cochrane House 247, 287
Tusquets, Oscar (b. 1941) 367

Ulm, Germany: Minster 101, 72
Upjohn, Richard (1802–78) 281
Urbino, Italy: Ducal Palace 132
Utzon, Jørn (b. 1918) 363, 425

Valencia, Spain: Lonja de la Seda 121, 139
Valladolid, Spain: Cathedral 167, 202; College of San Gregorio 165
Valletta, Malta 151
Van Alen, William (1883–1954) 322, 373
Vanbrugh, Sir John (1664–1726) 220–22, 253, 254
Van Brunt, H. (1832–1903) 283, 326
Van Campen, Jacob (1595–1657) 215, 244
Van der Meij, J. M. (1878–1949) 341, 399
Van de Velde, Henry (1863–1957) 337, 339, 394
Vanvitelli, Luigi (1700–73) 235, 252, 270
Vasari, Giorgio (1511–74) 136
Vauban, Sébastien Le Prestre de (1633–1707) 151

Vaudoyer, Léon (1803–72) 281
Vaux-le-Vicomte, France 207, 237
Vendôme, France: La Trinité 96, 96
Venice, Italy: Ca' d'Oro 123, 138; Doges' Palace 121, 137; Library of St Mark's 143, 159; Palazzo Grimani 141, 157; Palazzo Vendramin-Calergi 143; S. Giorgio Maggiore 147, 171, 190; SS. Giovanni e Paolo 114; S. Maria della Salute 178, 202; St Mark's 30, 18
Venturi, Robert (b. 1925) 362–63
Verberckt, Jacques (1704–71) 211
Verona, Italy: Palazzo Bevilacqua 141, 156; Pellegrini Chapel 141; S. Zeno 67, 62
Versailles, France: château 208, 211, 238; Pavillon Français 211; Petit Trianon 242, 281; Theatre 252
Vesnin, Aleksandr (1883–1959), Leonid (1880–1933) and Viktor (1882–1950) 318, 327
Vézelay, France: church 54, 45
Vicenza, Italy: Basilica 145, 160; Palazzo Chiericati 145, 162; Teatro Olimpico 145, 161; Villa Capra (Rotonda) 147, 164
Vienna: bank (Domenig) 361; Belvedere 184; Imperial Library 183, 208; jewelry shop (Hollein) 361; Kärntner Bar 319; Kunsthistorisches Museum (Museum of Art History) 289; Majolika House 294; Museum of Natural History 289; Neuer Haus Haas 367; Postal Savings Bank 294, 341; Schönbrunn Palace 183; Stadtbahn stations 294; State Parliament 237; Steiner House 319, 368; Zacherl Apartment House 352; CHURCHES: Karlskirche 182, 207; Maria von Siege 279, 323; St Stephen's Cathedral 101; Steinhof Asylum church 294, 342; Votivkirche 279
Vierzehnheiligen, Germany 192, 188
Vignola, Giacomo Barozzi da (1507–73) 137, 150
Vignon, Pierre-Alexandre (1763–1828) 230, 258, 264
Viipuri, Finland: library 324, 378
Villanueva, Juan de (1759–1811) 249
Viollet-le-Duc, Eugène (1814–79) 275, 280, 281
Visconti, L.-T.-J. (1791–1853) 287
Viseu, Portugal: Cathedral 112
Vitruvius (1st c. BC) 10, 22–23, 159
Vittone, Bernardo (1702–70) 180, 206
Vladimir, Russia: Cathedral of the Dormition 33
Voysey, C. F. A. (1857–1941) 301, 349
Vranov Castle, Czech Republic 183
Vredeman de Vries, Hans (1526–1606) 156

Wagner, Otto (1841–1918) 294, 318, 341–42
Waldsassen, Germany: abbey 191; Kappel 192
Walpole, Horace 271, 314
Walter, T. U. (1804–87) 274
Wanstead House, England 229

Wardell, W. W. (1823–99) 278
Ware, W. R. (1832–1915) 283, 326
Warkworth Castle, England 117
Warsaw, Poland: Lazienki Palace 244, 283
Wartburg, Germany: Castle 275
Washington, DC 237, 239; Capitol 237–38, 274; National Gallery 346
Waterhouse, Alfred (1830–1905) 275, 284
Webb, Aston (1849–1930) 289
Webb, John (1611–72) 179
Webb, Philip (1831–1915) 300–01
Weimar, Germany: Römisches Haus 244; Schloss 232; School of Applied Arts 339
Wells, England: Cathedral 90, 94, 88; chapter house 119, 134
Weltenburg, Germany: abbey church 193, 220
White, Edward Bricknell (1806–82) 259
White, Stanford (1853–1906) 290, 289
Wies, Die, Germany 192, 219
Wild, J. W. (1814–92) 284
William 'the Englishman' (12th c.) 79
William of Sens (12th c.) 79, 88
Williamsburg, Va., USA: College of William and Mary 223
Wilton, England: church 284; House 161
Winchester, England: Cathedral 58, 62, 98, 52; Hall 117
Wines, James (b. 1932) 361
Wohlmut, Bonifaz (d. 1579) 154
Wolff, William 279
Wollaton Hall, England 157, 175
Wood, John, the Elder (1704–54) 238
Woodward, Benjamin (1816–61) 306, 355
Worksop, England: Priory 64, 59
Worms, Germany: Cathedral 47, 33
Wren, Sir Christopher (1632–1723) 168, 216–19, 223, 271, 246–50
Wright, Frank Lloyd (1867–1959) 302–03, 349, 352, 407–09
Wroclaw (Breslau), Poland: Deutsche Werkbund Hall 337; Jahrhunderthalle 317, 367; St Mary on the Sands 103, 110; Town Hall 121
Würzburg, Germany: Residenz 184; Women's Prison 234, 269
Wyatt, Benjamin (1775–1850) 252
Wyatt, James (1746–1813) 228, 242, 271, 259

Yamasaki, Minoru (1912–86) 358
York, England: Assembly Rooms 230, 262
Ypres, Belgium: Cloth Hall 121

Zacatecas, Mexico: Cathedral 204
Zakharov, A. D. (1761–1811) 237, 257
Zamora, Spain: Cathedral 72, 73
Zaragoza, Spain: church of the Pilar 167
Žďár, Czech Republic 195, 223, 224
Zimmermann, Dominikus (1685–1766) 192, 219
Zohltovsky, I. V. (1867–1959) 344
Zwartnots, Armenia 20
Zwirner, Friedrich (1802–61) 280